The Writing of Innocence

SUNY SERIES
LITERATURE...IN THEORY

SERIES EDITORS

David E. Johnson, *Comparative Literature, University at Buffalo*
Scott Michaelsen, *English, Michigan State University*

SERIES ADVISORY BOARD

Nahum Dimitri Chandler, *African American Studies, University of California, Irvine*
Rebecca Comay, *Philosophy and Comparative Literature, University of Toronto*
Marc Crépon, *Philosophy, École Normale Supérieure, Paris*
Jonathan Culler, *Comparative Literature, Cornell University*
Johanna Drucker, *Design Media Arts and Information Studies, University of California, Los Angeles*
Christopher Fynsk, *Modern Thought, Aberdeen University*
Rodolphe Gasché, *Comparative Literature, University at Buffalo*
Martin Hägglund, *Comparative Literature, Yale University*
Carol Jacobs, *German and Comparative Literature, Yale University*
Peggy Kamuf, *French and Comparative Literature, University of Southern California*
David Marriott, *History of Consciousness, University of California, Santa Cruz*
Steven Miller, *English, University at Buffalo*
Alberto Moreiras, *Hispanic Studies, Texas A&M University*
Patrick O'Donnell, *English, Michigan State University*
Pablo Oyarzun, *Teoría del Arte, Universidad de Chile*
Scott Cutler Shershow, *English, University of California, Davis*
Henry Sussman, *German and Comparative Literature, Yale University*
Samuel Weber, *Comparative Literature, Northwestern University*
Ewa Ziarek, *Comparative Literature, University at Buffalo*

The Writing of Innocence

Blanchot and the Deconstruction of Christianity

Aïcha Liviana Messina

Cover image: *Recomposition 4, 2021*, by Susanne Doppelt. © Susanne Doppelt, 2021. Used with permission.

Published by State University of New York Press, Albany

© 2022 State University of New York

All rights reserved

Printed in the United States of America

No part of this book may be used or reproduced in any manner whatsoever without written permission. No part of this book may be stored in a retrieval system or transmitted in any form or by any means including electronic, electrostatic, magnetic tape, mechanical, photocopying, recording, or otherwise without the prior permission in writing of the publisher.

For information, contact State University of New York Press, Albany, NY www.sunypress.edu

Library of Congress Cataloging-in-Publication Data

Name: Messina, Aïcha Liviana, author.
Title: The writing of innocence : Blanchot and the deconstruction of Christianity / Aïcha Liviana Messina.
Description: Albany : State University of New York Press, [2022] | Series: SUNY series, literature . . . in theory | Includes bibliographical references and index.
Identifiers: LCCN 2021048869 | ISBN 9781438488998 (hardcover : alk. paper) | ISBN 9781438489018 (ebook) | ISBN 9781438489001 (pbk. : alk. paper)
Subjects: LCSH: Blanchot, Maurice. | Innocence (Psychology) | Nancy, Jean-Luc.
Classification: LCC B2430.B574 M47 2022 | DDC 194—dc23/eng/20220103
LC record available at https://lccn.loc.gov/2021048869

10 9 8 7 6 5 4 3 2 1

Contents

Acknowledgments	vii
Foreword *Serge Margel*	xi
Introduction: The Fall of Innocence	1
1. Law	27
2. Grace	45
3. Innocence	71
4. Apocalypse	89
5. The Deconstruction of Christianity in Nancy and Blanchot	105
Conclusion: The Innocence of the Stone	135
Notes	141
References	185
Index	193

Acknowledgments

This book took shape progressively from 2014 to 2021.

I would like to thank Ilit Ferber, Adam Lipsczyc, Andrea Potestà, and Nassima Sahraoui, with whom a small but durable research group emerged and has not only continued but has amplified over time. In this context, a very embryonic version of chapter one was presented in 2014 in a seminar called "Language and Violence" at Tel Aviv University, and a first version of chapter three was presented in Warsaw the following year in a seminar called "Space and Violence," after which we spent an entire afternoon commenting on a passage from Melville's *Billy Budd*.

A previous version of chapter one was also presented in Buffalo in 2014 at a conference organized by two extraordinary friends and colleagues, Rodolphe Gasché and David E. Johnson, whose way of cultivating friendship and thought allowed me to persevere in this book project. I'm infinitely grateful to them and to the whole audience that was present in Buffalo, and in general to the Department of Comparative Literature at the University at Buffalo where I have often enjoyed attending their excellent lecture series.

In November 2015, I presented an early draft of the first part of chapter five in an international conference on the thought of Jean-Luc Nancy titled "Jean-Luc Nancy, penser la mutation," organized by Jérôme Lèbre and Jacob Rogozinsky. I would like to thank them for their invitation, for their trust, and for this important moment of rigorous thought, but also for friendship, which they made possible. When the conference began, the audience and the speakers were still shocked by the terrorist attack that had just taken place in Paris.

In September 2015, I presented a first draft of the final part of chapter five in the city of Messina at an event on Nancy's book *The Disavowed Community*, organized by Caterina Resta, Rita Fulco, and myself.

Their collegiality and friendship doubtlessly keep me joyful in the world. I thank them, and I thank Jean-Luc Nancy who, besides being there with an invaluable generosity, commenced speaking in Italian without noticing, thus overcoming his own idea that he was not able to speak it. The content that became part of chapter five was also presented in the Eugenio Donato Seminars in Buffalo, organized by Rodolphe Gasché, whom I can never thank enough. I would like to extend all my gratitude to the audience for their insightful questions and many thoughtful reflections.

The last part of chapter five discusses an article co-written by Juan Manuel Garrido and myself that was published in *Cahiers Maurice Blanchot*. I would like to thank Danielle Cohen-Levinas and Michaël Holland for their invitation to write this article, which indeed was the occasion to clarify Nancy's difficult, important, and controversial book. I'm grateful to Juan Manuel Garrido, with whom I've shared many discussions and learned one important aspect of the Greek philia (friendship) in which philosophical differences have not only their place, but also their histories. I'm also very grateful to María del Rosario Acosta whose reflections, after she read this co-written article, have been decisive in the elaboration of chapter five. I also thank her for inviting me to give a seminar called "Deconstruction of Christianity in Nancy and Blanchot" at DePaul University, as well as the students who attended the seminar.

Finally, a less embryonic version of chapter one was presented at Emory University, in a talk organized by Matías Bascuñán in 2019, who has been, with Manuela Ossa, a formidable host. Their trust, their desire to think, their high expectations are indeed vital, constantly aiming to rethink academia and the university.

Enormous thanks also to Marcia Cavalcante, who edited the dossier on *History, Today* in *Philosophy Today*, where a first version of chapter four was published.

I also extend my thanks for the help I received either to edit this manuscript or to translate some portions directly, and to improve or complement some ideas.

Preliminary versions of some chapters were originally written in French and have been translated into English. Jonathan Cimon-Lambert translated a preliminary version of chapter one. Lena Taub translated a preliminary version of chapter four. Donald Cross translated the conclusion and has helped to revise chapter two. I would like to express my gratitude to them and to Cheryl Emerson, who not only helped to revise the whole manuscript of this book, but who has also commented on it and participated in its unfolding. I would also like to thank Luís Felipe Alarcón for his comments and careful reading of the first version of the complete manuscript and, in general, for the horizon his point of view manages to open—and for his unwavering friendship.

This work was made possible above all by the commitment, energy, and concern of the students, friends, and collaborators with whom I organized lecture groups and seminars on Blanchot. It's a formidable opportunity to be able to share such disarming writings in contexts where we can take the time to let writing question our categories of knowing and being. This has been the case in a reading group on *The Writing of the Disaster*, whose participants include Víctor Ibarra, Julieta Marchant, Amanda Olivares, Mauricio Oportus, Ricardo Perez, Rudy Pradena, Felipe Quintero, Marcela Rivera, and Cristián Rustom.

The last version of this book included a response to the commentaries formulated by the anonymous readers. I'm extremely grateful for their very important and insightful remarks, for their suggestions, and for their careful reading.

It's important to acknowledge that this work was made possible thanks to the support of the Chilean National Funding for Scientific and Technologic Development (Fondecyt 1210921) and of Universidad Diego Portales in Santiago de Chile.

I would also like to thank *The New Centennial Review*, *Philosophy Today*, and *Les cahiers philosophiques de Strasbourg* where preliminary versions of the first part of chapter one, of chapter four, and of a portion of chapter five have been published. A previous version of chapter one originally appeared in *CR: The New Centennial Review* (vol. 15, no. 3, 201–24),—published by Michigan State University Press. A previous version of chapter four originally appeared in *Philosophy Today* (vol. 60, no. 4, 877—92). A brief portion of chapter five originally appeared in *CR: The New Centennial Review* (vol. 17, no. 3, 63–80) published by Michigan State University Press and in *Les Cahiers philosophiques de Strasbourg* (no. 42, 153—68).

Foreword

Serge Margel

The Exposure of Innocence and the Desire for Inexistence

First and foremost, innocence does not exist. It is a state of grace, or a gift. It is a gracious state of an inexistence, before the opposition between life and death, generation and destruction, appearance and disappearance. "Before," that is before time, before history, before the time of history, before dialectics and its contradictions. Innocence represents this state of time within time, which shapes time until its loss, until its fall or its annihilation. Innocence is not the fall within time, but rather it is the fall of time itself, which comes out of itself, exceeds or reveals itself, going beyond its own limits and diverting its own dimensions, the past, the present, and the future. Without dimensions, without qualities, without duration nor eternity, the time of innocence constitutes the state of inexistence of time within time. It is the inexistence of Adam, which Adam was not able to preserve, or in which Adam did not want to persevere, as Saint Augustine writes. Adam is the name of that which tends toward existence, of that which wants to exist, to be there, to be something, to be a subject of attributions, to receive properties, to have qualities, to have intentions, to be conscious, to be affected, to act, to feel, to think.

Life surprised Adam in his desire for existence. Death took hold of him in his freedom. Life and death are accidents that Adam experiences as infinite falls in time, like the vertigo of passing toward existence, like the madness of becoming the subject of one's own affections. Adam is the name of the one who rejects inexistence, who refuses one's inherent inexistence at the state of innocence. He is that which wants to be something, a man, a woman, something that thinks, that desires, that desires to desire, even without desiring anything other than to exist. Adam is the name of the one who wants the impossible—*to exist*—to be his condition of existence. In this sense, Adam is the name of the impossible innocence. Aïcha Liviana Messina's book is an important work on innocence, but also on the impossible, as a condition of existence. This book is troubling by its audaciousness and by its caution. It takes a term, *innocence*, and constructs it into a concept, as the title of the opening chapter, *The Fall of Innocence*, and shifts it from its context of emergence in order to put it to the test, as if to expose it, as Adam does when he sees himself naked once he leaves innocence. Genesis, Paul's Epistles, the Apocalypse, Saint Augustine are all there, mentioned, commented. However, what is important for the exposition of innocence is Blanchot. It is Blanchot, reader of Hegel, of dialectics, of history, of the right to death, of literature, and of the power of the law.

The strong and audacious hypothesis of the book is quickly presented:

> Innocence is a key issue in Blanchot's writings. Although this notion is not recurrent and only rarely mentioned, Blanchot's thought is grounded in innocence since it stems from the impossibility of the subject. Blanchot's point of departure is not a fall that makes possible the subject and that structures it into guiltiness, but rather a fall from the condition of the subject and that questions not only its autonomy but also its unicity. Blanchot's thought assumes that what makes possible the subject—its condition of possibility—is also what implies its collapse. The condition of possibility of the subject is therefore, at the same time, its "incondition." Assuming Hegel's idea that the subject is not substantial but that it is the fruit of a process, Blanchot thinks that the subject is grounded on negativity, namely, on a process by which he is revealed to himself through the negation of its natural condition, a negation that is also the revelation of its spiritual content. Consequently, like Hegel, Blanchot thinks that the subject is not given as a natural entity, but shapes itself through experience. However, for Blanchot, negativity (or experience) is double-edged. Whereas negativity does shape the world and the humans into cultural forms, it is also faced with the fact that humanity, in the ultimate instance, is not grounded. For Blanchot, the negative does not have a spiritual content. (23)

Everything is presented and stated. Several pages into the book, we understand where it is going, where the author is leading us. Blanchot speaks little about innocence and does not make it a concept, nor an object of reflection. Yet, innocence is a key to his work. The key, clavis, is that which opens and closes, which at the same time gives and restricts access. A key allows one to go to the heart of something, to penetrate the intimacy while preserving its secret. This is the objective of Aïcha Liviana Messina's book: to enter, by way of innocence, Blanchot's profound and difficult thought, which is more or less closed, hermetic, disseminated, and which resists solutions, passwords, all keys to reading, and rules of interpretation. The book allows one to enter Blanchot's work through a notion, which is not strictly Blanchotian, but which gives access to his thought, or lets his thought open up to itself, to give access to itself, while secretly closing in on itself. It is innocence considered from the point of view of the "negative." The negativity of the negative is not simply negation, and Aïcha Liviana Messina, who reads Blanchot reading Hegel, presents this well. Unlike negation, which is opposed to affirmation, negativity is double. It is the immediate and simultaneous duplicity of the negative: the condition for the existence of something is determined by the negation of its own conditions of possibility. One could also say that negativity is an oxymoron conceived as a principle. And this is what innocence consists of, on which Blanchot's thought is anchored.

The approach adopted by Aïcha Liviana Messina's book does not consist in creating a list of occurrences of the term *innocence* in Blanchot's texts. It proceeds quite differently. With great philosophical erudition, this book creates a veritable concept of innocence. Through a reading of the Bible, of Judaism, of Christianity, with theological, philosophical, and literary notions, with the hypothesis that innocence appears throughout and influences Blanchot's thought from within, Messina remarks that, first and foremost, this thought concerns the question of the subject and its condition of existence as the "incondition" of possibility. For the subject, innocence constitutes its impossible existence, its fall, its loss, but also its chance. In fact, the conceptual key the book creates makes it possible to open several locks and to enter more than one thought. Messina developed this key itself as a set of keys of variable abilities, with which, by penetrating Blanchot's thought, she enters directly into Hegel's thought, but also that of Kierkegaard, of Levinas, as well as that of Saint Paul and his Epistle to the Romans, which seeks to deconstruct Judaism and the Mosaic Law. Messina calls this conceptual key "the ethical consequences of innocence thought as a fall and of the peculiar reading of Christianity it unfolds" (41). In her reading of Blanchot, she advances a new reflection on the Jewish question as a deconstruction of Christianity. Here, however, Judaism is mainly Levinas and the subject submitted to the law or to the face of the Other, and Christianity is primarily Hegel and the subject as the transgression of the law by love and freedom.

The ethical consequences of innocence constructed as a negative concern the notion of grace first and foremost. According to Saint Paul, it is through the law that I was able to know wrongdoing and sin, and grace alone can save me from them, or save me from the law of sin, and thus from the fall, from death, from the end. With this radical critique of the law, Paul seeks to accomplish two things, which, according to Aïcha Liviana Messina, can be found in the Blanchotian thought of innocence. On the one hand, Paul wants to show that the law itself or on its own cannot create justice. This is the Pauline deconstruction of Judaism and of the Mosaic law, of the commandments that impose and forbid. On the other hand, Paul affirms the necessity of a transformation of human being, or the birth of a new human being through grace, necessary for achieving justice. This is the creation of a new Adam, or of a new Adamic state of human being. However, for Paul, this is also the establishment of another true Judaism, which no longer depends on the letter of the law and its commandments, written in stone, but rather on the gift of grace alone and its spirit, which reigns within the heart. Messina compares Saint Paul and Blanchot on a specific but ambiguous point, which at the same time distinguishes them: grace does not overturn the law, nor does it abolish it, allowing instead a different relation to the law—a new human being too, and a new Judaism. For Paul, grace is salutary. It makes it possible to accomplish the law in spirit in order to defeat death. For Blanchot, grace is a chance. It makes it possible to divert the law by the love of death. In other words, Paul and Blanchot are alike in affirming the necessity for a new human being and another relation to the law, for a different apprehension of death that is directly related to the question of innocence. According to Paul, freeing oneself from the subjugation to the law, going beyond the law through grace, consists in creating a new Adam, another first man who did not impose the law as the condition of his existence. Not only did this new human being not know wrongdoing from the law, nor introduce death into the world as punishment for all of humanity, but he also and more importantly defeated death and saved all of humanity.

In his commentary of the Epistle to the Romans, Saint Augustine reminds us that Adam's freedom could have allowed him not to commit a sin, and thus not to die. It could have prevented him from dying, him, Adam, the first man, but it also could have prevented the to die, as an Adamic condition for all of humanity. He could have "persevered" in his state of innocence, preserved his *posse non peccare*, and thus acquired the immortality of the *non posse peccare*. This was a possibility for Adam, this was his freedom, inscribed in his nature or his essence. This was Adam, and only that. Adam's innocence was indeed this freedom; it was the possibility to be immortal, the possibility of impossible death. And this is where Blanchot's Paulinism distinguishes itself from Paul himself. Both of them diverge on the possibility of the impossible, on this negative or this oxymoron conceived as a principle of the existence of all of humanity. Blanchot is closer to Augustine in the sense that Adam, by desiring existence, chose death. As Aïcha Liviana Messina strongly affirms, for Blanchot, the "detour of grace" involves "the love of death" (90). This relentless search, this infinite expectation, this love of unconditional death entails neither wrongdoing nor punishment, but rather inexistence alone that is inherent to the state of Adam's innocence, and to his absolute freedom. The negativity of innocence is the conflict or the internal division of desire. It is the unbearable inexistence that drives Adam to choose death, to prefer existence, to desire it despite everything and despite himself. This desire, this love, "conditions" his freedom to choose a paradoxical, impossible death, or as Blanchot says, for "the impossibility of the to die." As Messina writes, "the detour of grace is the very detour of the 'to die' (mourir) that fails to come to term; that is, that not only fails to reach the limit but also makes it vain in its inertia" (102). For Adam, who is inhabited by this freedom, by this impossible desire, this desire for the impossible, everything begins with the end, everything begins by coming to an end. Genesis is the Apocalypse, creation is revelation, the first man is the end of the world, and the first book of the Old Testament is already the last book of the New Testament. The impossibility of the to die is the freedom of this inexistence, by which Adam will not have been able to persevere in his state of innocence. Yet, it is also what Aïcha Liviana Messina's book demonstrates, from which I will quote one more excerpt:

> Blanchot thinks of the Apocalypse in relation to the revelatory role of the end. If death (the negative) is undertaken in the work of meaning, then the end (death) has a revelatory role. The meaning that is made possible through the negative is necessarily apocalyptic since it implies the idea that the truth is revealed in the end; that the truth is revealed through the end. (164–65)

Introduction

The Fall of Innocence

> Hence, innocence amounts to non-action, like the being of a stone, not even that of a child.
>
> —Hegel, *The Phenomenology of Spirit*, 270–71

> Everything is innocence; and knowledge is the path to insight to this innocence.
>
> —Nietzsche, *Human, All Too Human*, 58

> Innocence: a sharp putting into question.
>
> —Blanchot, *The Step Not Beyond*, 125

Innocence is a dangerous topic. Whereas it could be reduced to a mere myth (located in an original paradise where it refers to ontological qualities), or to a mere negative determination (as when, in a juridical context, the innocent is the one who was not involved), there are fugacious but serious reasons to think that innocence has a form of existence that qualifies the human condition. In the first two cases, innocence is innocuous because it is nonexistent. It is either a myth[1] or a juridical determination that speaks of a *non-lieu* (the noninvolvement in a determined crime or offense). In these two cases, innocence makes sense negatively: it means the absence of guilt or of propension to guilty actions. In a way, the negativity of innocence is fundamental to the Western and, more precisely, Judeo-Christian conception of the subject. Any history of the autonomous subject would show that the birth of the subject requires the loss of innocence. An autonomous and responsible subject is necessarily a subject that can be held accountable for its actions, that knows the rules of society, and that has been educated to the difference between good and evil, or between right and wrong. The myth of the loss of innocence is indeed the basis of the Judeo-Christian tradition as well as of our juridical categories, but also of our understanding of the subject as historical. Indeed, innocent subjects are not in a condition to be held responsible for their actions. Moreover, they have no proper history precisely because they have not suffered loss. By contrast, the loss of innocence entails that subjects are able to acknowledge themselves as potentially guilty and hence as responsible. In addition, it is this loss that constitutes subjects as ex-sistent; namely, as opened individuals who are not immanent to an essence. In this sense, the loss of innocence is the beginning of history. Understood in this way, the myth of the loss of innocence is a structuring myth that explains the capacity to give an account of one's actions. It constitutes the structure of subjectivity in general. The myth of the loss of innocence puts at stake a lack that structures subjectivity and that defines the individual as existent, and therefore as historical.

Our point of departure, however, is that innocence is not a mere lack: a mere myth or a mere negative determination. Considered as a simple myth, innocence might have a structural dimension that permits the understanding of our ethical and juridical categories, but its understanding is only negative. The content of innocence remains outside of language, as something out of reach that has no more reality than a dream. By contrast, literature provides a multiplicity of innocent characters who show that innocence has a positive form of existence irreducible to ontological qualities (as if someone's nature could be qualified as innocent). In Dostoevsky's *The Idiot*, the "idiot" Prince Myshkin has the innocence of one who has not fully been fashioned by the rules of society. In Hugo's *The Man Who Laughs* (*L'homme qui rit*, 2013), Dea and Gwynplaine, the blind girl and the disfigured boy, are beyond the social conventions that would qualify the boy as monstrous and the girl as disabled. The blindness of the former and the artificial face of the latter, carved by a permanent laugh, render them innocent of the common way of seeing and of laughing, and of the violence both senses might entail when used conventionally. In these cases, *innocence is not a lack but a surplus*. It coincides with a certain eccentricity or even idiocy; with a certain particularity that does not conform to a determined way of being.

In a different way, there are also works of literature that focus on characters whose innocence is due less to their particularities than to their incapacity to judge. Melville's eponymous *Billy Budd* is a sailor whose actions, however criminal, are not intentionally so. By the same token, Meursault, the apparently cold character of Camus's *The Stranger* who remains without feelings on the day of his mother's funeral, has the same empty attitude on the day he faces trial for manslaughter. Interestingly, Meursault is not innocent because he has not committed the crime, but because he is structured in such a way that he seems to accept his actions without guilt. It is as if, albeit knowing the rules of society, he does not acknowledge the moral frame in which our actions make sense. Here, innocence could still be a form of ignorance. However, this ignorance is not a mere negativity that could be supplemented by knowledge. On the contrary, Meursault's ignorance does not result from a lack of knowledge, but takes place within it. It is in fact as if knowledge makes him indifferent, and hence, rather than making him different, makes him like any other person. Like Sorge, Blanchot's main character in *The Most High*, Meursault is not a "particular man"; he could be "anybody" (Blanchot 1996, 1). Meursault's apparent absence of feelings not only prevents him from being someone, a singular individual who has the capacity to account for his actions, but it also makes him anonymous, like anyone, giving birth to a sort of horizontal universality, as if Meursault's apathy were common because it is improper and hence irreducible. It is in fact as though his apparent apathy were like an atmosphere rather than an individual propriety, the strangeness of an epoch rather than a particular problem. *In this context*, thought of as a universal condition, *innocence is less (negatively) the ignorance of evil than evil as an irreducible condition of ignorance (and of indifference)*.

In all these cases and in very different ways, innocence stands not as a purity of the heart but as a sort of strangeness of the feelings. Rather than referring to a lost past, it questions social conventions to the point of jeopardizing the normative frames that determine human values and actions, their moral beliefs. It hence entails a change of perspective. However, in the case of Camus's *The Stranger*, innocence is not confined to the strangeness of a character; it speaks to the strangeness of social configurations in general. Unlike "the idiot" who is one singular man, Camus's "stranger" refers to a general condition of humanity. Here the innocent is not the idiot, the one who cannot overcome its particularity, but the normal, the one who is fully conformed to a frame and who hence cannot question their actions. While the idiot's innocence suspends judgment, the innocence of the stranger amounts to an impossibility of questioning in general. Like Arendt's (2006) analysis of Eichmann's case as embodying the banality of evil, Camus's "stranger" cannot become aware of his crime because he cannot question his actions in general. Such is the danger, or at least one of them, of innocence. In a world where systems have taken hold of everything, in which subjects have overcome their particularities in the name of universal motivations, individuals are no longer subjects but anonymous characters who function without judging. This innocence is neither a loss nor a myth in a remote and inaccessible past. On the contrary, it qualifies the human condition in general. Despite the foundation of the autonomous subject, despite the ideas of freedom and history at the core of Western thought, the freedom and historicity of the human condition might be only apparent.[2] In line with the main discoveries of structuralism, Camus's description of Meursault brings to light, as Levinas would say, that subjects are *acted* rather than actors: "Individuals are reduced to being bearers of forces that command unbeknown to themselves" (Levinas 1991, 21). In this condition, the foundations of the subject's responsibility and awareness are not guaranteed. The maturity of a subject's awareness, the "truthfulness" of its knowledge, are insufficient conditions for the assumption of any responsibility. It is why innocence can be considered as one of the issues of our contemporary world. Neither modernity nor postmodernity has managed to give birth to a subject that would not be trapped in innocence. Although defined by its autonomy and awareness, the subject remains mute and stuck in the incapacity to respond for its own actions. As Günther Anders says about the apocalyptical dimension of technique, what stands today as the end of the world is not the possibility of destruction but the fact that one might destroy the world in perfect innocence, as being a mere agent of the system. What Anders calls the "law of innocence" is the fact that we can enact our own destruction without being accountable for it. Paradoxically, technique—and hence science and knowledge—make humans all the more unable to imagine the consequences of their actions. This is why Anders writes: "If there is something that can symbolize the evil nature of our situation, it is this innocence" (Anders 2006, 53). Understood in this way, innocence is the condition of a humanity that can no longer be judged. It makes impossible all justice and all freedom.

❧

Innocence is a dangerous issue for a least two reasons, one moral and the other epochal.

First, innocence is not innocuous. On the contrary, precisely because innocence is associated with a form of unawareness, the innocent can mix with the worst crimes. The innocent ignores evil, unknowingly. Yet, this ignorance can be evil precisely in its radical form. This is the case of the eponymous character of Fritz Lang's movie *M*, where an apparently innocent man, ignorant of Good and Evil, cannot avoid raping and killing children. In this movie, streamed a few years before World War II—namely, before the legitimation of radical evil—what is interesting is that *M* is hunted by the officers of the law and also by the outlaws whose criminal activity is disturbed by this apparently innocent monster. At the end of the movie, *M* is judged by the criminals in an improvised trial before being arrested by officers of the law and in this way is "saved" by the police in order to have a supposedly legitimate trial. This scene reveals that legality and illegality go together, whereas innocence questions all juridical systems. As Blanchot (1992, 125) writes, where there is innocence, there is "a sharp putting into question." When evil is merged with innocence, we don't exactly know how to judge it.

Second, innocence cannot be overcome. Of course, thought in mythical terms as the quality of a pure heart, innocence is necessarily lost at the moment in which one becomes a subject of knowledge, or a subject of law. As soon as one becomes a subject through the use of reason and in the relation to others, as soon as one enters the sphere of language, which is also the realm of law,[3] one necessarily loses innocence. In this sense, innocence is always already lost. As previously stated, the loss of innocence is the beginning of the subject. For this reason, as Hegel believes, innocence does not properly exist: only a stone is innocent. But a stone is not self-aware. Hence, innocence is beyond the realm of awareness. It is not, or it is nothing.[4] Our only understanding of innocence is a myth. However, if innocence is not merely a lack of knowledge but can be its correlative, if, as Meursault's case shows, innocence is *rather an impossibility of being aware through knowledge than a proper lack of knowledge*, if it is a form of indifference that we acquire in the moment in which all particularities are overcome and one becomes anybody instead of someone, then *innocence is not lost by knowledge but rather produced by it*. It cannot be overcome by the birth of consciousness because it is its very shadow. In these figure-cases, innocence speaks of a human condition that abounds in crime without being able to account for it. *Innocence is the problem of responsibility in an area in which there are no subjects to account for their actions*. Innocence is dangerous in that it not only describes a stage of humanity that doesn't need to account for itself (this corresponds to innocence understood in mythical terms as the quality of a pure heart); it also stages humanity's condition as *unable* to account for itself (this corresponds to innocence understood as the shadow of awareness). As what cannot be overcome, innocence stages a subject that, albeit self-aware or at least able to reason and to acknowledge law, remains ignorant or indifferent to evil. In this configuration, it is not innocence that is outside of history (in that it would precede its birth). It is history that progressively relates to innocence as a form of ahistoricity that is inherent to it and that reveals evil as irreducible.

Albeit dangerous, innocence is promising. As stated, it gives birth to changes of perspectives than can open to new horizons and hence to new historical possibilities. In Dostoyevsky's *The Idiot*, for example, Prince Myshkin's innocence is not a limitation from a perspective that remains particular. The idiot's innocence (as well as innocence's idiocy) implies a suspension of judgment in general that questions individuals despite themselves and that can bring about radical and unpredictable transformations. The idiot's presence and persistent idiocy not only manage to force people out of their ways and to question their beliefs, but also to transform the social dynamics. It thus has a political impact (even if imperceptible and bound to disappear). In this sense, innocence is the necessary moment for any change in perspectives (in the Nietzschean sense) and hence of revolutionary situations. Indeed, innocence is impossible *as such* (as a moral quality based on an ontological propriety: the "pure heart"), as the propriety of a posited or of a self-aware subject. Yet, awareness would be trapped in itself if it couldn't be questioned, if it couldn't go through changes of perspectives, if it couldn't be detached from the horizon that guides it. For this reason, although there is no innocence that is aware of itself,[5] innocence is somehow a necessary condition of awareness.

Just as innocence is required for a change of perspectives, there would be no revolutions in general (e.g., political, moral, epistemological) without this instance of suspension, this positive suspension of knowledge. A revolution is such only if it is bound to the unknown. A revolution that would already know its results would in fact not be a revolution; namely, a radical transformation (of the material conditions of production of the world as well as of humanity). Hence, albeit innocence in its mythical acceptation is definitely ahistoric, history somehow requires innocence to be such. The desire for revolution can only happen as an innocent desire. In order to desire revolution, one has to ignore the object of its desire. By the same token, although innocence is contrary to morality (since morality requires a subjection to law and its acknowledgment), there would be no ethics without innocence. Without this instance of suspension of any secure values and of any determined knowledge, there would be no decisions, no singular affirmations, and, in this sense, no free judgment. As Derrida recalls in *The Gift of Death*, in order to be such, a decision cannot be a mere application of knowledge,[6] but rather happens as a rupture of the order of knowledge. It henceforth requires an instance of suspension. In the same way, a judgment is not a mere application of a rule, but its renewal. And in the wake of Kant, who has largely inspired Arendt's political thought, we can say that a judgment does not merely presuppose its criteria:[7] it produces its rule. Hence, although innocence (non-knowledge) is dangerously amoral, it is the condition of possibility of any creation of values, of decisions, of singular productions, and hence of newness, of history, of freedom. For these reasons, while it is irreducible to a knowledge, innocence has a transcendental[8] dimension. It is constitutive, but it cannot be constituted.

Innocence is indeed double-edged. It is either stuck in the ahistoricity of its myth, or it is the condition of any true radical change. It coincides with the impossibility of morality, but it is also a condition of possibility of ethics. It is indeed the negative of any awareness, or it is its failure; yet, it is also the condition of possibility of any free sight, perspective, and choice. This double-edged dimension makes of innocence an intriguing subject but also a difficult one since its meaning cannot be fixed once and for all. Innocence might never be what it seems to be and might not be where it seems to be located. Whereas innocence is a *sinuous* topic (that might never *be* what it seemed to be), when it is thought *without this sinuosity*—that is to say, as if innocence could *be* and could be put at stake as an objectifiable element—it becomes indeed very problematic. Innocence escapes subjectivity and puts it into question. When the subject becomes immanent to innocence, the latter can become an unquestionable monster. Therefore, while innocence has a transcendental dimension (it is the condition of possibility of revolution, of newness in history), can we be innocent of innocence? Can we innocently desire innocence, ignoring its dangers?

There are at least two ways of thinking about innocence politically that merit critical reflection. In some figure-cases, as in revolutionary projects inspired by Marx's idea of revolution, innocence is an unknown projected above knowledge.[9] Indeed, although Marx's idea of revolution has a scientific and a dialectical base, it is directed toward the unknown.[10] In this sense, albeit not based on faith, Marx's idea of revolution does have a Judeo-Christian inspiration: it aspires, if not to a redeemed humanity, at least to its complete renewal (which is a form of redemption).[11] But can this model still be desired *innocently*? Thought as the hope of a renewed humanity, revolution is still based on a dialectical model that separates knowledge and the unknown. Indeed, there is something romantic but also blindly violent in the innocence of revolution. On the one hand, as we know, these dialectical models end up justifying violence in the name of a Goodness that would transcend it. On the other hand, and correlatively, this idea of revolution seems to look for a purified humanity, as if humanity could and should start again, freeing itself not only from the possibility of evil, but also from the *memory of evil* and from its own history. Even while scientific, Marx's idea of revolution aims at redeeming humanity from its fallen condition, which is to say its alienation. Whereas in the first case we risk grounding revolution on a moral base rather than on a political one, in the second case, a humanity purified of its own memory of evil risks falling again into a form of innocence that is a mere unawareness of evil. Hence, albeit moral, this idea of revolution encloses the possibility of a complacency into irresponsibility.

In other figure-cases, innocence is claimed politically not as the necessity to save humanity from its fallen condition or from the different forms of its alienation, but rather to save the world from humans or, better said, from the anthropocentric dimension of politics. This is, for instance, the case of vitalistic thought where the ground of political claims is life and not the human being in common. In a historical moment in which the condition of possibility of life is put into question by climate change, life becomes evident (and crucial) as a new political objective. The latter can take the form of an affirmation of life's agonistic dimension, as in Esposito's (2008) description of a "positive biopolitics," or of a necessity to conserve life as in ecological claims that aim at saving the world from its end. These two claims, albeit different or even opposite (one is affirmative, the other is conservative), insist upon the necessity to overcome the human being for the sake of an innocence of life.[12] They both see in life a *value* that is affirmed for itself and the possibility to *overcome* the human and its endemic violence or forms of alienation and dominations.

Now, do these thoughts not again enact a redemptive scenario? The idea of a purity of life is indeed at the heart of the Christian idea of grace as that which saves from death. Although they claim to overcome the anthropocentric aspect of the Judeo-Christian legacy, these claims operate on the basis of a similar redemptive pattern. Inspired sometimes by a quick reading of Nietzsche's idea of life and of a "becoming innocent" (Nietzsche 1996, 59), these "positive biopolitics" that aim at elaborating a post-human politics stage a redemption from the Judeo-Christian background of Western history and from civilization in general. Moreover—and this is what is problematic—these redemptive thoughts entail new forms of alienation. Instead of affirming life for human purposes, humans should be serving life—as if life were a new God. Indeed, these postures posit life as pure, as if it were not a theoretical construction prompted to become an ideology. Now, as Heidegger (1991) has pointed out very clearly in his *Nietzsche*, rather than overcoming metaphysics, these vitalistic thoughts install new ones. They posit life as a truth above human artifice, as a Goodness beyond the human's essential involvement with evil. These "positive biopolitics" see in life an innocence that should be claimed against humanity's history of alienation. In all these cases, innocence is no longer sinuous. Its double-edged dimension disappears behind an ontology of life where innocence is posited as a metaphysical truth that could serve ideological ends.

Innocence is a key issue in Blanchot's writings. Although this notion is not recurrent and only rarely mentioned, Blanchot's thought is grounded in innocence since it stems from the impossibility of the subject. His point of departure is not a fall that makes possible the subject and that structures it into guiltiness, but rather a *fall from the condition of the subject* and that questions not only its autonomy but also its unicity. His thought assumes that what makes possible the subject—its condition of possibility—is also what implies its collapse. The condition of possibility of the subject is therefore, at the same time, its "incondition."[13] Assuming Hegel's idea that the subject is not substantial but that it is the fruit of a process, Blanchot thinks the subject is grounded on negativity; namely, on a process by which he is revealed to himself through the negation of its natural condition, a negation that is also the revelation of its spiritual content. Consequently, like Hegel, Blanchot thinks the subject is not given as a natural entity but shapes itself through experience. However, for Blanchot, negativity (or experience) is double-edged. Whereas negativity does shape the world and the humans into cultural forms, it is also faced with the fact that humanity, in the ultimate instance, is not grounded. For Blanchot, the negative does not have a spiritual content. As he writes in *The Writing of the Disaster*, "If spirit is always active, then patience is already nonspirit" (Blanchot 1995b, 40). The negative is rather the void that haunts any truth, any experience, as well as the human condition. Hence, in the process that gives it its shape, the subject undergoes its own void. The condition of possibility of the subject is also its condition of impossibility, its "incondition." The negative works (*œuvre*) and unworks (*désœuvre*). Subjects are the fruits of their works, of their experiences, and of their actions in the world. However, they are also confronted by an absence of meaning, by a void that dwells in these very works; by a form of unworking or inoperativity (*désœuvrement*) that threatens the subject's very condition of possibility. Therefore, what allows the subject to be self-aware and thus free is also what exposes it to what cannot be negated or overcome. It is what exposes it to the very void that dwells within it. What allows the subject to be at home, in the cultural forms it produces, is also what exposes it to a foreignness that is its own impossibility of being. It is what prevents it from being within itself as an autonomous subject, and, in consequence, to be still, to take place. It is hence what exposes the subject to what Blanchot calls the Outside (le Dehors); namely, not what is opposed to the interior, but what prevents any possible interiority, any possibility of being at home. In its ultimate instance, negativity leads to an irreducible wandering (*errance*) in which the subject is no longer an interiorized "I," master of itself. Destituted of the possibility of an interiority in which it feels at home, the subject is made anonymous, impersonal. In Blanchot, it is as in Freud, the unconscious that is foreign to consciousness in a duality that can eventually be overcome or at least be reflected on through analysis. Rather, foreignness dwells in consciousness, in the individuated subject: In the "I" dwells an "it" (*il*) that disarms the very possibility of the subject. In the determined individual dwells the anonymous. In the constituted human dwells what is no longer human. As *constituted*, the subject suffers its own loss. Blanchot's subject undergoes a loss of which it is innocent in that there is precisely no self-founded subject to account for it. Here, consequently, it is not innocence that is lost in order to acquire consciousness, as when Blanchot writes that there is a "loss of innocence that is itself innocent" (1992, 104). It is, on the contrary, consciousness that undergoes its own loss, a loss that is surely "itself innocent" since there is no subject to account for it.

It is very important to highlight that in Blanchot the subject is neither overcome nor destroyed, but doubled or confronted by the shadow of its loss. By contrast, considering that Blanchot merely assumes the "death of the subject" could lead to a merely dialectical understanding of Blanchot, where the subject is simply overcome by its negativity. However, in Blanchot, the void is the void of the subject, and there is no void without the subject's constitution. This has an important consequence since it means that instead of progressing toward maturity or self-comprehension, the subject faces his own enigma. He faces what he loses in order to *be* a subject. In this sense, this void that dwells in the subject and that puts it radically into question, as the ordeal of its historical condition, allows for the thinking that innocence is not an original condition from which one falls or departs, but that *innocence is a fall and even an endless fall.* If consciousness contains a void that leads to wandering rather than to a fully determined action, then one is doomed to innocence as the ordeal of the impossibility of awareness. Innocence is the void that haunts the subject. It is not what precedes the subject but what is concomitant to its beginning and that becomes more and more haunting during the process of awareness's history. Because it is concomitant with the unfolding of consciousness, innocence would be the destiny of the subject's history.[14] It is a fall that doubles the history of its mastery. The fall of innocence is history's inherent destiny and the reversal of any awareness (and of any *where*ness).[15] Rather than the entry into history, innocence is its fate. Better said: it is the fate inherent to our historical condition. But if innocence is an incondition rather than an original state, if innocence is a fall that entails the collapse of the subject's autonomy and not what the subject negates in order to become such; if, moreover, innocence is a fate that doubles the subject's history rather than an original condition from which the subject departs in order to constitute itself as historical, then is humanity trapped in irresponsibility and ahistoricity? Does the fact that innocence is before (in front of) the human rather than behind it mean that humanity is bound to the silence and immobility of innocence?

This nesting between the topics of innocence and the fall merits here a parenthesis on questions of the fall, innocence, and history such as elaborated in the Christian tradition and its philosophical legacy.

The topic of the fall is in fact a consequence of a Christian reading of *Genesis*. Now, it is interesting to observe that in a Christian perspective, the fall does not mean a declining movement from a spiritual life to a material one, such as described, for instance, in Plato's account of the relation between soul and body, where the body is a mere weight or tomb. On the contrary, Adam, the first man, or the first human being, is made of mud. Hence, the fall cannot relate to the mere materiality of the flesh. Rather, in a Christian reading of *Genesis*, the fall coincides with a relation to finitude and hence with a new experience of the flesh. More precisely, it coincides with an experience of the materiality of the body *as flesh*; namely, as vulnerable, as constituted by the possibility of temptation. God's warning in paradise is that if Adam, the first man, eats the prohibited fruit, he will die. As we read in the Douay Rheims Bible:

> And he commanded him, saying: Of every tree of paradise thou shalt eat: But of the tree of knowledge of good and evil, thou shalt not eat. For in what day soever thou shalt eat of it, thou shalt die the death. (Genesis 2:16–17)

It's worth noting that this warning doesn't mean that after eating the prohibited fruit, Adam will *be dead*, once and for all deprived of life. As emphasized by Augustine in *The City of God*, if Adam eats the prohibited fruit, he will not be dead, he will "die the death" (Augustine 1952, 304). This means that life will no longer feel its plenitude by union to the creation but that it will be crossed by death. Whereas the tree of life feeds Adam and Eve and maintains their connection to God's creation in its wholeness, the tree of knowledge disconnects life from the condition that grants this plenitude. Hence, *the fall means entering the time of death*; it means that life is no longer nourished. It means that life experiences itself as precarious. In this sense, to fall into disgrace means to experience life as separated from what connects it to the creation: it coincides with an exposition to life's fragility. Indeed, after eating the prohibited fruit, Adam's and Eve's eyes become opened to their nakedness (Genesis 3:7). They experience themselves as exposed, as finite. They are not only severed from the tree of life, but also exposed to the uncertainty of human will. To fall into disgrace is to experience the shivering of the flesh and of life's uncertainty. The tree of the knowledge of Good and Evil doesn't provide a theoretic knowledge but an existential one. It entails the shivering of the flesh that experiences finitude and is hence vulnerable. In this way, to fall entails an opening rather than a mere decline or a physical attraction toward the earth, as if the body were a dead weight. Indeed, in a Christian perspective, the fall is not due to the weight of the body but to a way of experiencing existence—the will and the way it dwells in the flesh—as finite. In this sense, Christianity is not the rejection of the flesh but its adventure, its adventure as fragile, or—said in Hegelian terms—its adventure as spiritual.[16]

Both Hegel and Blanchot could be two interpreters of this idea that the fall coincides with the entering of death into life. On the one hand, Hegel is close to the Christian idea that the fall is the entering of death into the world. For Hegel, death is the negativity that allows all becoming. If in paradise Adam and Eve are good in the sense that they can't be tempted, by the fall they can *become good*. By the same token, if paradise is the time of eternity, of a life that is continually nourished, by death life can *become immortal*, thus overcoming its own negativity, its finitude. Hence, the fall in Hegel is indeed a necessary condition for the human being's spiritual life. As Hegel says in his *Lectures on the Philosophy of Religion*: "It is said that human beings in Paradise and without sin would be immortal; they would be able to live forever. . . . On the other hand, however, it is also said that human beings will become immortal for the first time when they have eaten of the tree of life" (Hegel 2007b, 303). There is an immortality that can only be talked about as mythical (as when Hegel says "it is said") and another one that is the very work of knowledge and that hence coincides with the human's spiritual condition. This one, according to Hegel, can be factually described: "The fact of the matter is that humanity is immortal only through cognitive knowledge; for only in the activity of thinking is its soul pure and free rather than mortal and animal like" (304). Indeed, for Hegel the only true immortality is the one granted by the fall and by the history it makes possible, for this immortality is spiritual and not only animal. It is given to knowledge and as its own history.

On the other hand, Blanchot also shares this Christian pattern that the fall is concomitant to the introduction of death into life. *The Step Not Beyond* could in fact be a commentary of the thirtieth book of Saint Augustine's *The City of God*. As Blanchot says in *The Step Not Beyond*, and which Augustine beautifully explicates as a commentary on *Genesis*, death is not a mere end; it is concomitant to life. In Derrida's words, the fall coincides with a contamination that makes impossible the separation of life from death.[17]

This idea has numerous premises and consequences.

First, death is not merely exterior to life as an outside element. As Blanchot reiterates, citing a proverb (namely, words that seem to carry a truth without origin) rather than its author (who is supposed to give an origin), "as soon as one begins to live, he is old enough to die" (Blanchot 1992, 95). A "proverb" Augustine could easily be referencing in *The City of God*: "Thus, man is never truly 'in life' from the moment that he inhabits this dying rather than living body" (311). However, what matters to both Blanchot and Augustine is that if life is always already marked by death, then we seem to live the dying rather than a life. We dwell in a time out of time, rather than a linear chronology; in Blanchot's words: "Dying—dying in the cold dissolution of the Outside: *always outside oneself as outside of life*" (97, my emphasis).

Second, because we seem to inhabit "the dying" rather than life, death cannot be localized. On this point, Augustine's remark could certainly have inspired Blanchot in *The Step Not Beyond* when the latter speaks about the "unforseeability of death" (96): "For if a man is not 'in death' but is 'after dying' the moment that all life has disappeared, when can we ever say that a man is dead while he is dying?" (96). Indeed, if when death occurs, life has already disappeared—moreover, if we never really inhabit life but the "dying"—then death cannot be localized ontologically. But if death cannot be localized, then how is it possible to unify the different moments of time? Surprisingly, although Augustine hopes for redemption, for both authors death exists only as a gap that prevents any unification of time. In Augustine's words: "thus in the course of time we look for the present but cannot find it; for the passage from the future to the past is without space" (313); in Blanchot's words: "you die and yet you do not die and yet: thus, in a time without present, the dying that defers speaks to you" (107). In other words: death does not provide a directionality for time, but instead dislocates it. Now, because in Augustine the fall refers to an originary condition of innocence, there is a possible redemption, and hence a directionality to time. However, because in Blanchot the fall is not preceded by innocence, but rather coincides with it, there is no hope for a second Goodness, no hope for salvation, or to become a "second Adam."

If death is concomitant to the fall, and if death coincides with a dislocation of time, then the fall cannot signify the mere entry in a teleological conception of time. Indeed, the fall is neither a mere declining (from the soul to the body) nor a mere elevation (from an animal one to a spiritual one). Whereas *The Step Not Beyond* could be a commentary on the magnificent pages Augustine dedicates to the question of death in book thirteen of *The City of God*, Blanchot, as we have often emphasized—and this will differentiate Blanchot from both Augustine and Hegel—does not consider the fall as secondary regarding innocence, but rather as a fall of innocence. While for Hegel the fall, as being the introduction of death into life (in Augustine's case) and of negativity into the world (in Hegel's case) is the condition of possibility of time and of history, for Blanchot death has always already contaminated life and dislocated any possible unification of time. This preoriginary contamination entails that the negative (death) cannot be overcome. In this way, instead of giving birth to time, the fall of innocence attracts time *out* of time. More precisely, whereas the fall in Hegel entails the work of the negative, the overcoming of a negative condition, in Blanchot the negative is twofold: it works and unworks. It allows the constitution of time and at the same time pulls it toward the void of its foundation. Hence, in Blanchot, by virtue of the constitutive dimension of the fall, which constitutes time, there would also be a "fall of the time," precisely because of the void that constitutes it. As one reads in *The Step Not Beyond*: "there where time would fall, fragile fall, according to this 'outside of time in time' " (Blanchot 1992, 1). In brief, in Hegel and Augustine the fall has a teleological and constitutive dimension. It constitutes the human being into death and hence projects it toward its possible redemption. If the fall is a disgrace by which the human being knows its own propension to evil, by the fall the human being has to *become* good, which is now its responsibility. However, in Blanchot, because the negative is twofold, the fall at once makes possible and impossible the subject as well as history; the fall constitutes time but also attracts it out of time. In a way, the negativity of the fall, the twofold dimension of the negative or of death, is drawn toward innocence, its joyful cry, or its garden:

> All words are adult. Only the space in which they reverberate—a space infinitely empty, like a garden where, even after the children have disappeared, their joyful cries continue to be heard—leads them back toward the perpetual death in which they seem to keep being born. (Blanchot 1992, 19)

Indeed, in Blanchot innocence is a dangerous topic that seems to drive in a mute and atemporal paradise. Our issue should be addressed again: if innocence is not merely surpassed, but threatens the subject and its very temporality, doesn't this fall of innocence entail the destruction of any ethics? Where does Blanchot's inverted Christianity lead?

We can now return to the ethical issues addressed beforehand. Blanchot's important fragments on the question of responsibility in *The Writing of the Disaster*, as well as his correlative and explicit dialogue with Levinas's thought in this particular context, might suggest that Blanchot's thought of the subject amounts to the collapse of any ethics. First, because for Blanchot the "I" contains the specter of the anonymous, responsibility cannot be grounded on subjectivity or unicity, as is the case for Levinas. Hence, Blanchot writes in *The Writing of the Disaster*, "The use of the word 'subjectivity' is as enigmatic as the use of the word 'responsibility'—and more debatable" (27). Second, Blanchot's radicalization of Hegel's idea of negativity does not open to the thinking of a subject constituted by the Other, as is the case in Levinas's thought. Rather, the subject's "own" (or rather improper) otherness might lead to an indifference toward the others and even toward the Other. Whereas for Levinas, as Blanchot reads him, "It is the Other who exposes me to 'unity,' causing me to believe in an irreplaceable singularity, for I feel I cannot fail him," for Blanchot, and precisely because of the radicality of this exposition, "I'm not indispensable; in me, anyone at all is called by the other" (13). This is why for Blanchot I am the "un-unique, always the substitute" (13). The void that dwells in the subject constitutes indeed a threat to any possible ethics. As we read in *The Writing of the Disaster*:

> If responsibility is such that it disengages the me from me, the singular from the individual, the subjective from the subject, unawareness from consciousness and the unconscious, the better to expose me to the nameless passivity, and if responsibility achieves this to such a degree that it is through passivity alone that I can answer to the Infinite demand, then I can certainly call the response responsibility, but only abusively, naming it by its contrary, knowing all along that to acknowledge responsibility for God is only a metaphorical means of annulling responsibility (the burden that weighs upon one as the obligation to assume it), just as, once declared responsible for dying (for all dying), I can no longer appeal to any ethics, any experience, any practice whatever—save that of some counter-living, which is to say an un-practice, or (perhaps) a word of writing. (26)

For Blanchot, instead of constituting the subjectivity of the subject, its unicity, the exposition to the Other exposes one to the very vacuum that constitutes the subject and hence to its impersonal dimension. Whereas for Levinas responsibility is not grounded on the autonomy of the subject but on the way the encounter with the Other provokes its unicity, Blanchot suggests that the encounter with the Other happens as an encounter with the Outside in which the subject can no longer be an "I," or can be an "I" only by an abuse of language. For this reason, the focus put on the Other—as would be the invocation of God—only attests to the fact that there is no "I" to respond and, consequently, that "I can no longer appeal to any ethics," any secure way to ground responsibility.[18]

The discussion between Blanchot and Levinas on the problem of responsibility correlates to the problem of the relation between passivity and subjectivity. For Levinas, the exposure to the Other (*Autrui*) that is constitutive of responsibility is such that it makes the "I" unique because it is an exposure from which I cannot withdraw. Where I am passive, where I am powerless, I am the unique, the unsubstitutable. Passivity in Levinas is not the contrary of activity. It is a "passivity more passive than any passivity" (Levinas 1991, 14); namely, a passivity that *resists* the subject's activity and power and that exposes it as the unique. Passivity is individuating, whereas activity abstracts the subject from the core of its unicity. By the same token, in his early writings, Levinas describes the experience of suffering as individuating.[19] To suffer is the impossibility of being abstracted from oneself. It is an obligation to oneself. This is the reason why it is a moment of individuation. By contrast, for Blanchot, suffering is what empties the subject of all individuality. In suffering, the subject is no longer working. Consequently, it can no longer produce itself as a determined subject. Rather than being an individuating instance, for Blanchot, suffering makes individuality impossible.[20] This radicality in the experience of the passivity of suffering leads Blanchot to revoke the very idea of a fall into guiltiness as what would allow a form of individuation (only an individual can assume guilt). The subject structured by guiltiness, as is the case of the subject of the fall, the subject of the law, supposedly assumes (by an abuse of language, as Blanchot would say) a fault they haven't committed in order to elude the weight of innocence. Adam's well-known fault is the fault of any human being who is made a sinner by the sin of one sole man (Barth 1956). Adam's fault gives birth to humanity *as* structured by guiltiness. The condition of the sinner is the human condition. Now, as previously stated, because the condition of the sinner is subject to law, it gives birth at once to a responsible subject as well as to a subject open to its own history, to its redemption. However, innocence is a fall that exceeds the fall into the condition of sinner (of a vulnerable flesh, or of a finite will.) Innocence *exceeds* (and not precedes) individuation and redemption through guilt:

> Suffering suffers from being innocent: thus it seeks to become guilty in order to lessen. But the passivity in it eludes delinquency. Perfectly passive is suffering, safe from the thought of salvation. (Blanchot 1986, 41)

Indeed, Blanchot's understanding of the subject as dwelling in its own void constitutes a threat to all ethics as well as to a history (be it individual or collective); namely, to a salvation—or, more simply, to any possibility of a change. If innocence is the subject's impossibility, innocence promises not a becoming, but only a form a being stuck in one's own incondition. The fall of innocence that can be thought with Blanchot leads to the collapse of the philosophical subject—the subject of self-awareness, as well as of the Judeo-Christian subject—the subject opened to being rescued from the loss that constitutes it through the history of salvation.

This "disastered"[21] ethics does not, however, mean the end of all ethics. Interestingly, while Blanchot is critical of Levinas's understanding of responsibility and of a conception of ethics and Judaism as subjection to law,[22] his peculiar reading of Hegel gives birth to a new possibility to relate to ethics that proceeds also from a new understanding of Christianity and more precisely of its redemptive pattern. It is this new understanding of Christianity that defines and orients Blanchot's relation to ethics, as well as the way innocence, thought as an endless fall, opens to new ethical perspectives. In other words, while Blanchot's reading of Levinas in *The Writing of the Disaster* leads to an ethical impasse, it is Blanchot's way of reading Hegel that permits opening new perspective on ethics.

Hegel plays a central role in Blanchot, particularly in his early writings. It's the case of *Literature and the Right to Death* and *The Most High*. These two works assume Hegel's logic, but to the point at which it is made impossible. Blanchot assumes the idea that being is dialectical (and not substantial). However, since the negative is double-edged (it makes possible being, but is also its void), then the dialectic of being necessarily interrupts itself: it faces its own void that it cannot overcome. In the work of being dwells its unworking (*désoeuvrement*). Its condition of possibility entails its irreducible interruption—interruption that cannot be dialecticized and hence interrupted. In other words, Blanchot's reading of Hegel opens to being's nonbeing. It exposes the unworking of the work of the negative.

In a certain way, both *Literature and the Right to Death* and *The Most High* put at stake a certain innocence, a sort of Adamic consciousness inseparable from what Blanchot calls "the last man"[23]; namely, a consciousness that cannot be thought in terms of self-awareness but that constitutes awareness's ordeal. Whereas Blanchot recalls that for Hegel innocence is "nonaction" (Blanchot 1995b, 40)—and, in this sense, is nothing or is not—Blanchot puts at stake innocence (in opposition to Hegel) not as being, but, reading Hegel to its ultimate consequence, as the nonbeing of being, as the unworking of the work of the negative. It is interesting to observe that when Blanchot defines, as does Hegel, innocence as "nonaction," he quotes Hegel in order to locate his thought in the impossibility that grounds it. When Blanchot writes, as if it were a quotation: "Hegel: 'Innocence alone is nonaction' (the absence of operation)" (40), not only does he imperfectly quote Hegel, but he also repeats Hegel otherwise.[24] For Hegel, innocence is nonaction in the sense that innocence *is not*, is nothing that can be. For Blanchot, by contrast, *innocence is being as impossible.* It is nonaction in the sense of the unworking. Hence, the quotation of Hegel's understanding of innocence occurs not within Hegel's system, but within its interruption. As Blanchot states, just before quoting Hegel: "The *Aufhebung* turns inoperable, ceases" (40).

Blanchot's thought, either through an analysis of the question of writing or through the actual experience of writing, constitutes both a deepening of Hegel's thought of the negative, and, through this new reading—and experience—of the negative, a new approach to the Christian understanding of the fall: it is a matter of freeing the fall from any idea of "salvation." More precisely, because for Blanchot innocence is not before the fall but is concomitant with it, because innocence is not mere immobility but the unworking (what fails the work of meaning, the ground of the subject, mobility), innocence is "safe from the thought of salvation." It allows no exit, nor any teleology or end. It is henceforth nothing like a safe thought.

Let's see more closely how these two texts—*Literature and the Right to Death* and *The Most High*—through their peculiar elaboration of Hegel's thought allow a new way of staging the question of innocence and, while thinking of innocence not as a past or mythical condition but as an incondition, a new way of relating to this Biblical legacy and its ethical stakes.

In *Literature and the Right to Death*, Blanchot affirms that literature aspires to saying "the presence of things before the word exists" (1995a, 228); that is to say, before Adam's gesture of naming things and making them part of his world.[25] In this same line, for Blanchot "literature is concerned with the reality of things, for their unknown, free and silent existence" (330). Literature is said to be their "innocence and their forbidden existence" (330). However, literature relates to this silence of things through a language that reflects its own void of meaning and that, in such a way, becomes a meaningless thing (328). It is thus through language that a certain Adamic silence can be, if not reached, at least put at stake.[26] It is through history that the ahistoricity of innocence begins to haunt the subject. However, through literature, one is not made aware of innocence as if it could become an object of knowledge (innocence, by definition, escapes knowledge: one ceases to be innocent as soon as they become aware of it). Because literature relates to the void that is constitutive of language, it does not give itself as an object of consciousness. On the contrary, literature, writes Blanchot, is "my consciousness without me" (328). In *Literature and the Right to Death*, Blanchot shows implicitly how literature, because it radicalizes the dialectic of being, does not meet Hegel's Absolute Knowledge, but precisely its failure. It doesn't reach self-consciousness, but rather a "consciousness deprived of self" (328). It doesn't reveal the truth of things, but rather relates to their presence "before the world exists" (328). In following Hegel's dialectic and his dialectic of consciousness, we meet (without properly reaching it) Adam's silence—but we meet it only through the dialectic of consciousness and following its ultimate consequence; namely, its interruption.[27] We meet it only as the silence of "the last man"; namely, of the human being of the "end of history"[28] who copes with the impossibility of this end. In this sense, *there is no original and pure innocence; there is only an impure and secondary one*. Indeed, for Blanchot innocence would rather be the unworking than, as in Hegel, mere or stable "nonaction." Through his reading of Hegel, Blanchot gives a new account of Christianity's perspectives on humanity, an account that is not directed toward its redemption or—to speak here rather in Hegelian terms—to its divinization through its spiritualization. Its development is, on the contrary, a way of relating to its impossible origin, to an innocence that exists only by means of a fall: of its fall or as the failure of human being.

Blanchot's narrative *The Most High* addresses a state in which the transcendence of the law is overcome and where citizens are no longer subject to the law but rather embody it. This narrative again unfolds a Hegelian logic *to its ultimate consequence*, namely, to the point of its interruption. It combines Hegel's conception of freedom in *Elements of the Philosophy of Right* with the topic of the end of history and with the Christian topic of the overcoming of the law by love that Hegel had approached in his early writings (as in *The Spirit of Christianity and its Fate*). For Hegel (as is the case for Paul and for Luther), the exteriority of the law is alienating. Freedom coincides with the overcoming of this exteriority and hence with a form of appropriating the law. However, rather than seeing in the end of history the realization of humanity's freedom, *The Most High* stages this freedom as alienating inasmuch as it is exposed to the void that constitutes it. In *The Most High*, the end of history does not coincide with a promise of redemption or with the accomplishment of freedom. Rather, *The Most High* stages a situation of violence and chaos that recalls what Blanchot, in *Literature and the Right to Death*, described as a "lawless violence" (330), namely, innocence or the existence of things before their entry into the world, before their subjection to the order of meaning. It is thus as though the Christian or Hegelian-Christian overcoming of the exteriority of the law either through the immanence of freedom (as in Hegel's case) or through the immanence of love (as in a Christian context) were staged as impossible, and as if the "end of history" were rather the beginning of a certain innocence—a dangerous (lawless) innocence, and not a paradisiacal one.

These two texts of Blanchot that belong to his early production provide an interesting account of Blanchot's relation to Hegel and, through Hegel, of the relation of Blanchot's thought to Christianity. First, these texts that, according at least to standard nomenclatures, coincide with the literary critic (in the case of *Literature and the Right to Death*) and to literature (in the case of *The Most High*), and because of the way the negative is experienced through language, play to philosophy the same role that philosophy plays to religion in Hegel's thought: namely, they are correlated dialectically and represent moments in the history of consciousness—except for the fact that literature neither overcomes philosophy nor drives it toward a higher degree of consciousness. On the contrary, literature reflects the void that haunts Hegel's dialectic and that leads to the description not of a self-aware consciousness but of a "consciousness deprived of a self." For this reason, although (or, rather, because) these texts belong to literary studies, they are highly philosophical: they deal with the negativity that is constitutive of meaning, consciousness, and truthfulness. Second, by expositing negativity to its ultimate consequence, these texts stage the end of history, and consequently of the Christian idea of salvation as well as the Hegelian idea of Absolute Knowledge as carrying their own interruption and as exposing the void that constitutes them. In this manner, through literature's specific relation to the dialectic of being, the accomplishment of Christianity is undone. What Christianity pretends to overcome (namely, the exteriority of the law) relates to a failure.

These brief approaches to *Literature and the Right to Death* and to *The Most High*, as well as to Blanchot's reading of Levinas in *The Writing of the Disaster*, reveal that Blanchot's "disastered ethic" entails a gesture of deconstruction of Christianity—understanding here by deconstruction not a destruction but, on the contrary, a gesture that relates to the meaning of Christianity, but as its own impossibility, and as impossible to be mastered. It is hence as though Blanchot's writing was the reflection or the specter of Christianity's impossibility. Hence, deconstruction is not a destruction nor an overcoming.[29] Blanchot deconstructs what could be called in a very schematic—and Hegelian and Christian[30]—way the (Jewish) idea of a subjectivity and of a subjection to law (or to the Other) *as well as* the (Christian) idea of an overcoming of law's heterogeneity through love or through freedom, thought in Hegelian terms. However, Blanchot's relation to Hegel (and, through Hegel, to Christianity) reveals that *Christianity's impossibility persists as a rest*: in *The Most High*, as will be developed at length in the first chapter of this book, the overcoming of the law relates to the law's outside, which still acts as a law in that it presents itself as an irreducible rest. Christianity's impossibility is faced with a form of disturbance that could be a resistance to the end of history and even, as we will see in the fourth chapter of this book, an exigency to relate historically to this end. What interests Blanchot *through* literature is neither law (or the unicity or subjectivity that stems from it) nor its overcoming, but its rest. This rest is what puts ethics into crisis ("ethics goes mad," as Blanchot writes) because it is irreducible to any determined law and because it entails the failure of the subject, including the core of its unicity. However, it is still what, because it cannot be reduced, calls for a response. Even though in the failure of Judaism (thought in Paulinian terms) and of Christianity (thought as the overcoming of law), ethics "goes mad," responsibility has to be thought from what makes it impossible. One must "answer for that which escapes responsibility" (Blanchot 1992, 123), as we read in *The Step Not Beyond*.

Following this line, *The Writing of the Disaster* does not merely reject responsibility. It reformulates it according to its impossibility: "the responsibility with which I am charged is not mine and causes me not to be I" (1995b, 357). Whereas there is neither an adequate response (a response adequate to a rule) nor a proper subject that can, in its unicity, be summoned to respond, what there is to do is to give voice to the very failure of the response, as well as to the very failure that calls to respond. In *The Step Not Beyond*, Blanchot gives to this failure the name of the neuter: "In the neuter—the name without name—nothing responds, except the response that fails, that has always just missed responding and missed the response" (1992, 118). In this failure of the law's overcoming, Blanchot is not rejecting ethics. Whereas he is not thinking of an ethics grounded on subjectivity and on the law, nor on an ethics of the law, he is thinking of an ethics of the failed response. Christianity's rest entails, therefore, a complete reformulation of ethics that is neither grounded on a subject nor on the law, and that deals with its own madness or impossibility.

※

Several publications on Blanchot appeared in 2014, many of them related to his political thought, and many of them shedding new light on his so-called conversion from the right wing to the left wing during the period that separates his activity as a journalist in the 1930s and 1940s, and to his activity as a writer, which starts at the end of the 1940s. Among these publications, Jean-Luc Nancy's book *The Disavowed Community* returns to Blanchot's thought on the question of community, and in particular to Blanchot's *The Unavowable Community*, on which Nancy focuses exclusively. One of Nancy's theses is that *The Unavowable Community* contains literally an unavowable argument, one that resists being said and that for this reason remains hidden. For Nancy, the construction of Blanchot's book contains an ambiguity between a left-wing thought that Nancy associates with Blanchot's proximity with Levinas and hence with Judaism and its elaboration of the topic of the law—"the law is the properly Jewish factor," writes Nancy (2016, 64)—and a right-wing thought that Nancy associates with Blanchot's less explicit elaboration of Christian topics, in particular the topic of love or of the heart. It is more, for Nancy, the enigmatic character of Blanchot's book—enigmatic for its simplicity and way of being inconclusive rather than for the complexity of its argument—leaves the last word to what would be a rather right-wing thought rooted in Blanchot's way of staging Christian topics and related to the way the second part of the book, which focuses on the question of the heart, goes beyond the ethical dimension of the law (considered as "the properly Jewish factor").

Albeit most Blanchot scholars had interpreted Blanchot's thought as left-wing, a thought that had given birth to a new way of thinking justice, communism (Iyer 2004), and power, and that was in dialogue with Judaic thought (Fynsk 2013), Nancy (and with him, but for different reasons, other authors such as Surya, Brémondy, and Girard)[31] proposes a different approach to Blanchot's thought and to politics in general. What leads to the necessity to read Blanchot's political thought anew? Why would Blanchot's understanding of Christianity be relevant to understanding not only his political thought but political thought in general?

❧

The first part of the book analyzes the ethical consequences of innocence thought as a fall and of the peculiar reading of Christianity it unfolds. It argues that the topic of writing in Blanchot gives a new focus on the Paulinian problem of law's overcoming—namely, grace—and that innocence understood as the fall of the subject and of time allows for new views on responsibility and on the problem of the Apocalypse. The closing chapter of this book analyzes Blanchot's understanding of Christianity through the lens of the political stakes of Christianity's deconstruction. It argues that finitude, such as Nancy and Blanchot have thought it, constitutes a common thread of thinking of Christianity's deconstruction but also opens onto two different political conceptions of the world and of community. The construction of this book suggests that whereas innocence in Blanchot allows for a reformulation of ethics, brought to the political stage, innocence—and, more particularly, Blanchot's own gesture of deconstruction of Christianity—might indeed contain dangers.

Chapter one explores the relationship between the law, violence, and writing through a confrontation of Maurice Blanchot's thought with Giorgio Agamben's and Jacques Derrida's analyses of the structural violence of the law. The chapter's central concern is whether the violence of the law can be overcome, as Agamben suggests, following a Christian (Paulinian) vein, or if we are bound, if not to endure it passively, at least to enact it, as Derrida suggests, following an idea that law is irreducible. By interrogating Agamben's claim that life can deactivate the violence of the law, and by highlighting how Blanchot challenges Derrida's "double-bind" approach to legal violence, this chapter claims that although Blanchot rejects the idea of an overcoming of law's violence, his notion of writing as "passivity" allows us to conceive of the law as experiencing its own limits by playing its own game. For Blanchot, writing does not overcome the violence of the law; rather, it puts at stake the gratuity of its foundation. In this way, it makes possible a freedom that is not entirely defined by law and that in this sense relates to innocence. Writing affirms innocence precisely where it draws the law into experiencing its own limit, its foundation out of law.

Chapter two focuses on the topic of grace in the way that Blanchot elaborates it enigmatically in *The Step Not Beyond*, namely, not as a "gift of grace," as in Saint Paul, but as a "detour of grace." Through a confrontation of Blanchot's thought of the relation between writing, death, and law with Paul's conception of the relation between law and death, and with Nietzsche's call for "new tablets," this chapter proposes a new elaboration of the relation between grace and justice. Blanchot's thoughts on grace diverge from Paul's idea of a gift of grace that saves from the law in order to redeem humanity. Rather, Blanchot's understanding of grace is related to what fails the human. In this sense, it is closer to Nietzsche's proposal of departing from the land of the human. The "detour of grace" graces what fails the law, not the ones who, through law, are made human. Yet, albeit closer to Nietzsche than to Paul, Blanchot's understanding of grace is not oriented toward a writing of new tablets. The latter would entail a new relation to law, whereas what Blanchot calls "white writing" entails the effacement of law and a departure from the Book. In this frame, grace in Blanchot is articulated to an idea of justice that is not thought as individual righteousness but as hearing what's beneath the human and that requires breaking with the law of the Book.

Chapter three raises the issue of how to define responsibility if innocence is not what we lose in order to become a subject, but what threatens the subject of muteness. First, through a confrontation of Blanchot's thought with Hegel's and Kierkegaard's, this chapter analyzes and radicalizes Hegel's negative understanding of innocence as being nothing since only what is part of self-awareness can be positively determined. It argues that although innocence is nothing, this nothingness has an effect on awareness. Second, this chapter shows that innocence might constitute a threat to an ethics grounded on the idea of an autonomous subject. Third, thought as a failure (and not as an original condition), chapter three argues that innocence constitutes an ethics of the failure of law. In fact, this failure is what silently calls to respond to what is beneath language and meaning.

Chapter four argues that innocence thought as the subject's impossibility amounts to a new thinking of the Apocalypse. Thought not as an original condition, but as the impossibility of the subject, innocence presents itself in the form of an apocalypse that would not arrive as the end of times, the moment of the final judgment, but as the impossibility of time and of any judgment. In this problematic frame, the issue raised in chapter four is how to think time and history where innocence, conceived as what leads the autonomous subject to its collapse, prevents any form of assumption of oneself, and hence of change. Taking into consideration the way literary writing addresses the problem of the end, and through a confrontation of Blanchot's thought with Hegel's and Heidegger's views on history, this chapter argues that Blanchot's writing aims at making historical that which is left out of history. Hence, rather than being caught in an end of time where nothing passes and nothing arrives, Blanchot's writing inverts the relation between time and eternity: eternity doesn't end time but is made transient through writing. In Blanchot, the apocalypse is not the end of times but the temporality of the eternal. However, although Blanchot's writing prevents any form of immobility in an innocence where nothing would occur, this chapter raises the problem of the relation between writing and the question of the world. To write what is left out of history, to interrupt time in order to cause eternity to experience a form of temporality, might be a way of losing the world, thought as what requires time and history in order to take shape. If this is true, then Blanchot's ethics might lose the political.

The closing chapter of this book addresses the relation between Blanchot's deconstruction of Christianity and the political. It is centered on a confrontation between Blanchot's and Nancy's thought and seeks to give clues to Nancy's polemical book, *The Disavowed Community*. It first argues that Nancy's and Blanchot's conceptions of the deconstruction of Christianity are based on their understanding of finitude. For Nancy and Blanchot, finitude is infinite and permits the thinking of Christian topics such as eternity, resurrection, and grace in a frame where Christianity merges with an atheism. Secondly, it shows that although finitude is Nancy's and Blanchot's common thread for their thinking of the deconstruction of Christianity, their ideas on death differ in such a way that leads the former to think of death as part of the ontology of being-in-common, and the latter to think of death as an affirmation of a relation that breaks with the world. Hence, Nancy's relation to Christianity is related to his thinking of the world, while Blanchot's Christianity would rather be apocalyptical. Third, this closing chapter analyzes Nancy's political critique of Blanchot's *The Unavowable Community*. It argues that Blanchot's political thought is not anti-democratic as Nancy claims. However, where Blanchot seeks to affirm a radical democracy, he might lose the basis for any democratic thought: language as the possibility of a negotiation and of a plurality of posited voices.

Chapter 1

Law

Whether it is of divine or human origin, whether its function is to ensure order or to transform subjects through singular acts of interpretation, whether it is of the order of the police state that subjugates or of the hermeneutical responsibility that liberates, the law is inseparable from the test of violence. Indeed, as Derrida showed after Schmitt and after Montaigne, the sovereignty of the law stems from its unconditionality. The law has the *force* of law only if we cannot retrace its origin, nor explain to ourselves its ultimate foundation. Otherwise, if the law were to become fully explicable, it would become "human, all too human" (alluding to Nietzsche) and would no longer have the force of law. It would no longer impose itself and therefore no longer command respect. Thus, by dint of its very structure, the law is either secret or unjustifiable.

This violence specific to the law corresponds to what Derrida (1992), taking up Pascal, calls "the mystical foundation of authority" and to what Agamben (1998, 49) calls "the pure form of law," which is to say the law as a pure form divested of a signification, a meaning that could be understood. As in Kafka's stories where individuals are accused of an unknown infraction that they're incapable of understanding, the law that is supposed to give shape to reality—to order it and thus to give it meaning—can also expose a whole life to the absurd. Concordantly, in *The Trial*, K. spends his whole life defending himself in a trial whose limits and origin he cannot perceive, until the moment of death—and until he dies without understanding, "like a dog" (Kafka 2000, 953). While Derrida and Agamben agree that violence is peculiar to the law, they disagree on the answer to be given to this violence.

Whereas for the former this violence is impassable and constitutes the test of any juridical decision (Derrida 1992, 23), for the latter the violence of the law must be overcome (Agamben 1998, 57). While for Derrida, the ambivalence of the law is what brings into play, in any juridical decision, a part of the unknown that, without ever assuring us of the fairness of a decision, opens us to the future—to the "*à venir*"[1] (Derrida 1992, 60), for Agamben, the anomy peculiar to the law must be affirmed by subjects who will then no longer be bound to the law, but who will have surpassed it (Agamben 1998, 55). In other words, for Derrida the violence of the law structures our relationship to justice, whereas for Agamben justice consists in overcoming this violence—an overcoming that can take only violent form. For Derrida, the law has no ultimate, determined foundation. To this extent, any juridical decision is exposed to a double-bind: it requires the *simultaneous* application of a rule that pertains to what is known (in that it relates to a tradition) and also the reinvention of the rule by bringing into play the unknown of the law (opening itself to the future, to the *à venir*). For Agamben, by contrast, it is not a question of "negotiating" (1998, 54) with the known, with the rule, but of reclaiming the unknown force of the law—that is, of surpassing the order of the known by the unknown. In Agamben's (1998, 55) words, it is a question of making the state of exception not a "rule" (which is imposed on us) but a "task" (which we can fulfill). From Derrida to Agamben, the experience of violence is twofold, one being impure (since it requires negotiation) and always mixed with the violence of the law, and the other (being pure because it claims to free itself from the first). But in what way could there be a violence *free* of the law? Is it not always within a context defined by the law that violence occurs? Furthermore, is not the law that "establishes" violence—whether or not it takes the form of a state of exception in which the legitimacy of law is suspended in favor of the pure anomy—at least what makes it possible to measure violence, to become aware of it, and therefore to answer or acknowledge it? In other words, can we responsibly overcome the violence of the law?

Concerning this problem, Blanchot has indeed a singular position. On the one hand, as with Derrida and Agamben, for Blanchot reflecting on the law amounts to a thinking of the void or of the unknown that constitutes it. Yet, for Blanchot, the anomic nature of the law derives from the void that haunts language, from the fact that the foundation of meaning is haunted by its very collapse (1992, 97). In Blanchot's case, the unknown is therefore a test (*épreuve*) or the impossible experience of what is known. Knowledge is the ordeal of its very impossibility: the unknown is not exterior to knowledge, but stems from it. Thus, the strength of the law lies in its weakness. The law does not *only* expose us to a double-bind, to a decision that requires us to articulate the conditional and the unconditional. The weakness of the law, the void that haunts language, is, on the contrary, what draws us to the outside of the law, to the point of prohibiting the law to itself and making the moment of the decision impossible.[2] Thus, in *The Step Not Beyond*, Blanchot (1992, 95) refers to a "prohibited mocking of the prohibition" ("*l'interdit se riant de l'interdiction*"), which is to say a law that comes about only through self-derision. Rather than requiring a sovereign act, the law leads instead to what undermines sovereignty but does not necessarily characterize a just experience, an experience that overcomes the violence of the law. In other words, if the double-bind is for Derrida a test of the impossible, the weakness of the law for Blanchot does not constitute an overcoming of the impossible in the possible, but a subsequent ordeal of the impossible.[3] On the other hand, unlike Agamben, we do not find in Blanchot the idea of consuming or exceeding the law. To the extent that the weakness of the law is what bars it from posing as such ("the prohibited laughing at the prohibition"), the law for Blanchot can neither be fulfilled nor surpassed. Moreover, the Blanchotian idea of the "end of History" and the role that this motif plays in his literary narratives confirm this idea. Indeed, by situating his reflection at what he calls "the end of History" (i.e., not only the end of ideologies that arise as metaphysical meanings, but also the advent of a society that has overcome its contradictions and that, by so doing, has freed itself from the exteriority of the law), Blanchot shows that any claim to complete the law exposes us to its anomy. There is therefore no overcoming the violence of the law. *Because it is inseparable from the anomy that founds it, the law is, on the contrary, the experience of what does not end.*

How then, in this doubly "disastered" context—that is, of a force that is doubled by weakness and a completion rendered incomplete—can we think about our relationship to the law and the violence that is peculiar to it? By exposing the juridical decision to the impossible test of the impossible—that is, to the anomy as weakness and not as a strength—and by showing that the law, by virtue of the anomy that "establishes it," cannot be fulfilled, does Blanchot confront us with the inevitable violence of the law in an even more radical way than Derrida and Agamben have done? Or, by addressing the question of the law through language and the question of literature that makes of it a singular test, does Blanchot lead us to the experience of another test of the law and its violence?[4]

In a preliminary note to *The Infinite Conversation*, after placing the question of writing in the context of the end of History, where not only social contradictions would be overcome but also where the meaning of History would thus finally be present and the law (of meaning) fully revealed, Blanchot writes:

> Writing thus becomes a terrible responsibility. Invisibly, writing is called upon to undo the discourse in which, however unhappy we believe ourselves to be, we who have it at our disposal remain comfortably installed. From this point of view writing is the greatest violence, for it transgresses the law, every law and also its own. (Blanchot 1993, vii)

This sentence, for the time being enigmatic, allows us to formulate some hypotheses: For Blanchot there is indeed a "combat" to be waged against the violence of the law. It is therefore not a question of remaining in a single double-bind or, worse, in the radicalization of its impossibility. However, this fight remains inherent in the violence of the law. It is through writing, and therefore through a certain experience of language and of law, that it is possible to fight the law. Thus, it is not a question of opposing one violence to another as Agamben does, but of playing one violence against itself.

The Force and the Weakness of the Law

In Blanchot's work and from his early writings, law is not merely one topic among others. Rather, it is at the heart of the question of writing, and, to be more precise, it is related to what makes writing a topic (a topos). It is related to the topicity of writing; to what takes place or is taken out of place with writing. In fact, the question of writing, as Blanchot addresses it, is in many ways related to the twofold aspect of law that has been mentioned previously. Writing is essentially related to law inasmuch as it makes use of language, which is to say a system of meaning that *de-fines* a certain *order* of things: an order or a law. In this sense, writing enacts the law; it is not without relation to what Derrida calls the "force of law." It is through writing that the law can be inscribed, testified, made public, incorporated, and transmitted, as it is through writing that a sentence is ordained. When writing is used to enact the law, its force or its authority is as irrevocable as it is impersonal. Writing has the force of a decree that can be neither effaced nor discussed. But, viewed from another perspective, writing is not the mere application or inscription of a language. In fact, following Derrida once again, writing is not reducible to its alphabetic dimension. Before being a sign and the reproduction of a sign (of a word), writing is related to the very material mold that makes possible any inscription (and therefore the alphabetic writing). In Blanchot's words, before being a visible sign that is given to a reader as something that they can relate to, writing is the act of "[cutting] into a stone or wood" (1993, 422); it is a hole rather than a plain sign. Writing is therefore twofold: it gathers a linguistic dimension and a material one; a comprehensible and therefore visible dimension and an invisible one; a dimension that is part of a history and that contributes to its unfolding and a dimension that is necessarily doomed to forgetfulness. Writing belongs to the order of what is known (and hence ordered: subjected to a law) and to the unknown, to the silence that is subjacent to law's foundation. In this sense, what is called writing is not merely the reproduction of a language but the very traces that make possible any form of transcription. Taken in this broader sense, writing is at the same time within and without the whole defined by law. It indeed has something of the twofold dimension of the law: if, in order to write, one will have had to hollow out a stone as says Blanchot, then any transcribed meaning touches the meaningless dimension of this hole. In Derrida's words, any ideal meaning touches this material gap in order to be stamped, to be constituted and present. In this way, *any meaning produces its abyss*. It produces its impossibility that stems from its very condition of possibility. The materiality of writing therefore relates to this bifid side of the law that places us simultaneously inside and outside of it. Writing embodies meaning as ordered to a principle. It is the very reproduction of law and the exercise of its force, but it embodies this force within the very gap that its traces require in order to be marked, inscribed. Writing happens as a "limit experience," to use an expression that gives its title to the second section of *The Infinite Conversation*. It therefore happens not as a mere subordination to the law, not as the mere exercise of its force, but as an *experience of law in its bifid dimension*.

Blanchot addresses the ambivalent omnipotence of the law most explicitly in what we could call his last novel, *The Most High* (1996).[5] Alongside *Aminabad*, *The Most High* is a work of fiction that is—quite exceptionally, for Blanchot—structured as a story. Unlike his other "fictions," *The Most High* (as well as *Aminabad*) holds to a narrative structure. It has, somehow, a teleological structure, a beginning and an end. This literary aspect is interesting since it allows for the consideration of law as an epochal problem where what is at stake is not History and its different moments or stages, but its dissolution and, hence, the problem of narrating this dissolution. *The Most High* narrates, in fact, how law becomes omnipresent in the context of the end of History, where freedom coincides with the absence of any particular interest and, hence, where there is no longer any contradiction between freedom and obedience to the law. The end of History brings us to the moment when the contradictions are overcome—when law is both suppressed as a separate entity and, for this reason, omnipresent. In this context, the State is not an abstract or separate entity but that which is incarnated by every citizen, each having overcome their own particularity. Hence, the central character of *The Most High* is "anybody" (*un homme quelconque*) named Sorge. The novel's central character is "anybody" (1996, 1) incarnated by a singular man. This reinforces the hypothesis that there is an intimate connection between the topics of the end of History and of the law. Since at the end of History there is no more contradiction between the particular and the universal, between freedom and the State, the novel that unfolds at the end of History can only narrate law's omnipresence, and, in this narration, the narrator cannot be distinguished from his object: law. In other words, where the suppression of the law apparently overcomes the contradiction between the particular and the universal, law is omnipresent. It belongs not to the sovereign but to its dissolution. Sorge is not a particular citizen separated from the officials who enforce the law or from the sovereign of the State. He is, on the contrary, in his anonymity, in his way of being everybody and nobody, "the Most High." He is the immanence of the force of law and, in a way that will have to be described more precisely, the transcendence of citizenship.

In a way, Sorge has something of the twofold aspect of writing mentioned earlier. On the one hand, Sorge is fully conformed to the law. He embodies it to the point that his whole life is devoted to the law. Therefore, law and life coincide,[6] and this coinciding testifies to law's authority: because Sorge's devotion is absolute, because it fills up his whole life, there is no escape from the reach of the law, which is omnipresent by nature. It leaves no gap, no way out, no time to rest from its exigencies. But on the other hand, this inherent omnipresence of the law coincides with its emptiness. As mentioned in the context of the end of History, law is not guaranteed by the State as an exterior entity; it inheres in every citizen's anonymity. However, every citizen embodies the law not because the citizen has internalized its meaning or the details of each prohibition, but because they are predetermined by what constitutes its force (which, as will be seen, is concomitant to its weakness). In *The Most High*, law is never referred to as an ensemble of specific prohibitions. What makes each of us subject to both the law and an official of the law is the faculty of sight: namely, the fact that the light of vision defines both a space of control and a space of participation in such control; a space where one is controlled and a space where one is an agent of this control; a space where things happen and a space where nobody can be said to be out of this stage. It follows that the narrator of *The Most High* (Sorge) relates on different occasions not only the power but also the desperation that brings him his sight, which has the power both to make the law circulate and to create exclusions. While he stipulates that, because sight enlightens public space, it is enough to walk in the street in order to fulfill a duty, Sorge also describes this power of light as a void: "Knowing that anyone was thankful of my sight and that even the one that, on the other side of the barrier, condemned by my sight to isolation and destruction, were thankful to me for it, I couldn't help it, I couldn't bear it: this was deepening a void in my sight."[7] Light is synonymous with the law, with its space and its efficiency. In this sense, everyone's particular sight embodies law—everybody is one of its agents. But while law is nothing other than this light, this equivalence between light and law reveals the law's vacuity. In *The Most High*, law is a power that is exercised *in spite of oneself* ("I couldn't help it," says Sorge); it is therefore equal to an empty passion and, accordingly, to a passion for the void (the void being attractive)[8]. It is exercised passively, and this passivity comes from the impossibility of defining law as an object. It stems from the emptiness of law; from the emptiness that law is. In this sense, as already suggested, Sorge possesses something of the twofold nature of writing. Or, more precisely, thanks to Sorge, the reason why writing has this twofold nature can be explained. If writing can be both essential to the law and essentially transgressive, is this not a consequence of the emptiness of the law? Is it not related to the very nature of the law, which, owing to its emptiness, is everywhere and nowhere; or, more accurately, everywhere *because* nowhere? Is it not therefore because the legitimacy of law is empty, hence illegitimate? Because the frontier between law and its Outside—what is beyond law—is already erased?

It would seem that Blanchot's last novel is, precisely, a progressive description of the erasure of this frontier between law and its Outside. In fact, Sorge is wholly implicated with the law. His entire life is dedicated to the law, but at the same time, his life pulls him beyond the law. From the beginning of the novel, Sorge's illness keeps him away from both public space and public time. Having fallen ill, Sorge cannot go to work, cannot be among others, and cannot participate in the temporal space of the public sphere. In this sense, Sorge's life is as much dedicated to the law as it is isolated from it.[9] And we could even think that that which devotes him to the law is what makes him out of law. Sorge's illness, in fact, could be nothing other than Sorge's passion, than his passivity in its way of enforcing the law, of exercising it *in spite of himself*. Although the novel doesn't make this idea explicit, it does make clear not only that Sorge's illegality happens in spite of himself (as with Sorge's devotion to the law), but also that this illness, which progressively becomes part of a general epidemic, is what distinguishes him—not as the particular opposed to the universal, but as the "Most High," as the one who is untouchable, unnamable.[10] Sorge's illness relates in fact not to some sublime figuration of horror but to the *unlimited* aspect of suffering and of isolation. Moreover, illness is the experience of a passivity that breaks down the subject's powers and thus leads to an experience of the anonymous individual in the extreme. In other words, in *The Most High*, the force of the law coincides with its weakness:[11] legality is revealed to be outside the law. While the novel is still a tale of the erasure of these frontiers, it arrives at the point where the novel must cease, because in the absence of any frontier there is no longer a limit, no longer an end. Therefore, it is not by chance that Blanchot's last novel has for its central topic the coinciding of the law and its reversal, of the Most High and the plague. Indeed, on the back cover of *The Most High*, Blanchot writes:

> The Most High can be only his own negation. In a perfect society, where the plague is declared in a way that the plague-stricken become the only rebels, where aid puts in danger the supreme law, the Most High, beyond all divinity, is only a sick person that dies without dying, unless he becomes the "Thing" itself, the terrifying nothing, the truth that misleads and that is mistaken, the ultimate word which ultimately can only be heard by immortal death.

Hence, located at the end of History, *The Most High* shows that where law is supposedly overcome in its transcendence, where law is not embodied in determined rules but in every citizen as anonymous—as void characters attracted by the void—law is all the more sovereign. Said in Agambenian terms (although deviating from their arguments), the realization of the state of exception cannot give birth to any accomplishment of justice because it doesn't save from the force of law. Rather, it exposes the violence of its weakness. Said in Derridian terms, law's void is not necessarily a promise of the future (the *à venir*) because it makes impossible any decision, any awareness. It defines our being stuck in an endless end. Indeed, Blanchot's idea of law as an attractive void seems incompatible with any idea of justice, be it the justice that requires "infinite negotiations," as is the case in Derrida's thought, or the justice that requires a confrontation with the force of law, as is the case in Agamben's thought. However, although Blanchot's conception of the end of History seems reluctant to think in terms of Messianic time, it highlights the danger of Messianism when, as is the case in Agamben's thought, it stems not from a hope beyond reason but from its own realization. In such a case, the realization of the state of exception, the belief that the affirmation of law's void can indeed bring about justice, exposes the risk of a violence that is no longer limited by law—hence, to a violence that, deprived of limits, of frames, also precludes the possibility of naming it, and hence of fighting it.

> The messianic hope—hope which is dread as well—is inevitable when history appears politically only as an arbitrary hubbub, a process deprived of meaning or direction. But if political thinking becomes messianic in its turn, this confusion, which removes the seriousness from the search of reason (intelligibility) in history—and also from the requirements of messianic thought (the realization of morality)—simply attest to a time so frightful, so dangerous, that any recourse appears justified: can one maintain any distance at all when Auschwitz happens? How is it possible to say: Auschwitz has happened? (Blanchot 1995b, 143)

"The Prohibited Laughing at the Prohibition"

The Blanchotian treatment of the "end of History" shows that there is no completion of the law. The (Hegelian-Christian) surpassing of the law is, quite to the contrary, the moment when the law proves to be unsurpassable, omnipresent.[12] The society described in *The Most High* is a one that accomplishes the law only by exposing itself to the violence of its anomy, which prevents any form of interpretation of the law. In *The Most High* it is both the Derridean double-bind and the Agambenian consuming that are exposed to their impossibility. The realization of the state of exception to which Agamben refers—and which can be called, according to Lorenzo Fabbri, the "exception to the exception"[13]—is therefore not a solution to the violence of the law. Does this mean that we are destined for such violence in a definitive and hopeless way? Instead of making justice and freedom possible, would the structure of the law—its constituent anomy—only reveal (as in *The Most High*) unlimited injustice and alienation?

Whereas the Derridean double-bind risks confinement in the undecidable, and thus in the violence of the law, Agamben's proposed solution to the violence of the law raises problems on at least two levels. First, it is problematic from a theoretical point of view. By acting as if there could be an "exception to the exception" (i.e., a realization of the state of exception that excepts us from the exceptional, from the exceptional dimension of sovereignty), Agamben acts as if we could exist independently of the law, as if we were not constituted *by* the law, which is also to say, by language. In the wake of Benjamin, and by a rather mysterious gesture, Agamben proposes to overthrow the law and its mortality (its exposure to "bare life," without rights) by what seems to be an affirmation of a life free of the law, which would thus be able to complete the law. Indeed, in *Homo Sacer*, Agamben affirms:

> Law that becomes indistinguishable from life in a real state of exception is confronted by life that, in a symmetrical but inverse gesture, is entirely transformed into law. The absolute intelligibility of a life wholly resolved into writing corresponds to the impenetrability of a writing that, having become indecipherable, now appears as life. Only at this point do the two terms distinguished and kept united by the relation of ban (bare life and the form of law) abolish each other and enter into a new dimension. (1998, 55)

By a gesture that is both mysterious and dialectical, Agamben seems to affirm that it is possible to reverse the relationship between the law and life.[14] While under the law life is reduced to its nakedness and is finally exposed without rights—as happens in the concentration camp situation—once the state of exception is realized and thus the sovereignty of the law is surpassed (Fabbri's "exception to the exception"), life is affirmed independently of the law. Yet, as Agamben himself has shown, the law is not an entity independent of human beings and external to their lives. But if Agamben has shown the intricate relationship between the law and life,[15] his idea of an "exception to the exception" still relies on the Christian presupposition of a possible life outside the law.[16] However, this idea of a pure life, of a life free of the law, is problematic. Unlike Christianity, which accepts the idea of a life absolved from the law and therefore from death,[17] Jewish hermeneutics, and in particular the Levinassian conception of language, shows for example that language (and therefore the law) constitutes a "breath of life." As Levinas writes in the form of a question in *Otherwise than Being, or Beyond Essence*: "Isn't man the living being capable of the longest breath in inspiration without stopping and in expiration, without return?" (1998, 182). For Levinas, the Other is the one who opens me to language insofar as they are the one who literally inspire me (and thus give me the breath). Hence, for Levinas, the breath of life is inseparable from language and therefore from the law. In this context, the law does not determine life negatively, as bare life, life *exclusively* without rights; it is also what characterizes life as created; that is, as bearing the mark of the Other who carries it beyond itself, beyond its own limits.[18] Because language contains a part of the unknown, language is not only what normalizes existence, but also what animates it, what links it to "elsewhere" and thus constitutes the openness of the living.[19] It follows that life is never "pure" of language, of the law, and of the mortality it means for the living.[20] Moreover, as Derrida and Blanchot have clearly shown, life is inseparable from finitude.[21] It occurs only through the finitude that haunts it. Life is therefore separated from itself: this is its law. The idea of overthrowing the law with life, on the pretext that the law has total control over life, does not hold because it presupposes an untenable separation between the law and life. Furthermore, it is not tenable from a critical point of view: is it not precisely *because* of our relationship to the law and language that we can think of the violence of the law and of language? Agamben thus acts as if life were independent of death, of finitude; as if we are not created beings, bearing the mark of the Other (of the law, of others, of finitude) for which we are accountable.

Second, and consequently, the Agambenian idea of an "exception to the exception" is problematic not only from a theoretical point of view, but also from a practical perspective. Indeed, to free oneself from the law as an empty form, to free oneself from language and finitude, is to free oneself from the common and from freedom. As Nancy and Blanchot clearly show in works predating the publication of *Homo Sacer* (and which did not fail to interest Agamben),[22] to the extent that finitude constitutes life in incompletion (according to the idea of an "infinite finitude," to quote

Nancy), it is the heart of our openness to the common.[23] The fact that life is always already inhabited by language, the law, and death, is clearly the indicator that we exist in common, that we are constitutively open to each other. Furthermore, the fact that the experience of the law is also that of an anomy also constitutes the test of freedom. The anomy or absence of meaning that haunts meaning is what summons us to decide freely, without submitting ourselves to a preexisting norm. The constitutive anomy of the law is in this sense what calls us to be creators of meaning. Following the Levinassian schema, one could even say that anomy is what articulates freedom with responsibility: it is because we are constitutively affected by the absence of meaning (law's anomy) that we are free of meaning. We are creators of meaning in the same measure that we must respond to a meaning that is absent. This is our responsibility and also our hermeneutical vitality.[24]

Thus, to free oneself from the law by the idea of a *pure* life is to free oneself from politics *and* from ethics: from the common, from freedom, and from responsibility. The problem is that Agamben is looking for a solution to the aporia of the law instead of holding open its level of problematicity. In this, as we have already suggested, the Agambenian solution (which is quite mysterious) resembles the Christian solution on the wake of what Saint Paul had also described as the necessity to overcome the violence of the law;[25] namely, the idea of a community of individuals freed from the law by grace and thus freed from finitude. This solution, because it is a solution, is problematic: freed from finitude, are we still in common? Do we still have to answer to each other? Are we still alive?

In view of this problem posed by the idea of a reversal of the law by life—and of the violence of the law by the violence of life—the Blanchotian idea of writing and the type of trace it constitutes can open a path that Derrida most certainly opened but did not pursue in the same direction. Indeed, for Blanchot, as for Derrida, writing is not a simple transcription of language. It is, on the contrary, the test of meaninglessness. For Blanchot, writing is rather the test of what thwarts the work of meaning. In this sense, it is the paradoxical test of the collapse of language. Thus, writing consists in a *confrontation* with language once it is not a full form—to speak here in Agamben's language—that is, the reverse side of an empty form, without signification. Now, if language is not a full form, a pure meaningful content, it is not because there is a secret or a mystery outside of it. What empties language of meaning is, in a sense, also what constitutes it. In this respect, Blanchot references Hegel for thinking of the void of language (and hence of the law). Following this line, Blanchot pushes the question of the negative in Hegel to the consequence of its extreme. If meaning is the test of the negative—that is, of death at work—then at the origin of meaning there is death, nothingness. The characteristic of literature is to reflect the negative insofar as it does not work, as "unemployed negativity," in the words of Bataille (1998). In this way, what doubles the life of the spirit as a ghost is death, but an a-spiritual death, an unemployed death, a "cadaveric death," says Blanchot in *The Work of Fire*. Life is born in the wake of death, but from a death that is not an *end*; from a death that does not rise in a sense; from a death that (just as the corpse exposes us to the irreducibility of absence, to the presence of absence) does not pass; from a death that is the "impossibility to die," as Blanchot writes repeatedly. Reflecting law through language, literature, and writing allows the test of Agamben's understanding of the relationship between life and law by what Blanchot calls the "*mourir*"—the "to die." Instead of opposing life and law, Blanchot observes that law gives itself as its own impossibility, as the "to die."

Whereas Agamben proposes through life to overthrow the law and its violence (and by extension its mortality), Blanchot situates us in the place where life is inseparable from death. Whereas Derrida thinks of the double-bind as the articulation of the known and the unknown, of laws as we inherit them and of the singularity of each case, calling for a new interpretation of these laws (therefore of this heritage, of this past), Blanchot situates us in the place where language itself—by which reality takes shape and becomes known—becomes a test of the unknown, of the nothingness of meaning that constitutes it. Now, this does not only mean a blocking of the Agambenian "solution" and the Derridean aporia; it also entails a struggle. As has been tacitly emphasized, to the extent that writing is a test of that which defeats language, writing is a *confrontation* with the law from the void that haunts it. Without being an activity (since what defeats language is indeed the ordeal of a "passivity more passive than any passivity"), writing does take on a certain "combat"—to use a word that Blanchot borrows from Kafka—toward the law. Hence, the interest of Blanchot's position is that this is indeed a struggle that is thought of *from* the test of passivity that the anomy of the law exposes; from the inseparability of life and the law; that is, not from the idea of a pure life, but from what Blanchot calls the "to die." Thus, in *The Writing of the Disaster*, Blanchot refers to a "combat of the disaster," or a "combat of passivity" (1995b, 140). But if there is indeed, within this "passivity more passive than any passivity" a kind of fight, what exactly is the horizon of such a fight? Can a "combat of passivity" really constitute an opening toward what could be locked in a double-bind? By asserting only passivity, do we not finally get caught in the trap of anomy?

The Outlaw Writing of the Law

The many fragments of *The Step Not Beyond* centered around the question of the law show that the characteristic of the law is, paradoxically, to "forbid" itself. Indeed, even though the law is supposed to *set limits* and thus to make possible an orderly society, the very void that founds it makes these limits unstable. To guarantee order, the law establishes differences: it separates good citizens from criminals, daytime activity (legal) from nighttime activity (illegal), the living from the dead (relegated to cemeteries at the margins of the cities). However, because the basis of the law is illegitimate, its own borders are unstable. Thus, in *The Step Not Beyond*, Blanchot distinguishes between two types of transgression. One is to cross a line. This type of transgression is part of the law, within the legal framework it defines. Breaking the law also means confirming it. A criminal who violates a prohibition acts in collusion with the law. From this point of view, to quote Saint Paul, the law calls for transgression.[26] To violate it is therefore always to play the game of the law. The transgression cannot liberate from its authority. The other is a transgression that relates to the inherent emptiness of the law, to what, in this way, goes beyond the limit. In this respect, Blanchot's narrative entitled *The Madness of the Day* shows that the law not only stimulates distinct forms of sexuality by stipulating different sexual prohibitions, but the law is itself a sexual or rather erotic object insofar as it always escapes. Thus, in *The Madness of the Day*, the law is presented as a knee that one would be tempted to touch (Blanchot 1981, 16). Now, the image of the knee may indicate that the law is nothing more than "a nothing" (*un rien*) that attracts. In this second case, the law prohibits itself because it escapes from that which is part of a limit. It escapes the night as well as the day. It is part of what Blanchot calls "the neuter," which is not a neutralization of differences (a neutral position), but what makes them impossible and thus exposes the violence outside the law.[27] In this second case, the violation does not confirm the law. As we read in *The Step Not Beyond*: "Transgression doesn't transgress the law, it carries it away with it" (1992, 100). Although, as we can see, this second scenario is dangerous, it can also facilitate an experience of freedom that does not confirm the law.[28] In this second aspect of the transgression, it is not a question of playing the game of the law, of confirming its authority, but of *making the law play its own game*.

If, as we noted earlier, the theme of law is omnipresent in Blanchot's work, it is not only as a theme, as an object of thought, but also as what is concretely at stake in the very act of writing. Indeed, we can consider that Blanchot's entire writing is a way of making the law play its own game. In this sense, it follows entirely in the wake of the "combat." On the one hand, as Derrida clearly shows in *The Law of Genre* (2011), Blanchot's writing plays with the genre's own boundaries; that is, with the limits that the law is supposed to define. On this subject, *The Madness of the Day* is not only a narrative about the law, but also a narrative that brings into play the law of the narrative and exposes the narrative to the impossible.[29] In this way, writing *frees* from the limits the law imposes. This freeing does not negate law. In such a case, it would be tributary to what it negates. Rather, it puts at stakes what "prohibits the law to itself." Hence, it does not rely on an external term, as Agamben proposes. It makes the emptiness of the law the experience of what takes us beyond the law, but without freeing us from it (or without claiming to overcome it). In this sense, as Derrida shows very well, *The Step Not Beyond* does not take us into a beyond, as if a liberation were possible (2011, 33). Fragmentary writing proceeds on the contrary from what cannot be confined within a limit, from what cannot be consumed—from what Blanchot calls the "crossing of the uncrossable"—and opens onto the infinite. The fragmentary is in this sense the very spacing of the Outside. As Leslie Hill has shown effectively in *Maurice Blanchot and Fragmentary Writing*,[30] the fragmentary is not a unit closed onto itself, understood *from* the law. Rather, it is the writing of that which infinitely carries the law away and which, insofar as it constitutes an infinite ordeal, remains unfulfilled. The "combat of passivity" is then the affirmation of what Blanchot calls the "*entre-dire*" (the inter-diction):[31] of what separates the law from itself, of its power of unification, and therefore of control. This separation corresponds to the affirmation of the common as well as to freedom. The "combat of passivity" is a writing that *enter-tains* (as in the French word "entre-tient") itself—infinitely—with what resists the one, what constitutively defeats the law; what is therefore without hierarchy but also without possible finalization. Thus, *The Infinite Conversation* (which, at this stage, should be translated as *The Infinite Entertainment*[32]) "concludes" as follows: "The law is the summit, there is no other. Writing remains outside the arbitration between top and bottom" (Blanchot 1969, 636).

Let us return to the definition of writing found in the preliminary note of *The Infinite Conversation*:

> Invisibly, writing is called upon to undo the discourse in which, however unfortunate we believe ourselves to be, we who have it at our disposal, remain comfortably installed. From this point of view writing is the greatest violence, because it transgresses the law, every law and its own law. (viii)

Unlike Derrida, Blanchot does not think of the relationship to the law solely in terms of the double-bind because, by following the thread of the void that haunts language, the law radically carries itself outside the law, following the—infinite—wake of its own erasure. Unlike Agamben, Blanchot does not think of the relationship to the law in terms of consuming or emancipation because the Outside the law—its weakness—is also its strength, by which it inevitably imposes itself without our being able to understand it, to master it. But Blanchot's position is neither so far from Derrida's nor so far from Agamben's. Instead, it reformulates them in a different way, based on an experience of passivity that is paradoxically part of a combat.

As for Derrida, with Blanchot, we always speak two languages: the language of the law and the language of the void that haunts it. We are therefore in a kind of double-bind, but, as we have seen, in a double-bind radically exposed to passivity, to the outside. It is therefore a double-bind that runs on empty. However, this radicalization of passivity does not lead to a lack of decision, as I initially suggested. On the contrary, considered *from writing*—that is, from the "combat of passivity," that which defeats the subject entails a rupture, and in this sense a "cut" or a de-cision, regarding the order of meaning. Indeed, fragmentary writing is a writing of the cut (*la coupure*). It is a writing of what takes language outside of itself.[33] In *The Infinite Conversation*, Blanchot entitles a subsection of the chapter "Writing and Atheism: Humanism and the Cry," "The Break: Writing Outside Language" (1993, 260). In this writing where the meaning (the law) constantly forbids itself, what speaks is the other of the One (of the law or of language). Thus, all Blanchot's writing is *an out-law writing of the law*. It is the writing of what carries the law out of itself, without going beyond it. It is a writing of the enter-tainment (*l'entre-tien*), of what has always shared (or divided) the One. In this sense, it is the "combat of passivity"—a fight that is not *against* the law (this "against" only confirms it), but *for* the other, for what bans the law to itself, for the impossible, which is not so much its foundation as its threat. As we read at the beginning of *The Infinite Conversation*: "But why two? Why two words to say the same thing? It is because the one who said it is always the other" (1993, ix).

As with Agamben, Blanchot does not stick to a position of subjugation in front of the violence of the law. In this sense, while it is true that Blanchot does not depart from language (and thus stands in a kind of double-bind), neither does he fix himself in the same type of violence as the law exerts. The "combat of passivity" is a fight that seeks to liberate from the subjection proper to the law. However, unlike Agamben, it is not life that opposes itself to the law but what Blanchot calls the "to die" (the indifferentiation of the neuter, the exposure to the void of meaning that establishes meaning) that causes the law to be carried outside of itself—a carrying out (*emportement*) that, as we have seen, is not a consuming. In so doing, Blanchot does not overcome the law by life; he makes the law play its own game by putting into play the finitude (the "to die") that has always contaminated life.

Does this reformulation of the ordeal of the double-bind and the decision and problem of the completion of the law make of Blanchot a kind of new Hegel who synthesizes the impossible: Derrida and Agamben? Is Blanchot a neo-Hegelian who synthesizes what Hegel would have defined the antagonism between law (as irreducible) and its suppression, between Judaism—or law as being the "properly Jewish factor"—and Christianity (characterized, from a Paulinian point of view, as its accomplishment into love)?

With regard to Judaism and Christianity, Blanchot is rather the reverse of Hegel. He starts from what defeats the law and maintains its inaccessibility in what nevertheless bans it from itself. Thus, Blanchot does not keep us in eternal subjection to the law and in a relationship of constitutive guilt (where the law is inaccessible, we are constitutively guilty before it); but neither does he affirm the innocence of life against the constitutive guilt of the law. On the contrary, Blanchot's interest is not in the "innocence of life" (a metaphysical postulate), but in the "innocence of dying" (1992, 127); that is, in what does not succeed in being, in what occurs only by erasing itself and disturbing everything.

But if innocence is about dying—that is, about what prevents us from being our own, if dying is the task of a writing that combats not only the law but also its own law—does this writing not abandon us to the violence of chance that is without law? If the question of writing in Blanchot restores an ethical dimension to transgression by affirming the finitude that is at the heart of life and language, does this writing, which "remains outside the arbitration between top and bottom," constitute a possible political path? Does it not affirm freedom within the same terrorizing framework deployed by *The Most High*?

Chapter 2

Grace

Grace digs sin up by its roots, for it questions the validity of our existence and status. It takes away our breath, ignores us as we are, and treats us as what we are not, as new men.

—Barth, *The Epistle to the Romans*, 190–91

Oh my brothers, your nobility should not look back, but out there! You should be exiles from all fathers—and forefatherlands!

—Nietzsche, *Thus Spoke Zarathustra*, 163

Delving into the relation between law and writing has led to two results that are intertwined. On the one hand, we have seen that there is no overcoming the supremacy of law. Law, at least in a Hegelian (and Christian) perspective, might be fulfilled at the end of History, but this fulfillment still relates to law. It relates to the (decentered) "heart" of its sovereignty; namely, the Outside. On the other hand, the structure of writing, being twofold, allows for playing with law in such a way that law is driven to play its own game. In this game, law's foundation is revealed to itself as empty, with no reason, namely, as gratuitous. Law's sovereignty faces the sovereignty of chance, of that which happens without reason. Hence, the sovereignty of law might not be overcome; its authority happens to merge with the gratuity of a game. In this scenario, if we are (as in Kafka's *Trial*) always already guilty before the law, hence guilty in our very innocence, it is because the sovereignty of law is founded in the innocence of a game.

Since it has no proper foundation or meaning, *law can be fulfilled only by making one guilty of one's own innocence*. Thus, the fulfillment of law amounts not to overcoming it, but rather to discovering its irreducible gratuity. Yet, does this mean that the end of history abandons us to the gratuity of law? Playing law's game might open to a new thought and experience of freedom, but it seems to be incompatible with a demand for justice. How can there be justice where gratuity prevails? There where freedom is related not to others but rather to the Otherness of law, freedom might lead to terror rather than to a demand for Justice. As is the case in Kafka, at least, law's inaccessibility does not guarantee justice (and, in this sense, exposes one to endless violence). However, neither does playing with the law of law guarantee an alternative to its violence.

The ethical impasse resulting from this relation between writing and law leads to further inquiry into the relation between Blanchot's thought and Christianity. Indeed, the way Blanchot follows Hegel's thought of law at the end of History gives rise to a double relation to Christianity. On the one hand, Blanchot remains close to a Christian conception of law in that it is not given as a transcendent instance separated from the human being. Rather, as we have seen in *The Most High*, *law's transcendence is experienced in the paradoxical immanence of the Outside*. In a way, Blanchot adopts the Christian (and Hegelian) idea that divinity is incarnated and that this mediation overcomes the exteriority of the law. On the other hand, the way in which Blanchot thinks literature demonstrates the inoperativity (*désoeuvrement*) of this idea since the void of language does not allow the transcendence of law to be merely overcome. Blanchot's considerations on the ambivalence of literary language show that, in fact, the immanence of law transcends because its void cannot be located. Hence, in *The Most High*, law's immanence gives rise to violence and suspicion rather than to love and freedom. Overcoming law brings about another experience of the force of law that stems from its weakness. Thus, where law transcends and reigns from its very immanence, there is not justice but terror.

This divided relation to Christianity is crucial in Blanchot's thought of grace. He develops the topic explicitly in a series of fragments of *The Step Not Beyond*. There, Blanchot assumes Pauline thought concerning the notions of law and grace but separates it from its principle and consequences. In fact, in Paul's epistle to the Romans, law is associated with death, while grace is understood as a gift that saves from law's mortality. Law is associated with death since "I would not have known what sin was had it not been for the law. For I would not have known what coveting really was if the law had not said, 'You shall not covet'" (Romans 7:7). Because law is exterior to the individual, it marks the individual with a duality. Under the law, the subject is no longer determined by the spirit but now by the flesh. As can be read in *Romans* "For when we were in the flesh, the affections of sins, which were by the law, had force in our members, to bring forth fruit unto death" (7:5). Of course, as Paul says, one might "covet" even when not a subject of law. Although law by itself is spiritual, under the law, "I see another law at work in me, waging war against the law of my mind and making me a prisoner of the law of sin at work within me" (7:14). By contrast, grace redeems humanity from sinfulness in that it transforms human nature. Hence, while law is associated with death because it provokes sinfulness, grace is a gift of life that overcomes the very mortality of law: "The law was brought in so that the trespass might increase. But where sin increased, grace increased all the more" (5:20). Indeed, in *The Step Not Beyond*, Blanchot borrows from Paul the idea that "the law kills" (Blanchot 1992, 25). However, Blanchot speaks of grace not merely as a "gift"[1] that saves from death but also, and more precisely, of a "detour of grace," which, according to Blanchot, entails the love of death.

> The law kills. Death is always the horizon of the law: if you do this, you will die. It kills whoever does not observe it, and to observe it is also already to die, to die to all possibilities, but as its observance is nevertheless—if the law is Law—impossible and, in any case, always uncertain, always unrealized, death remains the unique falling due that only the love of death can turn away, for he who loves death makes the law vain in making it lovable. Such would be the detour of grace. (Blanchot 1992, 25)

Why does Blanchot speak of a "detour of grace" rather than a "gracious gift"? Does this change offer a clue to the ethical impasse with which the necessary void of the law confronted us? Or, again, does it deepen the idea that such a void gives rise only to terror? As Blanchot notes in *The Step Not Beyond*, grace lies between the rigor of law that demands in principle that a just ruling should be justified, and the luck that comes from chance—that is, for no reason. On the one hand, like chance or luck, grace is without explanation:

> Luck is only another word for chance. Good, Bad, it is still luck and, always, good luck. Similarly for grace, which can be

disgrace without renouncing the extreme good grace it owes to its "transcendence." (Blanchot 1992, 26)

On the other hand, grace is an exception with respect to the law that also confirms it. Grace saves from the terrifying decree of law while also confirming the law's transcendence. It is a sovereign gift:

Grace is unjust, an unjustified gift that does not take what is right into consideration, while confirming it nonetheless. (Blanchot, 1992, 24)

And to complicate even further this triangle where law, grace, and chance meet, law—like luck—is anonymous (it concerns everybody in the same way), while grace is always singular:

The law says "in spite of you" [*"malgré toi"*] familiarity that indicates no one. Grace says, "without you, without your being there for anything and in your own absence," but this familiarity which seems to designate only the lack of anyone, restores the intimacy and the singularity of the relation. (25–26)

While law kills because it is the neutral application of a rule that looks at no one in particular, grace restores the singularity of a relation. While "law kills," ignoring its subjects, does grace articulate a demand for justice by restoring "the intimacy and the singularity of the relation"? What does Blanchot call a "detour of grace," and what kind of intimacy or singularity does it put into play?

Grace as War Waged between Life and Death

Unlike the secular and juridical conception of grace, according to which grace consists in making an exception in relation to a judgment that should have been ineluctable, the Christian understanding of grace does more than except a subject from the contingency of a judgment. In fact, as noted previously, from a Christian point of view, grace entails a transformation of human nature. In Paul's epistles, grace refers to a new state of humanity wherein the latter, no longer under the law of the flesh, is now under the law of the spirit[2]—and, hence, no longer *under* the law (as if the law were an external entity) but *beyond* it.[3] Grace saves from the law in that it unifies the human being, which had been split into two by the very prohibitions that led it into temptation. From this view, law is unable to give birth to justice. For Saint Paul, as for revolutionary thinkers, *justice needs a transformation of human nature*. But unlike Marx, for instance, revolution for Paul does not stem from a previous transformation of human and material conditions. Rather, revolution happens by the power of faith, as a "gracious gift," a favor.[4] It is gifted. However, if grace intends to provide justice (the reign of the righteous) by attacking the causes of evil at its very root, do we not run the risk of reaching a state of goodness, through grace, in which we become deaf to the call for justice? Is justice the realm of the "righteous" (δικαίωμα); namely, the realm of "new humans" who are qualified for goodness because they are freed from evil? Or does justice take place in the space of a relation?

The beauty of Pauline thought is indeed rooted in what Marx would have called the "poetry of the future."[5] Paul's message is directed neither to reason nor to belief, but rather to faith. The "message of the cross is foolishness" (1 Cor 1:18), says Paul in the first letter to the Corinthians. In this sense, to use a Foucauldian frame of analysis, Paul's speech breaks with the *episteme* of the time. His message requires a kind of speech that breaks with the Jews' need of signs and with the Greeks' wisdom or rationality. In Paul's view, both postures have in common the fact that they base their convictions on explanation or proofs. This makes their aspiration human rather than divine. According to Paul, the Jews "ask for signs," whereas the Greeks "seek human wisdom" (1 Cor 1:22). By contrast, faith is a relation to the unknown. It does not require arguments or signs. Rather, it transforms the individual. To find grace is to be renewed in such a way that the "new human beings" are divine rather than human. Hence, Paul's letters can only be heard through the novelty of its message, as an unheard-of language, for they are addressed not to present individuals, but rather to those whose faith will transform them radically. Indeed, Paul's message belongs not to mere mortals, but instead to potential new humans. So, if the "message of the cross is foolishness," it cannot be heard by the community of men and women who are merely inhabiting this world; it can only be heard by those who are already a bridge, as Nietzsche would say,[6] and whose senses, breath, and thoughts—at least in their current form—will be taken away. In this sense, Saint Paul's grace is, in a way, equally close to Marx's idea of a "poetry of the future" and to Nietzsche's idea of the transformation of the human being by a call that can make sense only by revolutionizing the senses. As Nietzsche writes in *Thus Spoke Zarathustra*, "Must one first smash their ears so that they learn to hear with their eyes?" (2006, 9). But how can one hear this unheard-of message?

Paul's message, as well as the very idea of grace that he aims at diffusing, is based on the idea of a separation between life and death. As he writes at the beginning of his letter to the Corinthians, "For the word of the cross is folly to those who are perishing, but to us who are being saved it is the power of God" (1 Cor 1:18). Paul's message is foolishness for those who belong to the realm of death. By contrast, it can be heard only by those who are saved from death. In other words, Paul's message is inseparable from the action of grace.[7] The message he transmits is inscribed in the frontier that separates life from death; those "who are perishing" from those who "are being saved." For Paul, this not only means that a meaning is inseparable from an expression, but also that a message has a meaning only in a dynamical process of transformation, in what Karl Barth called "a war of life and death."[8]

To understand this point, let's recall that for Paul, as said previously, grace saves not only from law but also from the mortality of law. In his epistle to the Romans, Paul associates law with death. Law not only provokes death (as in a death sentence); for Paul, because law provokes the temptation to transgress, *death enters the world with law.* Law gives birth to sinfulness and, hence, to mortality. As Paul writes, "Once I was alive apart from the law; but when the commandment came, sin sprang to life *and I died.* I found that the very commandment that was intended to bring life actually brought death" (Romans 7:8–10, my emphasis). The death sentence is not therefore the consequence of the law's authority. It is not one condemnation among others. *To be under the law, subjected to law, to be made a subject through law means to be condemned to death.* Conversely, to be graced is not merely to be excepted from law's jurisdiction but also to be saved from death. Grace is therefore the action of a meaning that withdraws from death. While, still according to Paul, the command of law belongs to the "oldness of the letter" (Romans 7:6), grace entails entering into a lively language, a language of the spirit, as Paul says. Again, "if I speak in the tongues of men or of angels but do not have love, I am only a resounding gong or a clanging cymbal" (1 Cor 13:1). In this sense, law commands but only provokes division within the individual. The command of law belongs to the "oldness of the letter" because it maintains the individual in the realm of death. However, grace is a renewal. To find grace entails a radical—semantic, vital, temporal—rupture with life under law. Hence, Paul's message produces the addressee at the same time that it addresses them. It is a message that exceeds reason and any form of calculation that would aim at securing a belief. It does not impose itself as the tyranny of dogma. Instead, it requires the transformation of the individual who no longer acts and understands as a function of calculation. The language of reason or signs presupposes the division between flesh and spirit. By contrast, grace unifies the individual by them to what exceeds reason. Hence, Paul's message—grace—entails a war waged between life and death in that it is an action and not a mere theology confined to theory. Paul's fight is not with unbelievers. Rather, his message fights the mortality that prevents the action whereby grace renews the human and purifies the human condition of its contagion of death.

In its Christian meaning, indeed, grace names not a mere exception from the decree of law, but rather a transformation within our relation to law that aims at overcoming law's negative effect of dividing the subject. This thought of grace has the folly of a revolutionary aspiration that drives toward the unknown and aspires to a complete (and not merely partial) transformation of the human condition. Driving beyond the law (not in order to negate it, but rather to efface it),[9] grace *frees* individuals from their submission. They are no longer *under* the law or subjected to a commandment that—just as in Kafka's *Penal Colony*—always already condemns them to death independently of their conduct. Excepting from the law, grace is an action of saving; that is, of renewing the individual in such a way that they are no longer subjected to law, to the flesh, and hence to death. The action of grace thus brings about political perspectives; it entails a change in the very idea of "reigning." In grace, the individual is not *under* law. In this sense, they are free. They become righteous not by submitting to the law's commandment but by incorporating its meaning otherwise. In a secular or merely juridical perspective, grace amounts to the sovereignty of law. Grace—understood as an exception—can only be given by a sovereign whose sovereignty entails the power to suspend law. However, *in a Christian perspective, grace modifies the idea of reigning since it aims at creating a community beyond law*.[10] Yet, as I have suggested, from such a perspective grace responds to an idea of freedom rather than justice. If, through grace, new men and women are righteous because they are transformed, do they even hear a call for justice? Can a message that aims at transforming the individual still be heard as a language? Does it still have the exteriority of a language that, like that of law, always comes from elsewhere and might in fact be the condition of possibility of relating to another? In a community of righteous men and women, is there a need for justice? There where men and women are saved from death, there where life can be conceived as separated from death, is there any possibility of relating to any exteriority? Without exteriority, doesn't righteousness simply mean the immanence of the individual to themselves, and hence to their incapacity to reflect on the possibility of evil? Even though new men and women do not exactly coincide with the innocence of Adam,[11] it is uncertain whether their righteousness doesn't confront the same silence that drew Adam into sinfulness without even knowing it.[12]

The folly of grace has indeed the beauty of a revolutionary aspiration, but it entails the risk of deafening the individual.

The "Detour of Grace"

As previously suggested, Blanchot's *The Step Not Beyond* assumes a Pauline understanding of law to the point that the former will also risk an articulation between law and grace. However, in those fragments, Blanchot diverts from the very principle that determined the Pauline understanding of grace as an action that transforms the individual. In this chapter, I will follow the thread of this deviation in order to bring to light the new articulation Blanchot proposes between law and grace, as well as the way the question of writing in Blanchot and its relation to law raises the issue of the risk of deafness under grace.

Following Paul's Logic to Foolishness

In order to understand what is at stake in Blanchot's evocation of law and grace in *The Step Not Beyond*, it might seem necessary to comment line by line upon this long fragment where law and grace appear most directly. However, a linear reading of Blanchot's writing would presume that it follows a progression, which is not the case. Instead, I will first focus on its apparent nucleus in order to discover the fractured logic contained in this fragment, thus making any idea of unity impossible. What could be called the "central" passage of this fragment seems in fact to repeat Paul's argument about the relation between law and death. Blanchot argues not merely that law condemns to death, as if the death sentence were a mere sanction, but rather that "law kills" or that law is "death itself wearing the face of law" (1992, 24–25). Moreover, Blanchot bases his argument on the dialectical relation that exists between law and sinfulness, which Saint Paul had explicitly developed in his letter to the Romans:

> The circle of law is this: there must be a crossing in order for there to be a limit, but only the limit, in as much as uncrossable, summons to cross, affirms the desire (the false step) that has always already, through an unforeseeable movement, crossed the line. The prohibition constitutes itself only by the desire that would desire only in view of the prohibition. (Blanchot 1992, 24)

In this passage, Blanchot is indeed repeating Paul's logic (which, at this stage, is folly neither for believers nor for sages!). If it is true that law is given because there has been a first act of transgression (which led to Adam's fall), it is nevertheless only by law that a transgression can exist *as such*. Conversely, because the prohibition gives birth to transgression, the latter does not free from the former. On the contrary, it confirms it. In these few lines, Blanchot is therefore assuming the idea that law produces division in the subject. For this reason, as in Paul, law not only kills in the sense that it condemns to death: it *is* death. Finitude is correlative to law: it exists with law.[13] However, the repetition of this Pauline logic is immediately subverted not by another logic but by this same logic driven to its ultimate consequences:

> And desire is the prohibition that frees itself in desiring itself, no longer as desire itself forbidden, but as desire (for the) forbidden which takes on the brilliance, the amiability, the *grace* of the desirable, even if it is mortal. (Blanchot 1992, 24)

Whereas transgression confirms the prohibition and is therefore defined negatively, the desire that pushes one to transgress is now not only a desire for the prohibited object, but also for the prohibition itself. In other words, the desire is desire for the limit and not for what is limited by the limit. The negativity of transgression is thus converted into an affirmative movement. Transgression is not a movement that aspires to go beyond a limit, but rather the very experience of this limit.

So far, Blanchot is only unfolding a logic—Paul's logic that, insofar as it is a logic, contains no foolish ideas. However, by thus pushing this logic to extremes, Blanchot now brings us to its foolishness. In fact, the first occurrence of the word *grace* in the passage from the fragment under analysis indicates that for Blanchot, grace is not what drives *beyond* the law: it entails another relation to the law. While for Paul law has the negativity of death, Blanchot describes law as the *positivity* of death by apparently turning Paul's logic on its head. Indeed, if transgression ceases to be negative when experienced as an experience of the limit, if desire is free in the moment in which it is not a desire of the object forbidden, but rather a "desire (for the) forbidden," then law—as death—ceases to be negative the moment in which death is not feared but loved. This passage, a portion of which I've cited above, continues as follows:

> The law reveals itself for what it is: less the command that has death as its sanction, than death itself wearing the face of the law, this death that desire (against the law), far from turning itself away from it, gives itself as its ultimate aim, desiring until death, in order that death, even as death of desire, is still the desired death, that which carries desire, as desire freezes death. The law kills. Death is always the horizon of the law: if you do this, you will die. It kills whoever does not observe it, and to observe it is also already to die, to die to all possibilities, but as its observance is nevertheless—if the law is law—impossible and, in any case, always uncertain, always unrealized, death remains the unique falling due that only the love of death can turn away, for he who loves death makes the law vain in making it lovable. Such would be the detour of grace. (Blanchot 1992, 24–25)

This second part of the passage I am analyzing is amazing since it not only subverts Paul's logic in the very process of unfolding it, but it also subverts the very terms of this logic. In fact, as already noted, Blanchot does not call grace the movement that drives *beyond* law, in a form of fulfillment that also effaces law (or in a form of effacement that fulfills it); rather, he calls grace the desirable, as if grace were a gift given not from the exterior that elevated one beyond the flesh, but were, rather, *another experience of the flesh that happened from within the desire*. By the same token—but through a slightly different gesture on which I will comment later—Blanchot says not merely that law is death (law is "less the command that has death as its sanction") in that the prohibitions split the individual; he *also* says that death is law ("death itself wearing the face of the law"), just as if law were a secondary name given to the inaccessibility and irreducibility of death.

Now, this change in meaning does not happen casually; it is the consequence of the dialectical logic that relates law to transgression. Indeed, Blanchot's thought does not unfold *another* logic, but rather one sole logic split into two. This logic, followed to its ultimate consequences, drives its own terms to their constitutive ambivalence, as if two stories—two Histories—were correlates of one unique thread: one in which grace is a gift that elevates *out* of death's realm, *above* law; another in which grace names an affirmative relation to death; namely, love. Thus, the foolishness of grace is not exterior to law's logic—it stems from what splits that logic into two.

Grace as the Impossibility of Law

Let us interrupt the close reading of this fragment for a moment in order to situate this passage on grace and law within Blanchot's thought more generally.

Blanchot's conception of grace in *The Step Not Beyond* has to be understood in the context of his deconstruction of the border that separates life from death.[14] As we have seen, for Saint Paul, grace is a war waged against death. His thought of grace as the only possible means to fulfill (and efface) law relies completely on a separation between life and death. By contrast, whereas Blanchot does affirm, in Pauline fashion, that "law is less the command that has death as its sanction, than death itself wearing the face of law" (1992, 24), which thereby associates law and death, he also shows that death is impossible *as such*. This impossibility, as we will see, also calls into question the border that separates life from death. Consequently, grace in Blanchot will not be thought of in terms of salvation (from death). The "grace of the desirable" does not define the movement of a return (e.g., to Adam's innocence) or an overcoming (of human's sinfulness through a divine nature) but rather a "detour." This change in orientation throughout Blanchot's deconstruction of the border that separates life from death calls for explication.

For Blanchot, and this is a crucial argument that structures his entire thought and practice of writing (this point will be further developed since it is not without relation to the question of how to *hear* the message concerning grace), death thought of as a limit that separates life from death never occurs as a determined moment *within time*. When "I" die, I am not there to witness my own death. Hence, death is without witness. Nothing true can be said about death. Correlatively, death conceived as a limit or a determined moment is only a construction. Understood as the interruption of life, for instance, death can be certified only afterward, once a heart has ceased to beat, but not within the course of life.[15] If death is an interruption, it cannot be located within the course of time, which refers necessarily to a continuity, to what is measurable. In such a context, to associate law with death, in a gesture that seems to repeat Paul's thinking, *might be a way of rejecting his argument by making it impossible.* Law is associated with death in that law and death are conceived as limits or limiting powers. However, if death cannot be posited as such, then the limit between life and death, as well as the possibility of tracing a limit and of instituting a law, is called into question.

Blanchot expresses this double questioning (of law's possibility and of the separation between life and death) in numerous fragments of *The Step Not Beyond*. On the one hand, if death is impossible as such, then there is no clear limit that can separate life from death. On the contrary, the impossibility of locating and determining death has for a consequence the fact that death is disseminated and, thus, has already contaminated life. Death being impossible to determine in time, its temporality belongs to an "always already" that does not cease because it does not begin. Because death has no place, to live is always already to die. To live is always already exposure to a loss that is immeasurable. As Lacoue Labarthe (2015) says, it is an unending agony. Hence, Blanchot speaks of the infinitive verb "to die" rather than of the substantive noun "death." The infinitive refers to what has not started, does not end, and cannot be correlated to a determined subject. It bespeaks the infinity of that which does not happen in time, of a loss that cannot be correlated to a subject because it happens as the impossibility of being a subject (of death) and thus of appropriating the loss. Correlatively, if life cannot be clearly partitioned from death, then there is no such thing as an appropriated life. Hence, to live is, rather, to survive;[16] that is, to be kept in life "without life" (without a life of one's own that can be properly *delimited*, partitioned, from death). In this sense, Blanchot writes:

> To survive, not to live, or, not living, to maintain oneself, without life, in a state of pure supplement, movement of substitution for life, but rather to arrest dying. (1992, 135)

This co-contamination of life and death, which leads Blanchot to speak not of life as a substantial movement of appropriation (as would be the case in Hegel and Saint Paul) but rather of surviving, and not of death as a determined moment but rather of the impersonality of the "to die" as an " 'inert infinitive'" (1992, 107) of what does not take place in time, has important consequences regarding Blanchot's understanding of Saint Paul's message. More generally, it gives rise to another understanding of the Christian conception of time in derivation from the fall and oriented toward redemption. In Blanchot, the impossibility of death gives birth not to the time of the fall, where time is precisely the sign of a loss of eternity, but rather to a fall *of* time;[17] that is, to a loss of time that, having no end, becomes eternal. Hence, in *The Step Not Beyond*, for instance, Blanchot speaks of a "death of eternity" (1992, 30) or of the "perpetuity of dying" (131). In this way, recalling my description of the fall in the introduction, the fall in Blanchot is not a fall into time; it is a fall of time. Eternity in Blanchot refers not to a plenitude of time, to a fully self-determined present as in Hegel, but rather to the absence of time that the "to die" generates.[18] The fall does not take place in a structure where two states of humanity—such as the one characterized by innocence and the one characterized by sin—could clearly be differentiated. The fall, rather, is an erasure of the borders. Hence, the fall of time and the fall of innocence are connected to death by way of its impossibility. They allow the description of a completely different relation between time and eternity. Death being irreducible to a finite moment, not only does loss exceed any present, but it also loses the very possibility of the present and therefore of time. Hence, in Blanchot, eternity is not beyond death: it is, rather, the absence of time that derives from the infinity of the eternal "to die."[19] This explains why grace is described as the love of death. *Blanchot's grace lies within finitude and does not aspire to overcome it.* This means, as already suggested, that grace doesn't save (from death). The detour of grace is the very detour of the "to die" (*mourir*) that fails to come to term; that is, that not only fails to reach the limit but also makes vain its inertia. Rather than overcoming or fulfilling the law, the "detour of grace," or the "to die," "ignores" law! This peculiar relation between grace and law might indicate what Blanchot means by grace as a *detour*.

Blanchot's idea that death is impossible as such is indeed a way to invalidate any playing with the supremacy of law. As already mentioned, Blanchot assumes Paul's reading of the law in the wake of death. However, if death is impossible as a limit, as a determined moment, then, as said in the previous chapter, the law is made "vain" by what defines it: the power to institute a limit. If, on the one hand, law is not only the power to condemn to death but also "death itself wearing the face of the law," and if, on the other hand, death is impossible as such—that is, if as a limited moment death has always already failed in the "inert infinitive" of the "to die"—then *law transgresses itself in the very moment of its enunciation*. The infinity of the "to die" has always already—passively, without looking for it—transgressed the limit that death claims to be. Hence, law is disavowed by itself, by the very content (eternity) that its fulfillment would promise: "*Transgression*," Blanchot writes, "*this lightness of immortal dying*" (1992, 111).

This passive transgression, which Blanchot calls an "empty transgression" (1992, 106) because it has neither a subject nor a content, exceeds the dialectical relation that I previously established between law and transgression. In the wake of Saint Paul, Blanchot recalls that the law calls for transgression and that transgression therefore confirms the law. However, the transgression of the "to die," of this "inert infinitive," does not confirm the law since it happens in the wake of its own impossibility. Thus, as shown in the previous chapter, we find ourselves confronted with the case of a transgression that "makes the law vain" (1992, 25); that is, a "transgression [that] does not transgress the law" but instead "carries it away with it" (101). Unlike the "gift of grace," which fulfills the law while effacing it, the "detour of grace" stems from a transgression that takes place because of law's own impossibility and, hence, because of the law's void and that only meets this void. Now, this void does not entail the effacement of the law in the sense of its fulfillment. As shown in the previous chapter, the void of law that the "to die" meets is precisely its irreducibility.

This reversal of Paul's dialectic is expressed in one of the fragments of *The Step Not Beyond* in the form of a "conversation" in which two voices speak of the split inherent to the instituting moment of law. This fragment suggests, on the one hand, that it is death that originates law (law being thus "death itself wearing the face of the law") and, on the other hand, that law—because death is impossible—is prohibited by what makes it necessary. In other words, if law cannot be fulfilled, it is not because it splits the individual into two and separates life (the spirit) from death (the flesh), but rather because it is itself split, therefore making both life and death impossible. Law is simultaneously a limit and what makes the limit impossible. This fragment (which I have slightly shortened in order to make its movement more apparent) enunciates the law's own prohibition within a logic or a mode of argumentation that consists in splitting itself in such a way that its very content is forbidden:

> "It is forbidden."—"It is inevitable."—"Still, always to be avoided according to the movement of duration and as if there were no present moment appropriate for the falling due."—"From

this comes the need, without justification, to have always to gain an extra moment, a supplement of time, not for life, but for dying that does not produce itself in time."— . . . "To die is not declined."—"This inert infinitive, agitated by an infinite neutrality that could not coincide with itself, infinitive without present."—"So that one could affirm: it is forbidden to die *in the present*."—"Which also means: the present does not die, and there is no present for dying. It is the present that would in some way pronounce the prohibition."—"While the transgression of dying, which has always already broken with the present time, comes to substitute, in the unaccomplishment proper to it, for the trinary duration that the predominance of the present unifies, the time of difference in which this would always take place because it has always already happened: dying, coming again."—"The prohibition remains intact: one does not die in the present."—"It remains intact. But, in as much as it is the present that pronounces it and in which the transgression is unaccomplished in a future-past time, removed from any affirmation of presence, the transgression has always already withdrawn the present time of its pronouncement from the prohibition: has prevented it or prohibited it in dislocating it."—"Thus a time without present would be 'affirmed,' according to the demand of the return."—"This is why even transgression does not accomplish itself." (Blanchot 1992, 107–8)

As already suggested, in a movement that inverts Paul's understanding of the relation between law and death, this fragment assumes the idea that law does not provoke death (a split subject), but rather that death gives birth to law. Death, being impossible, is the very content of the prohibition. Therefore, *law is not exterior to what it forbids*: what forbids itself (death), what subtracts itself from presence, is the law! From this perspective, law for Blanchot is neither divine (such as when law is merely transcendent) nor human (such as when law becomes immanent). Law stems from the experience of the impossible and, thus, from what makes both divinity and humanity impossible.

While Blanchot is here subverting Paul's logic by questioning the relation between death and law, he is also drawing completely different consequences for the relation between grace and law. In Paul, grace overcomes law but does so in order to fulfill it. By contrast, in Blanchot, the "detour of grace" stems from a logic according to which what institutes law (death) is also what leads to its transgression (the infinity of the "to die"). Law is law in that it is a forbidden realm, in that it is inaccessible. Just as in Kafka's *The Trial*, what makes law inaccessible is also what leads to its transgression: death, as a limit, is always already transgressed by the "to die." However, in Blanchot, the transgression does not confirm the law; it "makes it vain." Law is prohibited by what makes it necessary such that nothing can be properly delimited as legal in opposition to something illegal. Death as impossible, prohibited, has always already disrupted life. What is prohibited is not beyond, as an inaccessible realm. *It has made any realm impossible.* Hence, law calls for a transgression that never ends because it stems from the impossibility of instituting any limit and of constituting any realm. This indeed constitutes an explanation of the split dimension of this fragment: on the one hand, "the prohibition remains intact: one does not die in the present"; on the other hand, death's impossibility has also made impossible the present and, hence, any inscription of law:

> It remains intact. But, in as much as it is the present that pronounces it and in which the transgression is unaccomplished in a future-past time, removed from any affirmation of presence, the transgression has always already withdrawn the present time of its pronouncement from the prohibition: has prevented it or prohibited it in dislocating it. (Blanchot 1992, 107)

Here, *law does not split the subject into two*, as if there were an original unity to which this division would refer. On the contrary, *law is the original split that prevents any unity*, any form of fulfillment, and thus any unified discourse (in this sense—I will come back to this idea—the impossibility of law explains the fragmentation of writing). However, because law is originally split, because it is a limit that is always already transgressed by what makes it necessary, law is maintained not in its transcendence, but rather in the immanence of a transgression that never ends. Blanchot's reconsideration of the relation between death and law displaces the challenge implied in the problem of law's unaccomplishment or unfulfillment. In Blanchot, law is removed ("made vain") by itself. However, this suppression maintains its inaccessibility. Hence, whereas law is not the "ultimate authority," the grace that deviates from law does not save from the death that law brings forth. Because law is made vain by what makes it necessary, individuals are not primarily *subject* to the law, which seems to be the case in Kafka (although in Kafka, as we will see, it is not only a matter of submitting to the law's authority but also of embodying what the law cannot bind). Insofar as law prohibits itself, a form a freedom can be envisaged. However, as already suggested, because the law's own prohibition still maintains a form of prohibition, because transgression can never be fulfilled, such a freedom is closer to the savagery of terror than to a true liberation (from what bounds to evil).

THE TWO TABLETS AND THE TWO WRITINGS

Blanchot twists Saint Paul's thought in two ways. On the one hand, he follows Saint Paul's internal logic to the point of madness. In this sense, the folly of grace dwells not in any sort of irrationality, but rather in the very rationality of law. Law's own effacement engenders grace in relation to finitude. On the other hand, Blanchot inverts Paul's proposition that law gives birth to death in that it splits the individual. For Blanchot, law is structurally split because death—which is impossible *as such*—originates it. Because death is impossible *as such*, as a limit, law has somehow always already been transgressed. The impossibility of death (which is the prohibited) entails a loss that has always already happened as that which makes life (which is the legitimate and even the source of righteousness, in Paul's view) impossible. The "to die" in Blanchot is the nonending dimension of a loss that is "contemporary" to life (although speaking of a contemporaneity, namely of a simultaneity, is problematic, since the time of the "to die" is that of a differing that makes the present of time impossible) and that makes life *as such* impossible. Thus, in Blanchot, time is not the correlate of any possible redemption. There is no original fall into time. Rather, there is an immemorial fall *of time* that prevents any end and, consequently, any salvation. Life cannot be redeemed, simply because life exists only insofar as it is always already contaminated by death. Life's eternity is given in the form of a survival maintained on the impossible verge of death or according to the infinity of the infinitive "to die." Hence, in Blanchot, grace is the love of death that nonetheless diverts law from any form of fulfillment. In this sense (and I will come back to this point), Blanchot's grace is somehow a *dis*grace.

Blanchot's double twist of Pauline logic sheds new light on the relation of Blanchot's thought to the Christian tradition, as well as to the way Christianity has enclosed Judaism in a reductive conception of the law. In fact, one cannot consider Blanchot to be a *merely* Christian thinker since his thought of grace is a diversion (a detour!) of Paul's preaching. But neither can one consider Blanchot to submit to an idea of ethic thought of as a subjection to law, and to a law thought of as merely binding, as would be the case in the Judaic thought (at least in a Paulinian conception of Judaism).[20] As with Saint Paul, law for Blanchot is the correlate of transgression. Unlike Paul, however, the transcendence of law cannot be overcome because the transgression is empty. Hence, what Blanchot deconstructs is the very hermeneutical premises that constitute the Christian understanding of the idea of a "Judeo-Christian" tradition, of the very hyphen—as Nancy and Lyotard would say—that entails the idea of a unification of these two traditions.[21] Following the (Paulinian/Hegelian) logic that unified them (law's overcoming by grace), he deconstructs this very unity and opens therefore to new hermeneutical possibilities. Whereas Paul's understanding of grace aims at fulfilling the "Judaic" law through its effacement as an external entity, Blanchot locates grace in the unfulfillment of the law, which leads to an affirmation of the love of death, the love of the inaccessibility of law. However, Blanchot relates to transcendence within the very movement that aims at making law immanent. In this context of a deconstruction of the hermeneutical background that defined the "hyphen" of the idea of a Judeo-Christian tradition, my previous question can be addressed more emphatically: To where does this "detour of grace" lead? How can such grace—thought of as a "love of death"—be connected to a demand for justice?

The question of writing in Blanchot and, in particular, its connection with law in both its biblical and secular meanings can help delve into these questions. Unlike Nietzsche, who proposed substituting "New Tablets" for "Old Tablets,"[22] Blanchot searches instead to deactivate law's supremacy without, however, submitting to another law that the idea of "New Tablets" might represent, and without aiming to fulfill the law in a movement that provokes its effacement. Actually, Blanchot proceeds backward. He does not aim at effacing the law—that is, the law as an "old letter" (in Paul's words), as a writing that belongs to the past and is unable to give birth to a new individual. Rather, he starts from the question of the (self-) effacement of law in order to show how this effacement determines a new idea or a new exigency of writing. In fact, if law is effaced by what makes it necessary and hence impossible to fulfill, then law's effacement, as I have frequently said, still acts as a law. Even when suppressed in the immanence of love (in a Christian context) or freedom (in a Hegelian context), the law still transcends. However, the demand implied in such an effacement defines what is here understood by law and by writing otherwise.

Let us begin with the similarities between Nietzsche and Paul. Nietzsche coincides with Paul in at least two ways: On the one hand, he suggests that law prohibits what it also provokes.[23] Thus, he observes that law cultivates guilt and pain rather than "innocence" and "enjoyment."[24] On the other hand, he sees that the law's commandments contradict the impulses of life.[25] Thus, in a way, for Nietzsche as for Paul, law divides the individual. It has a mortal effect. However, Nietzsche's thought aims not simply at a recovery of life through grace or a "new human being" through salvation; rather, Nietzsche aspires toward *leaving the land of human being* by relying on will as a creative task rather than on life as what is given. Indeed, Nietzsche's message in "On Old Tablets and New Tablets" is not to create a new individual on the basis of the original man (Adam), but rather to leave "the country of man" altogether: "But whoever discovered the land 'human being' also discovered the land 'human future' " (Nietzsche 2006, 172). Hence, *those New Tablets are tablets of this departure, this radical rupture*: with Christ as well as with Adam, with the New Testament as well as with the Old.[26] Yet how do we break with such a legacy? What "new tablets" can provoke the rupture with the land "human being"? Do tablets not still imply a writing and hence a form of legacy and even of death at work?

In the last chapter of *The Infinite Conversation*, entitled "The Absence of the Book," Blanchot develops the idea that writing exists in a necessary tension with law. In fact, if on the one hand writing is a trace, not a signifying sign but rather the movement of tracing prior to the production of any signification, and if on the other hand law is what calls for signification (an interpretation), then there is not only a tension between writing and law. Because law also requires writing for its inscription, it necessarily exists in tension with its condition of possibility. Hence, Blanchot writes: "The illegitimacy of writing, always refractory in relation to the law, hides the asymmetrical illegitimacy of the law in relation to writing" (1993, 431). According to Blanchot, writing obeys a double and contradictory "movement":[27] it either "*slackens*" (431)—that is, "accepts taking form in language" and, in this sense, is subordinated to a law—or it is refractory to meaning and, in this sense, pushes "out of language"[28] and out of the Book in which meaning is inscribed and institutionalized.[29] According to this other "movement," writing "remains foreign to legibility" (431). It designates a "(pure) exteriority, foreign to every relation of presence, as to all legality" (431). It is important to assert that writing as a *pure* exteriority—that is, as what would subsist outside of law—*cannot be attested*. It is only through law, through a system of signification, that we can relate to what resists signification. However, because writing is twofold, as shown at length in the previous chapter, the destiny of the Book in which law is inscribed allows the description of a double and "contemporary" (although dropping into diachronic) "movement": a movement in which law historically fulfills itself through its progressive understanding; a movement that drives out law, drives out the Book in which law is not only inscribed but also developed, understood, and fulfilled. Hence, Blanchot writes:

> The exteriority of writing, laying itself out and stratifying itself in the form of the book, becomes exteriority as law. The Book speaks as Law. Reading it, we read in it that everything that is, is either forbidden or allowed. But isn't this structure of authorization and interdiction a result of our level of reading? Might there not be another reading of the Book in which the book's other would cease to proclaim itself in precepts? And if we were to read this way, would we still be reading a book? Would we not be ready then to read *the absence of the book*? (431)

The structural interdependence of writing and law, as well as the duplicity of writing, entails that law, which takes place in the Book ("the Book speaks as Law"), has a double destiny. If it is bound to unfold through the Book, it is also doomed to be effaced in the Book's effacement. Writing is "black" *and* "white," to use Blanchot's formulation in *The Infinite Conversation*.[30] It is black in that it is not only legible but also serves legibility; it is white in that any legible sign bears a void of signification. The white writing is thus not separate from the black writing; one follows the other as its shadow. The black writing is meant to make law legible by giving it an interpretation. In this case, the law's void is "'legalized'" (433). All that is exterior (or unnamable, such as God) is *related* to an interior. It participates in the progressive relation of the law's meaning and leads to its fulfillment. The white writing is the void echo of the black writing. It not only prevents law's fulfillment, but it also calls for its effacement. Hence, in *The Step Not Beyond*, one reads this prophetic sentence: "everything must efface itself, everything will efface itself" (Blanchot 1992, 53). Now, this sentence could indeed be written in a Pauline vein.[31] The idea of effacement, in fact, entails the idea of overcoming the law of the Book (and of the Book as law). However, this effacement departs from the Book by virtue of the twofold dimension of writing. The white writing, which is inseparable from the black writing, entails a distortion or a detour from the Book's history that leads to its totalization and its fulfillment. But the white writing never exists *as such*. It exists only as a double, an echo of the law's legibility. Indeed, it *does not properly take place*. Otherwise, the exteriority of writing would be part of the Book. It would acquire a signification through the book.[32]

These pages on the exteriority of writing and the quasi-prophetic announcement of the "absence of the Book" define another twist that, in this case, Blanchot gives to Nietzsche's idea of "New Tablets." While Nietzsche seems to oppose two different Tablets and two different principles of writing (the writing of man—or of the human being—and the writing of the "overman," which is a bridge to a land that would leave behind the land of human being), Blanchot shows that it is the twofold aspect of writing that moves beyond the land of the human, to the "exile from all fatherlands" for which Nietzsche calls in *Thus Spoke Zarathustra*. Whereas the black writing is the writing of "human being," the white writing, always correlative to the black writing, is the writing of what *fails* humanity. It does not refer to a separate realm, as would be the realm of the "overman." The white writing refers not to a new system of signification but to what fails the realm of meaning. Hence, it threatens signification or language with "collapsing."[33] This is why Blanchot speaks of a "writing outside language" in *The Infinite Conversation*. Although this "outside" is never reached (for, if it were, it would belong to truth; it would belong to the history and legitimacy of the Book), it undoes our system of legibility (and legitimacy), thus relating to another region where neither meaning nor "human" reigns. Using Blanchot's formulation from *The Step Not Beyond*, one can say that the white writing is the "refusal to discourse" (1992, 116), which elsewhere Blanchot also calls the "cry" (1993, 262). It does not refer to any kind of animality; that is, to any kind of nature. On the contrary, it provokes a defection from nature. It moves beneath[34] rather than beyond. Hence, Blanchot is not writing "New Tablets" that necessarily amount to *another law*, precisely; another system of writing or of producing meaning. Rather, through the double dimension of writing (in and outside law), Blanchot relates to a movement that breaks with *all laws*. On this point, let us recall what Blanchot writes in the preliminary note of *The Infinite Conversation*, which ends with the chapter titled "The Absence of the Book": "Writing is the greatest violence, for it transgresses the law, every law, and also its own law" (1993, xii). Indeed, in this transgression, there is neither an overcoming of law as in Paul, nor a demand for New Tablets as in Nietzsche: "The law is the summit, there is no other" (1993, 434). Whether immanent or transcendent, law cannot be definitively suppressed. But there where law cannot be suppressed, writing relates to the vanity of law, to the very void of the law that has always already split it. Writing relates to this region of contamination between life and death, legality and illegitimacy, from which there is no exit (as when grace is thought of in terms of salvation) but that escapes all hierarchies and implies a detour from the history of the Book. Whence the concluding words of *The Infinite Conversation* and "The Absence of the Book," which I commented upon in my previous chapter: "Writing remains outside the arbitration between high and low" (1993, 434).

Grace and Disgrace or Redeeming the Other than Human Being

Blanchot's understanding of death and writing gives birth indeed to a new fold in Paul's conception of the relation between law and grace.

First, whereas in Paul grace *justifies* life by saving it from death, in Blanchot grace can only be thought of as the love of death. It is an affirmation of finitude rather than its negation. It's important to highlight that in Blanchot the "love of death" is certainly not a passion for suicide since death is affirmed as impossible. In this sense, the "love of death" is paradoxically a critique of suicide. But nor is the "love of death" its overcoming and thus annulation, as in Hegel's logic. In Hegel, and more generally from a Christian point of view, death is a path toward eternity.[35] However, in Blanchot the "love of death" should rather be understood in Nietzschean terms: as a passion for the impossible, for what cannot be overcome, in a way, for fate.[36]

Second, although grace deactivates the supremacy of law in Paul, this suspension coincides with a form of fulfillment. Grace in fact brings righteousness since it transforms the individual. By contrast, in Blanchot, grace does not suppress law: it relates to the outside of law, to what escapes its very measure. What "remains outside the arbitration between high and low" is indeed what escapes the hierarchies of law or law conceived as an ordered society. Hence, in Blanchot, grace amounts not to the sovereignty of God but rather to chance; that is, to what remains without explanation and, in this sense, what does not belong to a law. If, however, chance happens randomly, unpredictably, it still acts as a law. Chance still transcends the individual. It is in fact the very structure of transcendence since, by trying one's luck or—as we say French—*en tentant sa chance*, one surrenders absolutely to randomness, to the unknown. In this sense, as says Blanchot himself, grace is indeed a disgrace: "grace, which can be disgrace without renouncing the extreme good grace it owes to its 'transcendence'" (1992, 26). The transgression of *all law* that the preliminary note calls for as the very demand of writing can simply restore another law:

> Prohibition strikes the law. This is a scandalous event. The law strikes itself with prohibition and, thus, in the most deceitful way (the august deceit of the law), restores another law, higher, that is, more other, in a more decisive relation with otherness, from which the prohibition is then supposed to come. Chance—either luck or grace that puts the law in parentheses, according to the time outside of time—is then reintroduced under the jurisdiction of *another* law, until, in its turn, this one—then, in its turn . . . (26; my emphasis; Blanchot's ellipses)

Indeed, contrary to Paul, Blanchot will never abandon the idea that "the law is the summit, there is no other." This might be a clue, then, to the relation between Blanchot's thoughts on grace and the problem of justice. For Paul, to be in grace means to be excepted *from* finitude. Such a state of grace, such a *Reign* to which grace is a means, might deafen the individual. In Blanchot, by contrast, grace means to be excepted *by* finitude. Here, grace does not save. It is always more proximate to a disgrace according to which one is no longer *under* a law comprised of prohibitions, but rather bound to *affirm* the law of randomness where nothing is written. In the law of randomness, one is bound to affirm the unknown, the unpredictable, that which is neither divine nor human. As in the "throw of the dice," the law of chance puts the law of law into play. In this sense, randomness is not a law that calls for submission. Once again, we see that Blanchot puts the game of law into play and, hence, affirms freedom. But this anonymous and hence terrifying freedom can indeed connect to a demand for justice. In fact, while the gift of grace in Paul concerns only humanity and aims at restoring to human nature its divinity, the "detour of grace" in Blanchot relates to the other than human being. Although such a detour does not save, we can say that it articulates a demand for justice because it opens the space for "new relationships" (Blanchot 1988, 56). Disgrace (of grace) therefore has the grace to give birth to new relations that are not defined by the concept of unity, which is the case in Paul's preaching, according to which we are all one in Christ's body (1 Cor 12:12–27). The disgrace (of grace) follows the law's original split that drives it to madness. Such disgrace (of grace) ends up gracing the disgraced, those who are not bound to the law, because they belong to the failure of language.

If grace does not save, if it's closer to a disgrace, why does Blanchot maintain the idea of grace?

Blanchot is neither contradicting Christianity in a movement of negation nor articulating a new idea of Christianity. Rather, he is writing this history otherwise by taking into account what it excludes, but also what resists or fails the historicity of this legacy. For Paul, grace supposes faith in Christ's resurrection: it presupposes his death and hence the limit that separates life from death. Blanchot writes this history otherwise, taking as a point of departure the impossibility of death as well as the frontier that separates life from death. *The "detour of grace" is therefore the formula of a deconstructed Christianity.* It is not its negation but, as Nancy will say in *The Deconstruction of Christianity*, its "disclosure,"[37] its opening to another history or to the otherwise of History.[38] In this "otherwise," grace describes a relation to death rather than a war waged against death, to use Karl Barth's words. But this writing otherwise has to be heard in a literal sense. In fact, what is otherwise is not only the object of writing but also the very act of writing. In Blanchot's view, the Book is historical in that it has given a legitimate frame to what fails to be signified. Through the Book, a *relation* is established with what is beyond language. However, Blanchot's writing undoes what the Book unifies or that to which the book relates (religiously) beyond language. In this sense, instead of "broken Tablets" that call for infinite interpretations, as in Jewish hermeneutics,[39] Blanchot's writing would break language infinitely. Instead of commenting ("black writing") on what is fissured ("white writing"), Blanchot's writing gives voice to the fissure of the Book. In this sense, Blanchot's writing is not characterized as that which would efface the Book in a movement that suppresses it (and that hence suppresses the law that unfolds in the Book that it always presupposes). Blanchot's writing, rather, is *a writing of effacement*. It makes the effacement audible. Hence, it historicizes Christianity otherwise and correlates grace to *another way of hearing* rather than to the fulfillment of law into Law. Here, though not to the extent of Paul, we might be confronted with a writing (and not a predication) that transforms. But the "white writing" doesn't aim at restoring human nature or at divinizing the human. Closer to Nietzsche than to Paul, Blanchot could conceive this writing, which subtracts itself from law (and from its own law), as the cry that—in the words of Nietzsche—transforms or graces (!) our very senses: "Must one first smash their ears so that they learn to hear with their eyes?" (2006, 9).

Hearing with one's eyes might be the exigency not for the "new man" but rather for the "other than man (the other than human being)." However, in order to hear this call, we might not need "New Tablets" that would still be written with a human writing. We need a writing—or a law—that writes its own effacement without ever reaching an end or, hence, a truth. In this effacement, what we hear might not differ from the content of Kafka's singing mouse Josephine, whose song is not properly a song. What we hear might be simply nothing, but a nothing that, beneath the human limit (and any limit since limits always amount to humans), calls for an exigency of justice that requires not so much "new men" as new relations.

Chapter 3

Innocence

> One had to draw him into a fault, one had to reinvent for him alone the lost sense of what a fault was.
>
> —Blanchot, *The Last Man*, 6

Because law refers necessarily to an illegitimate dimension that secures its sovereignty, one can be outside the law even while obeying it. This is what happens to Sorge, who progressively embodies law's illegitimacy, the very weakness that makes it sovereign. Because the language that we speak and that makes us human is haunted by a void, to be a subject of language might entail the experience of a silence that deprives one of humanity rather than secures it. This is what happens to Kafka's most disturbing character, Gregor Samsa, this obedient son who wakes up one day in the body of an animal who possesses the capacity for thought, but who cannot express them. Hence, because of the twofold aspect of law and writing, humanity seems to be caught in a form of guiltiness that is simultaneously innocent since it happens as the collapse of the subject of language. In this context, humanity cannot be redeemed from what makes it guilty because there is no one to properly assume a fault. However, whereas there is no grace that allows for the renewal of the human condition, in Blanchot, grace happens as that which gives voice to what escapes the human or the legal realm. Hence, while there is no personal redemption and no proper redemption for human kind, the relation between law and grace in Blanchot opens a space of thought for what fails the human condition. It claims justice for that which is beneath the human and that which prevents humanity from conforming to its essence. In this sense, the fall of innocence gives innocence its chance. It does not describe the entry into language, into that which binds to law, and hence into what properly defines humanity. Rather, it takes place as the failure of language, as what prohibits humanity and precludes responsibility. In this failure, innocence doesn't belong to anybody. It is rather the impersonality that threatens anyone who pretends to be made one by their subjection to language. It is the silence that haunts anyone who pretends to be made human through the dominion of language.

But what can it mean to give innocence its chance? Are we here facing an "innocence of becoming innocent," as in Nietzsche; namely, a complete redemption not of humans in their finitude but of the human in its very condition as human? Do we not risk, as we saw in the introduction, in innocence, in a realm free of language and of law, pure amorality or the brutality of vitalism? Or can innocence, an innocence that is a failure rather than a quality, an impossibility of the human rather than a new ontology, be the measure of a new kind of responsibility?

To think innocence as the failure of the human and not as an original, paradisiacal, and mythical condition is indeed worrying and even anguishing. It means that innocence, rather than being past and lost, is a remainder that resists any form of appropriation. More radically, if innocence happens as the failure of the human within what grounds humanity—language and law (or language as law)—then innocence is the experience of a loss of language and of an impossible responsibility. Within language, one can stutter, one can experience the loss of its humanity. This is what occurs in Herman Melville's novella *Billy Budd*. When the beautiful Billy, a good-hearted young sailor falsely accused of conspiracy to commit mutiny, seeks to defend himself against the charge, he begins to stutter and, instead of proving his innocence, becomes filled with emotion and accidentally kills his accuser. Here, instead of standing for mere unawareness, innocence is figured as the condition that makes it impossible for Billy to be a secured self, a posited subject. Billy Budd, the character of Melville's novel of the same name, perfectly embodies the idea that innocence is a state not of plenitude but of failure. Rather than designating the condition of the one who does not possess language, it reveals itself in the condition of the one who cannot speak,[1] and hence who cannot vindicate themself. Rather than being paradisiacal, rather than describing a state of happiness, innocence is indeed anguishing. Within its stuttering, one happens to experience one's own impossibility, one's own destruction as a subject. In Billy Budd, innocence is experienced as a loss that is destructive. Happening as a stutter, it refers to a realm that escapes the opposition between myth and logos, between the paradise of innocence and the fall into sin where one is a subject of law.

Billy Budd's stutter recalls an unidentified character of one of Blanchot's "novels,"[2] *The Last Man*, where what is at stake is the end of human being, and hence of a language that can signify this end. In *The Last Man*, the "last man" is a sick man, most probably a writer, whose presence is characterized by fragility and silence. In this context, the "last man" is characterized as innocent. Although having little of Billy Budd's spontaneity, the "last man" resembles Melville's young sailor in that he does not dominate language and is therefore doomed to irresponsibility. Like Billy Budd, the innocence of the "last man" dwells in its inaccessibility, its removal from the common world:

> For some, he was curiously easy to approach; for others, he was surrounded by an innocence that was marvelously smooth on the outside, but on the inside composed of a thousand tiny edges of very hard crystal, so that at the slightest attempt to approach him he risked being torn by the long, fine needles of his innocence. (Blanchot 1987, 8)

And, like Billy Budd, the inability to speak characterizes the innocence of the "last man," as well as his lack of responsibility:

> When someone stops speaking it is hard not to go looking for the missing thought, but even though his thought often called out to us, one couldn't do such violence to him, he fell silent with such great innocence, such obvious lack of responsibility, he fell silent absolutely and entirely. (Blanchot 1987, 9–10)

In *The Last Man*, innocence takes place as a stubborn silence, as something that, within the realm of signification, signifies its opacity. Instead of enabling transparency and communication, it sustains their inaccessibility. Hence, in *The Last Man*, innocence is not, as in Nietzsche's idea of a "becoming innocent," a goal to be reached. Rather, *it is the impossibility of reaching a goal*. Because innocence is a silence that haunts signification, giving rise to its stuttering, it makes "man" or the "human being" impossible—and it also relates to this impossibility as that which cannot be overcome. Unlike what Nietzsche calls the "last man" in *Thus Spoke Zarathustra*, in Blanchot the "last man" is not the figure of a resented humanity that should hopefully be overcome by the "overman" (Übermensch).[3] It is the experience of "man," or, rather of the "human" being's impossibility.[4] It is henceforth an experience that has no end. Thus, rather than being a goal that announces a realm freed of humanity, innocence is an anguishing experience in which humanity feels its fragility but cannot overcome it. Thought not in terms of the pure heart but *as* human impurity, as humanity's failure, innocence is indeed not a condition of happiness. It is—and this drives us closer to Kierkegaard than to Nietzsche—an anguishing in-condition.[5]

In what follows, I would like to analyze this shift in the meaning of innocence in Blanchot's and Kierkegaard's thought and, more precisely, in the association that both make between innocence and anguish.[6] Kierkegaard and Blanchot each associate innocence with "anguish"; namely, with a feeling of nothingness that is a disturbance rather than a state of peacefulness or serenity. As Kierkegaard stresses in *The Concept of Anxiety*, the "profound secret" of innocence is that "it is at the same time anxiety" because it is a condition of ignorance (1980, 41). For Kierkegaard, the state of ignorance that is innocence coincides with the experience of a void that explains the step from innocence to guilt.[7] Innocence produces anxiety, and this anxiety thwarts the realization of any state of peacefulness and leads to the fall.[8] In Blanchot's *The Step Not Beyond*, we encounter a definition of innocence that has an obvious but curious Kierkegaardian echo. In one of its fragments, in fact, Blanchot writes: "Supposing that dread (*angoisse*) is innocence itself, an innocence apparently unknown, man feels guilty for not being able to bear innocence, guilty of this innocence that anguishes him" (1992, 67). Is this a repetition, here, of Kierkegaard's conception of innocence, or does Blanchot's repetition of this Kierkegaardian association between innocence and anguish entail a shift in the conception of innocence? To speak of innocence as a state of anxiety that leads to guilt may, in fact, be different than to speak of anxiety as a state of innocence about which one feels guilty.

The current chapter will therefore focus on Blanchot's repetition of Kierkegaard's conception of innocence *as* anguish. My idea is that in making the association between dread and innocence, Blanchot aims at engaging the philosophical and ethical consequences of innocence conceived as incapacity, a failure of the subject. Indeed, in Blanchot, innocence does not constitute a goal and hence cannot be correlated to an idea of becoming or of redemption (both ideas being teleological). Innocence is rather a state in which humanity is stuck. But since innocence coincides with a failure of the law (and not to a paradisiacal state pure of sin and ignorant of Good and Evil), I will argue that it allows for the thinking of an ethics that arises from the failure. Simply put, if innocence is a stutter, a silence that haunts language, one still must respond to this silence.

The Nothingness of Innocence

Innocence is most predominant in Blanchot's works that deal with the topic of the end. Blanchot's novel *The Last Man*, for instance, stages innocence not as the condition of the first man, such as the biblical Adam, but as a condition (an "incondition") related to the impossibility of ever reaching an end. The topic of innocence is also present in Blanchot's fragmentary writings, such as *The Step Not Beyond* and *The Writing of the Disaster*. Although very scattered, we find several fragments on innocence in those two works of Blanchot that indicate above all that there are no clear frontiers between guilt and innocence. In *The Step Not Beyond*, Blanchot speaks, for instance, of a "loss of innocence that is itself innocent" (104). As mentioned in the introduction, in *The Writing of the Disaster*, paraphrasing Hegel's *The Phenomenology of Spirit*, Blanchot writes: "Innocence alone is nonaction (the absence of operation)" (40). Here, again, we are in a perspective not of reaching an origin but rather of what is described throughout Blanchot's work as the impossibility of dying, which is to say the impossibility of reaching an end. Along these lines, Blanchot writes in *The Step Not Beyond* of the "innocence of dying" rather than the "innocence of living" (127), referring to the fact that one is made innocent by what prevents one from living and from being an "I." Indeed, for Blanchot, *innocence is the figure of humanity confronted with its own impossibility.* In Blanchot's writings, innocence emerges when humankind is no longer in a relation of power and therefore can no longer be appropriated to itself or to an essence. Rather than think that innocence is what *precedes* the constitution of humanity—of humanity as aware of itself—Blanchot here thinks of innocence as the failure of this constitution. In other words, keeping in mind Kierkegaard's conception of innocence, Blanchot, rather than defining innocence as ignorance, defines innocence in relation to what escapes the power of knowledge through which humanity constitutes itself. *Innocence would be the state not of the one who lacks knowledge but of the one who no longer possesses the condition of knowledge.* But if innocence is either ignorance or the impossibility of knowledge, how can we pretend to even speak about it? Isn't it precisely that innocence remains beyond the grasp of speech and, to speak in Hegelian terms, beyond the logic of the spirit?

As we have said, in the wake of Kierkegaard's *The Concept of Anxiety*, Blanchot relates innocence to the experience of anguish (*angoisse*). In associating innocence with anxiety, both Blanchot and Kierkegaard argue against Hegel. In fact, for Hegel, since innocence is a form of immediacy deprived of any reflexivity, it is, properly speaking, nothing (Hegel 1995, 244).[9] For Hegel, everything begins with reflection, with knowledge. In this context, it is logically impossible to speak of anything that is not part of the process of knowledge. Thus, innocence exists only as a myth. But for Kierkegaard and Blanchot, the trick of this approach consists in thinking that nothingness would not question knowledge, that nothingness would be a mere nonbeing that can in no way disturb the work of being. Now, in associating innocence with anguish, Blanchot and Kierkegaard both acknowledge that the nothingness of innocence is precisely something.[10] While, as Kierkegaard said, anticipating Heidegger, anguish defines a state of anxiety that has no object,[11] it occurs as a relationship with nothingness. In that sense, the nothingness of innocence produces anguish. Said another way, the absence of knowledge—the ignorance—that qualifies innocence is not a pure logical category, but rather a psychological state. In saying "supposing that dread (*angoisse*) is innocence itself, an innocence apparently unknown," Blanchot, like Kierkegaard, rejects Hegel's reduction of innocence to a logical category. Anguish or dread "is innocence itself" in that one has no knowledge about it, no mastery of it. Anguish is an experience that precisely reveals no subject, and hence fails to be experienced.

We can therefore trace the consequences that follow from the impossibility of reducing innocence to a logical category. The nothingness of innocence can be negated and appropriated to the constitution of knowledge only if this nothingness can be measured by it. The nothingness of innocence is a logical category only insofar as it belongs to the system of the constitution of knowledge. But innocence is not necessarily the opposite of wisdom. In acknowledging that its nothingness produces anxiety, Kierkegaard confronts us with the fact that *innocence is simply heterogeneous to knowledge*. If, as Kierkegaard says, innocence is ignorance, this ignorance has precisely nothing to do with the system of knowledge. Rather than being purely and simply nothing, *it is something that no knowledge can seize*. The fact that knowledge destroys innocence is insufficient for negating the existence of the latter. The fact that innocence is indeterminable does not suffice for it to be proclaimed that innocence can exist only in the form of a myth. *Because the nothingness of innocence is heterogeneous to knowledge, it questions knowledge.* Even though it is always out of reach, it has, somehow, a philosophical dignity.

It implies the distinction of nothingness from pure nonbeing. But while Blanchot and Kierkegaard share the idea that the nothingness of innocence is irreducible to nothingness, is there not a difference between the idea that innocence *produces anxiety* and the idea that anxiety is "innocence itself"? In *The Concept of Anxiety*, innocence is described as a stage *before the Fall* and therefore as an ethical category—but what exactly is the role of innocence in *The Step Not Beyond*?

Guilty Innocence

To approach this question, we need to deepen our sense of Blanchot and Kierkegaard's critiques of Hegel's system. Even if both Blanchot and Kierkegaard question Hegel's negation of nothingness, they approach this issue from different angles. Interestingly, from Hegel to Kierkegaard, and then from Kierkegaard to Blanchot, the question of innocence is radicalized to the point that it puts into question the condition of possibility for both philosophy and ethics. In fact, as we will see, in *The Concept of Anxiety* what is at stake in distinguishing innocence from any logical category is the acknowledgment of innocence as an ethical issue.[12] Conversely, in *The Step Not Beyond*, the problem of innocence seems no longer to be an ethical concern. Let's see in what sense anguish allows for a different conception of the issue of innocence.

Kierkegaard's critique of Hegel in *The Concept of Anxiety* has, in fact, an ethical dimension. While for Hegel, innocence is lost with the mediacy of reflection, for Kierkegaard, innocence is lost through a fault, which requires dealing with the aporia of original sin.[13] Innocence, in a purely logical conception, disappears in the immanence of the system. By contrast, an ethical conception of innocence requires thinking of the difference between innocence and guilt as a distinction between two heterogeneous stages. What here allows the thinking of the distinction between logic and ethics, and the conferring of an independent status to ethics, is precisely the fact that innocence is *something*. For Kierkegaard, and this is a central point in his critique of Hegel, innocence conceived as immediacy is already annulled by the mediation of reflection, without which it would be impossible to speak of immediacy.[14] The work of mediation in fact provides the only possibility of immediacy. But for Kierkegaard, "innocence is something that is cancelled by a transcendence, precisely because innocence is *something*" (1980, 37). Because innocence produces anguish, it is not merely dissolved in the work of mediation that constitutes reflection. Now, for Kierkegaard anguish is not merely a paralyzing psychological state. On the contrary, anticipating Heidegger, Kierkegaard thinks of anxiety as a relationship with nothingness that characterizes freedom.[15] "Anxiety," writes Kierkegaard, "is freedom's actuality as the possibility of possibility" (42). Anxiety can be thought of as what opens up the space of freedom, because in producing itself as a relationship with nothingness, it defines existence as opened to possibilities a priori. In that sense, freedom qualifies not the power of a subject but rather the structure of existence as opened. "Anxiety is the reality of freedom," in that freedom is the opening of possibilities. Consequently, the anxiety that produces innocence allows the concept of the Fall to be explained without resorting to a mere dialectical schema. If innocence produces anguish, and if anguish is the reality of freedom, then it is possible to understand the fall into sin neither as a necessity willed by God nor as a mere dialectical relationship with the prohibited that would inherently call for transgression (38–39).[16] It is because innocence produces anxiety that the prohibition, although not understood as such (for it can be understood as prohibited only for a subject of knowledge, for a subject who has lost innocence), can appear as a possibility. Kierkegaard can therefore write: "But he who becomes guilty through anxiety is indeed innocent, for it was not himself but anxiety, a foreign power, that laid hold of him, a power that he did not love but about which he was anxious. And yet he is guilty, for he sank in anxiety, which he nevertheless loved even as he feared it" (43). Conceived as anguish, freedom is based neither on knowledge nor on power. Therefore, he or she "who becomes guilty through anxiety" is not accountable for his or her acts. In this sense, he or she is "indeed innocent." However, because innocence produces anxiety, the state of innocence is not a peaceful condition protected from sin. On the contrary, anxiety has already disturbed innocence. Can we not say, indeed, that anguish is the disturbance of innocence, the disturbance that innocence is?

Kierkegaard does not properly develop this last point, which for Blanchot is essential. In "supposing that dread (*l'angoisse*) is innocence itself" (67), as Blanchot writes, innocence is indeed not a peaceful state—it arrives and can be thought of only as a disturbance. Unlike Kierkegaard, Blanchot does not think of innocence as a state of ignorance that precedes knowledge. More specifically, Blanchot speaks of non-knowledge rather than ignorance: of the impossibility of knowledge rather than its absence. In one of the numerous fragments of *The Step Not Beyond* dedicated to non-knowledge, Blanchot associates "non-knowledge" with a double operation (or, more accurately, a double "non-operation": "*désoeuvrement*"; namely the failure of any activity, rather than as simple inactivity). In Blanchot, "non-knowledge" has to do with what makes impossible the condition of possibility of knowledge. In dialogue with Hegel, Blanchot observes that while for Hegel, death or the negative is the condition of the possibility of knowledge, in Blanchot, the negative doesn't work but instead gives birth to unworkingness or the inoperative (*désoeuvrement*). In other words, while for Hegel, to know entails an operation of negation in which consciousness is made foreign to itself and reappropriates itself (being hence redeemed from death, from negation), in Blanchot, consciousness faces a negativity that cannot be appropriated and that hence is confronted with what escapes power. The concept of non-knowledge in Blanchot is henceforth related to what we could call, in Hegelian terms, a negative without negativity and that we can understand by returning to the topic of death. As already said, for Blanchot, because one cannot witness the instant of one's own death, it does not belong to a moment of time.[17] Hence, what Blanchot calls non-knowledge derives from the impossibility of having the knowledge of death, of witnessing death in the moment it occurs. Consequently, non-knowledge is not beyond knowledge. It is not a point located in the future that no knowledge could anticipate. It is what prevents knowledge from coinciding with itself: a failure of knowledge. As we read in *The Step Not Beyond*: "I know less about it than I know about it; it is over this being behind itself of knowledge that I must leap to reach—not attaining it, or ruining myself in it—non-knowledge" (62, translation modified). Non-knowledge is not something that is located beyond a limit: it is the impossibility of knowledge. Beyond any given limit, non-knowledge would still be defined by knowledge. It would be one of the moments of knowledge or its figures. "There is an 'I don't know' that is at the limit of knowledge, but that belongs to knowledge" (62), writes Blanchot. Using Kierkegaard's terminology (especially that of *Fear and Trembling*), such non-knowledge, being posited in relationship to a limit, could be reached through a leap; namely, through a suspension of knowledge that Kierkegaard calls faith.[18] In leaping toward it, one would still have knowledge as a ground. But if non-knowledge is "this being behind itself of knowledge," then one cannot even imagine it being accessible via a leap. Non-knowledge is not the negation of knowledge. It is not the absence of knowledge, as ignorance would be. It is the impossibility of knowledge. In that sense, and coming back to our initial quote—"supposing that dread is innocence itself"—we can say that if Blanchot does not rely on an ignorance separated from knowledge, and if non-knowledge is the impossibility of knowledge, then *anxiety is a vacuum stemming not from ignorance but from knowledge*. What produces anxiety is the fact that knowledge, within itself, is impossible. This fact has two consequences. The first is that while anguish stems from the impossibility of knowledge, it has no truth and makes vain any pretension to distinguish truth from error.[19] The second is that "supposing that dread is innocence itself," innocence is not a stage opposed to knowledge or consciousness: it is the impossibility of knowledge or consciousness. It properly belongs not to Adam, considered as the first man, but—and I will come back to this—to the "last man," considered as the human being's impossibility. Anxiety being neither truth nor wrongness, and dread being "innocence itself," innocence is the impossibility of such an "itself," of the idea of truth that such an "itself" presupposes.

The main differences between Blanchot's and Kierkegaard's conceptions of anxiety/innocence (of anxiety as innocence and of innocence as anxiety) are now made plain. Whereas for Kierkegaard, innocence can be described in terms of anxiety, the study of which belongs to psychology, for Blanchot the study of anxiety cannot be limited to psychology, because anxiety stems from the lack that knowledge is. Now, for Kierkegaard, innocence, considered as the impossibility of knowledge, is an ethical issue. However, conceived as the impossibility of knowledge, does innocence not simply destroy the possibility of ethics?

The Innocence of Guilt

Blanchot and Kierkegaard both see that innocence is not the opposite of guilt, that guilt already inheres in innocence. The disturbance or anxiety of innocence is, *in a way*, guilty. But only in a way. It is guilty inasmuch as it is innocent. It is guilty in the sense that no one is to be held accountable for a particular fault. This conception is reflected in another fragment of *The Step Not Beyond*, where Blanchot writes: "*declared always and everywhere guilty, and, for this matter, unconcerned* (hors de cause)" (105, translation modified). Innocence breaks the law without knowledge and because of non-knowledge; it remains unaccountable for ("unconcerned" with) this rupture of law, for this guilt. Yet by associating innocence with knowledge and not with ignorance, with the non-knowledge that stems from knowledge and not with an absence of knowledge, Blanchot goes further than Kierkegaard in conceiving the impossibility of differentiating guilt and innocence. In fact, as we have seen, Kierkegaard analyzes innocence as what one loses through an act of error, a fault. The loss of innocence is therefore the entry into the condition of sin and the condition of possibility for subjectivity. While in innocence, one is still in a dream state,[20] not fully aware of oneself, in sin, one is under the regime of law, assigned to be oneself. Everything changes, though, if innocence is no longer associated with ignorance. *If innocence is associated with the impossibility of knowledge, then the guilt of innocence is principally what makes subjectivity—and therefore any assumption of the law—impossible.* If innocence is the impossibility of knowledge, then one does not lose innocence in order to become a subject: it is innocence itself that loses the subject. Hence, Blanchot's fragment containing the words "*declared always and everywhere guilty, and, for this matter, unconcerned*" entails not only that innocence is not accountable for its fault, but also that *the primary guilt of innocence is to disavow fault, to impeach any assumption of guilt*. This extension given to the guilt of innocence indicates that Blanchot reads and repeats Kierkegaard's motif of innocence in order to reverse it, and thus to invert the modern and contemporary assumption of the relationship between guilt and subjectivity.

This inversion strengthens indeed the hypothesis that Blanchot's conception of innocence destroys the possibility of ethics, an idea that several fragments in *The Writing of the Disaster* make explicit. Recall certain fragments, cited in the introduction to this book, that put into question Levinas's conception of responsibility in relation to subjectivity, where Blanchot negates the possibility of a subject made *unique* in front of the Other. Where subjectivity fails, "I can no longer appeal to any ethics, any experience, any practice" (1995b, 26). This line of thinking is later confirmed when Blanchot alludes to an ethics that "goes mad"—"as it must" (27)![21] In fact, the radicalization of such guilt entailed by innocence concerns more than Kierkegaard's understanding of ethics: at stake is the very possibility for a grounding of ethics. By a thinking of innocence as what makes the subject impossible, Blanchot rejects not only ethics as grounded in a subject that is master of itself, but also the idea that subjectivity derives from the assumption—be it impossible—of guilt. Therefore, contrary not only to Kierkegaard but also to Heidegger and Levinas, Blanchot would not make the assumption that subjectivity is created via a debt, be it the debt one contracts with the past, as in Heidegger, or a debt contracted with the Other, as in Levinas.[22] Blanchot's departure from these other thinkers is what one of the fragments of *The Writing of the Disaster* oddly confirms. In fact, as mentioned in the introduction to this book, Blanchot relates innocence to the passivity of suffering; namely to what cannot be endured and thus exceeds the subject's power to offer any possible testimony about it. Recall what Blanchot says about the relation between innocence and guilt: "Suffering suffers from being innocent" (41).[23] The suffering caused by such innocence would be relieved if one were to become guilty; it would be part of the economy of the subject that aims for redemption. This is why, Blanchot continues, "thus it seeks to become guilty in order to lessen." But because innocence is the impossibility of subjectivity, it is precisely what destroys such hope of "salvation": "But the passivity in it eludes delinquency: perfectly passive is suffering, safe from the thought of salvation" (41). Hence, not only does innocence's "imperfection" (Schneider 2005) lead to guiltiness; innocence renders guiltiness itself impossible, which is its primary guilt.

The Spacing of Innocence

Because innocence is guilty and because its guilt "elude[s] delinquency," innocence not only breaks the law (as Billy does in *Billy Budd*), but it breaks the law of the law; namely, our hope in a possible redemption from our subjection to law. In more general terms, innocence, conceived as what "eludes delinquency," paradoxically compromises our salvation from death. It compromises humanity as structured by the history of its salvation, as what can possibly be redeemed. Therefore, we may ask again the question initially posed in this book: If innocence is thought of as either the failure of law or as the failure of what grounds the humanity of the human being (a mere destruction of Judeo-Christian theology, of the meaning of its eschatology—or of its meaning tout court), can an ethics emerge from this double guilt? Although the fragments in *The Writing of the Disaster* are explicit not only about ethics' madness but also about the necessity of this madness, can we not think, precisely because of this *necessity*, that this destruction opens to an ethics? In fact, if ethics is by *necessity* mad ("as it *must*" be, writes Blanchot), it is itself produced as law: its madness belongs to a *must*, a duty or a necessity; namely, to a law. Therefore, it cannot be considered merely as a destruction of *any* law. *Innocence is outside of the law inasmuch as it belongs to the law of the destruction of the law.*

In order to face the question of the law of this destruction, let us attend to the consequences of this shift. For Kierkegaard (and this could equally be applied to Heidegger and Levinas[24]), the guilt of innocence explains the birth of subjectivity. As already mentioned, guilt, assumed innocently, is what binds the subject (to the law, the Other, or the past).

Had it not been contracted innocently, the subject would remain within itself, master over its own reason.[25] Therefore, guilt would not be binding. However, because guilt binds without reason, without one having caused this subjection (innocently), it not only gives birth to subjectivity: it also maintains its openness. In fact, guilt constitutes subjectivity in the opening to what it is bound to (the law, the Other, or the past). Therefore, because subjectivity is constituted by the guilt of innocence, subjectivity is opened to its own historicity. Its constitutive guilt is what calls for its transformation and redemption. To reiterate, this explains how the loss of innocence is at once the entry into historical time.

By contrast, it is striking that Blanchot's innocent guilt coincides precisely with the *loss* of time. Innocence, as the impossibility of being, is not, as in its myth, a plenitude of time. Being an unlimited lack, it is also the impossibility of any limits, and therefore of time. Hence, in Blanchot, innocence coincides rather to a disorientation than to a paradisiacal state where everything and everyone seems ordered to goodness. Rather than describing a state of plenitude, of happiness and of harmony, innocence thought of as what fails human being is a space of wandering where what prevails is precisely the absence of any rules and goals that not only fix limits but also define beings. This "spacing"[26] or this wandering (*errance*) can be illustrated through the disorientations produced by Blanchot's main character in *The Last Man*. The "last man" is as fragile as he is unseizable. His fragility makes him paradoxically present through being absent, present as dis-tracted; namely, not fully *there*. But this distraction is not a finite "lack" or fault as with *Billy Budd*'s eponymous protagonist, who still has the grace of spontaneity and therefore of presence. On the contrary, it is what makes Blanchot's "last man" at once infinitely distant and infinitely attractive. *Innocence's lack decenters the space* and yields a game of proximity and distance that no longer has limits. It hence gives birth to disorientation. This is why "one had to draw him into a fault" (1987, 6), for guiltiness would at least fix limits, reintroduce a form of orientation. In this sense, although Blanchot *seems* to say almost exactly what Kierkegaard had asserted, the shift of innocence operative in his thought has, indeed, the opposite consequences. While Kierkegaard still thinks of the loss of innocence as the entry into time and thus the possibility of redemption, Blanchot thinks of innocence as a loss of time that plunges into unlimited wandering (*errance*) or disorientation. Yet, would a space that bears no time, a space of unlimited wandering, not be a pure inferno?

In order to answer this question, let us return to our description of innocence not as what is prior to the fall but as its very failure. In a biblical sense, the Fall, as we have said, is concomitant with the beginning of History. It is a fall *out* of innocence (which also designates an inaccessible time or a time accessible only through myth) into time. In Blanchot, as remarked throughout these chapters, the Fall is not a fall *out* of innocence; it is the fall *of* innocence that is also the fall of time.[27] The fall of innocence is, in fact, this gap, this non-knowledge that makes impossible time and space as horizons for a subject, as they are commonly defined. Blanchot's thought of innocence therefore describes the exact opposite of the biblical Fall. It is as though, in following innocence's non-knowledge, Blanchot were following a deviation, the trace of what has (necessarily) been left out of history: innocence. By thinking innocence as non-knowledge, as this passivity that disturbs both the possibility of knowledge and the constitution of time, by thinking innocence as a spacing that impeaches the subject's assumption, Blanchot indeed suggests that innocence resembles an inferno rather than a state of paradise. In fact, innocence conceived as the impossibility of being accountable for oneself can be pictured as an anonymous state in which no one can make any difference at all. Indifference reigns. Indeed, this conception seems to correspond to hell as defined as the state from which there is no way out.[28] Whereas the ones who are redeemed are the ones who are *saved* from time by virtue of their *historicity*, to be condemned to hell is *to be condemned without end*, in a time that bears no more difference (and is therefore not a time) and to a space without issue. Blanchot's deviation is therefore not a salvation *from* law. As seen in the previous chapters, law is not only "the summit, there is no other" (1993, 433), but grace allows neither an overcoming of the law nor its accomplishment. On the contrary, since this spacing of innocence erases any limit—and hence any law—it can be assimilated into what Agamben describes as a state of exception.[29] Rather than being the sole "violence of law" that imposes limits, that violently decides the jurisdictions over territory, this spacing, in erasing all limits, exposes the very core of law's violence, which is its suspension. Along these lines, not only does this thought of innocence seem to break with any ethics—with any law—but, in this rupture, it is exposed more radically to law's violence. It is the abandonment—without rescue—to an absence of issue.

Failure as Law

But if innocence is a deviation from the law of history, if innocence (and not the state into which humanity has fallen) is what fails, does this deviating line really have an unequivocal meaning? What deviates from the law can only be such—a deviation—if it deviates from itself; namely, if it doesn't become law: a continuous line that would give birth to an unequivocal meaning and that would define unequivocally a condition. Several arguments allow us to doubt that the spacing of innocence (namely, this fall of time) is at once the impossibility of any ethics and a condemnation to hell.

First, returning to *The Writing of the Disaster*, we can observe that Blanchot calls for responsibility where law seems to be refused. One fragment of *The Writing of the Disaster*, for instance, insists that the absence of obligation (and therefore of law) is not equivalent to the absence of responsibility. More precisely, this fragment makes explicit the idea that *there is responsibility where there is no law*. Such fragments refer to "that to which without obligation one must nonetheless answer (*répondre*)" (1995b, 34). In this sense, like Levinas, Blanchot is challenging the foundations of ethics. Like Levinas, for Blanchot responsibility does not require a self-positioned subject; namely, a subject whose activity is warrant of their consciousness and whose consciousness is warrant of their responsibility. For both Blanchot and Levinas, responsibility is anterior to consciousness because it stems from the subject's exposure, which is necessarily passive. In this sense, responsibility is not grounded but is without base, and at the same time is conditioned by a "passivity more passive than any passivity" (Levinas 1998, 14). Yet Blanchot seems indeed to go further than Levinas. In fact, the rupture between Blanchot and Levinas is located precisely around the notion of the law, of the binding, of the relation (the link or the line). While for Levinas the exposure of the subject comes from the face-to-face with the Other (Autrui) to which I am *bound* in spite of myself, for Blanchot the exposure of the subject breaks the bond of any relation, relating therefore to what is out of all bounds: what is outside of law. In *The Step Not Beyond*, Blanchot speaks, for instance, of a "relation with the non-concerning" that is neither "suffered" nor "assumed" by a subject (1992, 123). As previously stated, contrary to Levinas, this sort of passivity entails for Blanchot a rupture with the unicity of the "I" who suffers instead of assuming, as well as a rupture with the alterity of the Other to whom the "I" is bound, unavoidably and unconsciously linked.[30] Yet this rupture does not put an end to all responsibility. On the contrary, it redefines its origin and its task.

This rupture with Levinas, which marks a "step beyond" Levinas's notion of responsibility, leads us now to our second argument regarding the relation between innocence and ethics. Although Blanchot makes explicit the idea that this space without a subject (what we have called the spacing of innocence) breaks with any ethics,[31] he searches for the origin of an injunction, a call, that not only takes its source from outside of the law but obligates beyond it. In *The Writing of the Disaster*, Blanchot associates, for instance, the "failure," the "fall," and "law." It is as if law could now signify not the limit (that links and binds), but its erasure or failure—*as if law coincided not with the fall into sin but with the fall of innocence (the fall that innocence is)*. Recalling the proximity between "*falloir*" (which indicates an obligation: to have to) and *faillir* (which indicates a failure, a lack toward an obligation), Blanchot finally affirms in one fragment that "in its very failing the law commands" (1995b, 44). Since Blanchot is here pointing to a law that is maintained in its very failure, it is worth quoting the whole fragment:

> between falloir (be necessary) and faillir (fail)—I also say, it lacks, falls short, deceives. Such is the beginning of the fall: in its very failing the law commands, and thereby saves itself as law. (44)[32]

What does this fragment indicate regarding the problem of the relationship between innocence and ethics? What conclusions can we draw from reading it? If innocence is the failure of the subject, its impossibility (and therefore, the impossibility of any ethics), *it never ceases to act as law nonetheless*. In this sense, innocence can be associated to a fall, just as law can be associated to a fall. Innocence is not what is pure of law; it is rather an impurity (a fall) that acts as law. It is not the ignorance of law; it is law as what can never be known, as the very content and dimension of our ignorance. For this reason, we can even say that innocence expresses what, after Schmitt, Agamben, and Derrida had described as the ambivalence of law: what defines law's sovereignty is precisely that law is outside of the law. It is not founded, grounded, or explained. It does not belong to any law. But here, Blanchot puts at stake both the dialectical relationship between law and transgression that Saint Paul had already described in his Epistles and the aporia of the fall into sin that can only be explained by innocence (since before the Fall there is not a *subject* bound to law). The fall of innocence, this innocent guilt and this guilty innocence, delivers the space that best allows us to understand what in chapter one of this book was described as the "force of law" (Derrida 1992): its unfounded foundation (its "mystical authority," as Derrida would say, in the words of Pascal) outside of law. The fall of innocence, the failure as innocence, is what calls without properly binding. It is what cannot be avoided but that cannot be inscribed. It is hence this void of law—and this void that law requires, this void that law is—that is always already transgressed but that, because it remains unidentified, stays "unconcerned."

So, is the spacing of innocence the immobilization into hell, into an inferno? Whereas in Kierkegaard's thought the Fall could still open historical perspectives that would lead to redemption, can the "spacing of innocence," the fall *of* innocence, constitute any kind of promise?

Interestingly, when Blanchot seems to depart from any ethics, to the complete failure of ethics, he happens to repeat again a Kierkegaardian topic, but he does so in order to distance himself from Kierkegaard.[33] In *Fear and Trembling* (1985), Kierkegaard had criticized ethics, reducing it to legality; namely, to the mere application of rules. If I do no more than apply a rule, I may be acting legally, but I am not a self. I am just anybody. I am an anonymous bureaucrat who acts but doesn't think, and who therefore doesn't decide. Ethics (for Kierkegaard) being an anonymous sphere, Kierkegaard thinks of a sphere beyond ethics (defined as the mere application of rule) where the subject would recover their singularity. As we have seen, the "spacing of innocence" is precisely a space of wandering where the subject is made impossible and where anonymity reigns.[34] Yet now we can say that this anonymity is not pure indifference: it calls, it is this "Outside" (outside of the law), this "unconcerned" *of which* "one" has to answer, *although* no *one* in particular is called or concerned. Hence, Blanchot distinguishes the dissolution of the self that makes of anyone "anybody" from Kierkegaard's critique of anonymity: "There is no name anymore for a 'self,' but this namelessness is not the crude anonymity defined by Kierkegaard," writes Blanchot (1995b, 120).

Anonymity for Blanchot is not the absence of the self. It is rather the *otherness* of the self. It is its failure and therefore what *both threatens its relation to the law and also entails it*. This might now permit us to understand what is at stake in Blanchot's repetition of the concept of anguish, and of anguish thought as innocence. In Kierkegaard, innocence (as it causes anguish) leads to guilt; such is its innocence, because its fault was committed without knowledge. In Blanchot, innocence (as anguish) erases guilt; such is its guilt, because at play in this erasure is the (im)possibility of *any* ethics and therefore the risk of eternal impunity, the reign of evil. But if, for Blanchot, innocence destroys guilt because it destroys the unicity of the subject, it does not destroy the *feeling of guilt*: "man feels guilty for not being able to bear innocence, guilty of this innocence that anguishes him" (1992, 67). This means that outside of the law, there where there are no bounds, no limits, no obligations, one is still convoked to respond. But how can we define the content of such responsibility if, at its source, there is neither a subject nor an object? Since it is the failure of the law that is calling, what one is responsible for is the rupture of the law. One's task in responding is therefore not to leap beyond ethics, as in Kierkegaard, in order to exceed its generality, but to affirm the rupture of any law. Therefore, the fall *of* innocence does not constitute a promise of redemption. Nothing can be reached with such responsibility. No limits can be definitely crossed. Instead of a promise of redemption, the fall of innocence calls for constant rupture. At stake here is the necessity to respond not to what is beyond law (God, the sovereign) but to what is *beneath law*, to what doesn't accede to law: to the stammering of Billy Budd that makes him *less than a man*, to what escapes language but doesn't cease to murmur, to make noise. Indeed, by thinking of innocence as this non-knowledge that breaks the law, Blanchot is not seeking to reach the paradise of the innocents as if paradise would save from evil. Neither does he intend to accede to the truth of the Adamic myth. Rather, he seeks to give voice to what is beneath language, which has the power to link and therefore stands as law. This is why innocence is not what is left behind in the moment when we accede to speech and consciousness. *Innocence echoes language as its meaningless rest*. Rather than being the language we speak, the truth we can possess, it is the murmur that defines the content of our responsibility and that we cannot avoid. For this reason, far from leading to the abandonment of ethics and of philosophy (conceived as the problem of knowledge), the spacing of innocence defines anew its task, its exigency. As we read in *The Step Not Beyond*:

> Behind discourse the refusal to discourse speaks, as behind philosophy the refusal to philosophize would speak: speech not speaking, violent, concealing itself, saying nothing and suddenly crying out. Each is responsible as soon as he speaks, responsibility so heavy that he refuses it, but always in vain, it weighs on him before any refusal, and even if he sinks under its weight, he drags it down with him—responsible, in addition, for his collapse. (1992, 116)

Chapter 4

Apocalypse

> The belief that we might be the gleaming signs of the fire's writing, written in everyone, legible only in me, the one who answers. . . .
>
> —Blanchot, *The Last Man*, 64

> The other history would be a feigned history, which is not to say that it is a mere nothing, but that it is always calling forth the void of a nonplace, the gap that it is, and that separates it from itself. It is unbelievable because any belief in it would have to overlook it.
>
> —Maurice Blanchot, *The Writing of the Disaster*, 139

Conceived as a fall and even as the very failure of the subject, innocence prevents any thought of an origin. In Blanchot's texts, we have discovered that innocence is not a plenitude but the very impossibility of time, and that innocence is not a state of paradise but rather an inferno in which one risks being stricken with an inability to speak and to act according to reasons; where one is reduced to stuttering, which is a form of muteness, and hence confined to immobility. In this scenario, innocence not only coincides with the destitution of the mythical idea of an origin, but also with the impossibility of history and hence not only with an idea of progress, but also with the idea of change. Does this mean that with the topic of innocence thought of as the failure of the subject, we are facing a new idea of *apocalypse*—not an apocalypse that would take place *within* the course of history in order to end it, but an apocalypse *of* history that would sustain as immobility: an apocalypse where what would end is the possibility of the end and hence the possibility of deciding and judging?

The theme of the apocalypse—that is, of the revelation of the meaning of history—has experienced several types of interpretations: religious, literary, and philosophical. However, in each of these areas of thought, the apocalypse itself plays the revelatory role of disclosing the context of the times during which the interpretations were written. The Apocalypse of John, for example, can be understood in the context of persecution in which it was written.[1] But it also accounts for the Christian view of history as a whole; of the meaning of Christianity. If the twentieth century also has its own apocalypticians, it is not only due to the end-of-the-century atmosphere that haunts every century. The theme of the apocalypse found in Günther Anders, for instance,[2] speaks of a context characterized by certain events (the atomic bomb and thus technological development) as well as a certain status of philosophy: the influence of nihilism[3] on the question of meaning and, thus, of a certain end of history. But the worst of the apocalypses might not be the one that judges us, but rather the apocalypse that justifies our inertia to history. If we have nothing to fear in facing the apocalypse, it is because we have accepted all evils. In this context, we no longer need to respond to our action.

The fact that there may be apocalyptic theses during every era does not mean that their content (what they reveal) should be identical each time. While John's Apocalypse is flamboyant and arouses hope or fear (in the announcement of the end of the world, but also, and more importantly, in the final judgment), Anders's apocalypse is neither desirable nor undesirable. It speaks about a mutation of humanity, which has become immune to judgment; about a time that is without end or intensity (as is the case of judgment). For Anders, if we have indeed entered the end of time, it is not only because the atomic bomb can cause the physical destruction of the world. In fact, the atomic bomb reveals that the *world can end without judgment*. Moreover, the development of the technique is such that we could be automatons and not the ones responsible for the end of the world.[4] Consequently, facing the imminence of the end, we are not summoned in person. Anders's grim description is not about those who are potentially to blame, who fear judgment and hope for justice. On the contrary, it shows that the development of technology has immediately rendered evil innocent.[5] What is apocalyptic in the contemporary apocalypse is that it reveals none other than its own emptiness, which sets us back into an inertia (an absence of combat) that is immediately justified.[6]

In addition to these two extremes, there is another figure of the apocalypse that emerges from this nihilist climate: the apocalypse of Blanchot. In contrast to Anders, for Blanchot the apocalypse is not only a "phenomenon" determined by the context of the times; rather, the end is what occurs in every instant. Insofar as life is structurally finite, death is not a future event; rather, it prevents life from having frontiers that belong to it. Therefore, for Blanchot, the end is always already there, from the beginning. Now, by virtue of the contamination between life and death, between the beginning and the end, Blanchot leads us to think—and from different angles—that the end of the world has in a certain way already occurred. Death, having already befallen with life, makes us rather survivors for Blanchot. As we read in *The Step Not Beyond*, "to survive" is "rather to arrest dying, arrest that does not arrest, making it, on the contrary, last" (1992, 135). Likewise, since the beginning has always already been initiated by the end, for Blanchot, the world is rather a surrogate (a resemblance of a world) than a grounded and stable entity. In a way, since for Blanchot the end has always already taken place, time is none other than the eternal return of the end; of that which prevents the meaning of being forever present, unifiable, and therefore able to be grasped within a story. In this sense, there is neither the world nor meaning, nor, consequently, progress, but an eternal return of the end. Then does this mean that Blanchot forbids us to think *before* history? If the end is present from the very beginning, is it not rather high time to make history out of this end? Is it not time to take the apocalypse seriously?

The Shadow of the Apocalypse

While the theme of the apocalypse is seldom present in Blanchot's work—at least as a theme[7]—neither is it marginal. Rather, the apocalypse is like a question at the crossroads of fields whose borders are shaken by Blanchot's work: philosophy, the tradition of the Book, literature. Considered in a philosophical or biblical sense, the Apocalypse occurs as a revelation; that is, as a certain way of manifesting the truth. It coincides with the end of history, or even of the world, precisely in that the end is the very mode of this revelation or self-presentation of truth. The revelation is in fact an immediate presence: it cannot stand in time. It coincides, thereby, with the suppression of time and history. But what exactly is the point of view of literature on the Apocalypse? Literature, insofar as it develops in the world of fiction, is in a way the opposite of truth. We may ask, then, if it might not be the best critical weapon *against* the Apocalypse—that is, against the end of history and of the world—required by revelation.

Even if the question of the apocalypse is not treated as a main theme in Blanchot's work, it is still ubiquitous. It coincides with its narrative thread, haunted by the imminence of the end. Therefore, from *The Most High* to *The Last Man*, the apocalypse is present in its multiple facets: it coincides with the topic of the end of history in *The Most High*, with the theme of resurrection that appears in *Death Sentence*,[8] in the way in which the imminence of the end structures Blanchot's complete works, in the question of knowing if the end coincides with a revelation, and finally, in the question of knowing how to grasp this end in the language we possess, which is, precisely, the temporal and historical device through which communication is possible.

These various facets of the apocalypse are not, however, a simple thematic dissemination of a biblical topic that Blanchot would reproduce without alteration. Blanchot's text "Literature and the Right to Death" suggests, in a way, that literature maintains an essential and specific relation to the Apocalypse. In this text, the question of literature is evoked through the themes that are themselves apocalyptic: death and (revolutionary) terror, for example. Yet, there is a difference between the philosophical and biblical approaches to the Apocalypse, as opposed to a literary approach. Indeed, on the one hand, and in a very Hegelian sense (filtered through Kojève's reading of Hegel), Blanchot thinks of the apocalypse in relation to the revelatory role of the end. If death (the negative) is undertaken in the work of meaning, then the end (death) has a revelatory role. The meaning that is made possible through the negative is necessarily apocalyptic since it implies the idea that the truth is revealed in the end; that the truth is revealed *through* the end. In this way, philosophy and religion (defined here by the tradition of the Book) share a certain point of view on the Apocalypse. Yet, intriguingly, in this text Blanchot does not situate this shared knowledge at the end of times, but rather at the origin; that is, at the beginning. This idea is particularly present in Blanchot's conception of language that supposes the annihilation of the thing; namely, the idea that death—the end—is at work in the beginning. In a crucial passage in "Literature and the Right to Death," Blanchot begins by recalling an idea that is common to both philosophy and the tradition of the Book: the correlation between language and being. As for Hegel, things of the world and therefore the world itself befall by way of a spiritualization (e.g., as cultural objects). In *Genesis*, the coming to light of things does not precede the language that names them. It is by naming that Adam becomes master of the world. Thus, Blanchot quotes Hegel, who affirms that "Adam's first act, which made him master of the animals, was to give them names, that is, he annihilated them in their existence (as existing creatures)" (Blanchot 1995a, 323). By recalling the dialectical dimension of their being, Blanchot also recalls the dialectical dimension of the human being. Both things and human beings are befallen by language. Yet, this dialectical spiral has various consequences. On the one hand, it must be stated that the role played by language in the coming to light of things is not *innocent*. To name is in fact to annihilate. By representing the thing, the word also entails the absence of the thing. As Blanchot writes, "A word may give me its meaning, but first it suppresses it" (1995a, 322). Therefore, if the coming to light is made possible by language, and if in language annihilation is at work, then the end of the world (annihilation) is at the beginning. To quote the Hegelian commentary on *Genesis* is to say that we must think of the apocalypse in its coming to light of the world and not only in its eclipse. It is to say that the end is in the beginning; that it is coextensive with that which makes the present possible, and thus with time and therefore history.

Now, if annihilation is at the beginning, then our experience in the world is also a time of captivity. The human being who becomes master of the world through language, the human being whose language recalls their historical condition, is also the one who becomes a prisoner of that which they dominate; prisoner of a beginning that abandons them to the end of a history that is already destiny. Blanchot writes:

> God had created living things, but man had to annihilate them. Not until then did they take on meaning for him, and he in turn created them out of the death into which they had disappeared; only instead of beings (*êtres*) and, as we say, existants (*existants*), there remained only being (*l'être*), and man was condemned not to be able to approach anything or experience anything except through the meaning he had to create. He saw that he was enclosed in daylight, and he knew this day could not end, because the end itself was light, since it was from the end of beings that their meaning—which is being—had come. (1995a, 323)

In Blanchot's comment on his Hegelian reading of *Genesis*, the specific rapport between literature and the Apocalypse is played out. Recalling—in a

Hegelian way—that the end is in the beginning, Blanchot pits Hegel against himself and moves from the biblical Apocalypse (as well as from a certain structural homology that can be found between the dialectical conception of being and the Christian idea of the Apocalypse) to the literary apocalypse. If the end is in the beginning, as Hegel shows, then the beginning is impossible. The correlation between language and being shows that since human being wants to create *the* being—to become master, affirm their freedom, and therefore make history (by which they break their subjection to destiny)—they confirm their belonging to being, to nothingness, to the end, to death. So, *their entrance into history is their immobilization by history.* The human being who becomes such by giving themselves a beginning is in fact the human being of repetition (*recommencement*), the human being who becomes a prisoner of their own system: the human being who cannot start, who cannot be human. The human being who makes themself human by rendering themself master of the world, belongs from the beginning to the end of the world and of the human. Hence, while the tradition of the Book and the reading suggested by Hegel focus on the story of *Genesis*, literature focuses on its impossibility, on the inertia of the beginning, on *an end of the world that is concomitant with the possibility of the world.*[9] But why would literature, specifically, have another point of view on the apocalypse?

Blanchot's shift from the theme of the beginning to that of the apocalypse is a *step backward* or even a movement that is *immobile*. More precisely, the theme of the apocalypse in Blanchot holds onto this backward movement, a movement that is also immobile, a way (as in wandering) of staying put while advancing. Now, this immobility is in one sense the matter of literature. In a contemporary text on "Literature and the Right to Death" titled "Reality and Its Shadow,"[10] Levinas noted that the novel has its own time, which is not historical time; that is to say, the time of becoming, of transformation, of the influence that the human being has on the world.[11] Since the characters of a novel cannot speak (they are spoken for, they are that which the author of the book makes them say), they cannot transform their fate. The time of a novel is thus the temporality of fate, the time of the inexorable, of that which cannot change: of immobility.[12] But this difference in time should not be understood from a clear division between the realms of fiction and the real, which would belong to history. It is in fact inherent to the dialectic of being and ends up corroding this border between realms (of fiction and the real). Indeed, if being only emerges through its own negation, then it ends up welling like nothingness. Moreover, the dialectic of being equally implies the dialectic whereby being is made possible; that is, language. While language implies the negation of something in order to make it present in the form of an idea (re-present it), the history of the dialectic equally implies that for the being to be understood within all its moments, language must be negated to be re-presented. In this sense, "literature attempts being the revelation of what revelation destroys" (1995a, 328). This is the abyss from which literature emerges. If in everyday life, language is a means for accessing things (the element of negation: the negative at work), in contrast, in a work of art, language is presented as that which it is: it does not erase before the (absent) thing, but the thing is presented as absence. In this sense, literature is not foreign to the dialectic of being, to reality in its historical dimension; rather it is inherent to this dialectic up to the final moment of reflection. But from the moment that language is reflected upon, it cannot be negated, apprehended, mastered, since what appears with this last reflection is the nothingness that it is: the being as nothingness. This is why Blanchot writes that "the ideal of literature could have been this: to say nothing, to speak in order to say nothing" (1995a, 324). The immobile movement described by Blanchot when he shifts from the theme of genesis to that of the apocalypse is thus a movement inherent to the dialectic of being. However, it prevents this dialectic from being embraced, negated, and reflected in its truth. This immobile movement is the movement by which philosophy (whose movement is always assured in its recovery, in the possibility of its reflection in itself) stumbles in literature. It is the movement through which the being shifts into the nothingness that it is and that only comes to light when language is represented; that is to say, by the language of literature.[13]

What does this dialectical spiral of the being—which rather than self-realizing is found entangled in the language of literature, in words that have become things, as Blanchot writes—have to offer in respect to the question of the apocalypse?[14]

By connecting the end to the beginning, and by showing how the beginning is entangled in repetition (in a movement that reverses rather than advances), "Literature and the Right to Death" describes, in a way, *two apocalypses*. On the one hand, the apocalypse is concomitant with the way the truth manifests itself, occurs, or comes to light. In this sense, the apocalypse is not a purely irrational theme: philosophy belongs to its history. The Apocalypse of John, which is full of flamboyant images, corroborates (before time) a Hegelian conception of the spirit, which occurs as a fire. If what is true proceeds through annihilation, it can be compared to fire, which sheds light while destroying. The spirit that is embodied in the world in order to reveal meaning is fire. The world, in the Hegelian tradition, is true insofar as it is spiritual; that is, to the extent that a fire constitutes it. Since truth always occurs through certain destruction, its work ultimately joins the Apocalypse (a revelation that is also a destruction). On the other hand, the same fire reveals its power only by revealing its impotence. As Blanchot writes, since it is through language (the power of annihilation, of fire) that things come to light, the human being becomes the master of things by becoming the prisoner of the day. If they have power over that which can be denied, they have no power over the being that becomes synonymous with nothingness, which imposes upon the nothingness that makes it be. Thus, as we have seen, in the beginning, the human being annihilates the beings created by God, but this annihilation through which the human being creates a history for themselves is in fact a prison for the human being. He "saw that he was enclosed in daylight, and he knew this day could not end, since the end itself was light, since it was from the end of beings that their meaning—which is being—had come" (1995a, 323). The other apocalypse described by Blanchot, without necessarily being a subject of study, is that of nothingness revealed: of the day from which there is no escape, of the history that becomes fate once again. This apocalypse, which shadows the biblical Apocalypse, describes *an end of the world that is inherent to that which renders the world possible, as well as an end of time that is inherent to history*. This has to do, therefore, with a "work of fire" that has no home in truth or in the spirit, but which ultimately consumes (reflects) the spirit without allowing this consumption to come to term—that is to say, without coming to an end. The flame that animates literature is not the flame of life, where death is at work. Rather, the flame of death reveals nothing more than some nothingness that remains meaningless. Therefore, this apocalypse is not homologous with the biblical Apocalypse. Instead, what is present in this apocalypse is "the being which protests against revelation" (1995a, 330), which is to say, the being that refuses itself in the fire of truth.[15] How, then, can we understand this apocalypse, which only doubles the fire of truth as a shadow? Would the finding of an end of the world that would always already be there not simply increase the risk of immobility demonstrated by the various theses on the end of history and the world? Moreover, would the fact that the end of the world has no other consistency than that of being the shadow of reality, the shadow of the fire that makes the world in its truth, not absolve us even more thoroughly of any responsibility before history? What judgment and what justice can be expected of a shadow apocalypse?

The Other History or the Mobility of the Immobile

The relation between the language of literature and the end of the world evoked in "Literature and the Right to Death" allows us to articulate the end-of-century ambiance that appears in reading some of Blanchot's texts. *The Last Man*, for example, a text published almost ten years after *The Work of Fire*, returns to the question of fire, but in such an enigmatic way that one cannot tell if the theme of fire corresponds to the prophecy of the end of time, if it is performative, or if it is nothing more than a way of avoiding its announcement, its truth. In fact, in this two-part text, the second part blurs any hints that would allow the reader to locate an event, a subject of enunciation, and to delineate a theme. Furthermore, what could be the subject of the second part of the text is less a discernible event than a narrative voice that gradually ceases to narrate in order to address itself, thwarting the reader's ability to identify either the narrator or the subject that it narrates. It is as if the story of the "last man" were the story of the metamorphosis of the narrative and language; as if one could not think of the end (of man or, rather, of the human being and of history) in a language that is no longer that of the human being and its history. In the first place, a narrator speaks of an Other in the third person (he). Here, although this "Other" (an extremely fragile man, as observed in the previous chapter) may be very confusing, the narrator still has grounds from which to experience this detour and to formulate his astonishment. Secondly, the narrator seems to speak from another shore, as if after death (without allowing one to discern whether it is his death or that of someone else). In this second instance, the narrating subject is no longer in the position to give an account of that which barely happens. He is no longer in the position of the story, but rather of the *rapport*: of addressing (you), or even of prayer. It is as if the second part of the text were about a time after the end of time, but told in a language that is not precisely the secular language that can still be shared between finite and eternal time: between the present and beyond and which is constituted on the base of negativity; namely, of the end as a possibility. Can we deduce that this is a story for a time beyond time, that "after the end of the world" there is still a history? In this sense, contrary to Anders's prediction, can we think of a story of the end of history and the world?

The theme of the end of the world not only recurs in Blanchot's thought; it is a *point of departure*. This means that although this theme could very well place us at an impasse (the risk of complacency in immobility), it translates for Blanchot into the promise of *another movement* that allows the thinking of what Blanchot once called "the other history" (1995b, 138–39). But this movement can be another only if it disobeys the traditional patterns from which we think and act. To understand the theme of "the other history" in Blanchot, we must understand how we can think anew the question of the relationship between time and movement, and how, for Blanchot, a movement is still possible in the end. In this regard, Blanchot has two interlocutors.

The first is, of course, Hegel, for whom history consists in the dialectical synthesis of two movements: the temporalization of the spirit (that is embodied in the world) and time (whose history is spiritualization) becoming eternal. Since for Hegel the real is spiritual, not only does the spirit pass the test of contingency (i.e., of time), but also does so by acquiring meaning, contingency rises to the eternal. But we have seen that for Blanchot, these two movements, far from making possible the equilibrium between time and eternity, meet in a sterile eternity, immobilized by the end that it claims to subsume. Historical time tilts into the perpetual repetition; that is, into destiny: wandering without a goal. Thus, the immobility that Blanchot notices does not consist in an absence of movement, but rather a movement that does not advance, that is caught in its own trap.

The second interlocutor is Heidegger, for whom, as for Hegel, history is turned toward its own end. However, for Heidegger, what makes meaning possible is withheld, so that no access to the source is possible without a return toward what has been concealed. In this sense, there can be no authentic beginning other than that which has been held back, if what comes from oblivion can be unobscured. Heidegger's thought then describes a movement that aims to make present the immemorial, the origin. This is a return movement that institutes a new beginning. For Blanchot, if it is true that meaning is constituted in the oblivion of its condition of possibility, there is no access to this oblivion simply because that which is a condition of possibility is also the ordeal of a collapse of the possible. As we have seen from Blanchot and from Hegel's reading of *Genesis*, the negative, which is the condition of possibility of meaning, also coincides with the test (the ordeal) of its impossibility. The meaning revealed by the negative is also a void of meaning, an abyss.[16] Therefore, if appropriating the origin, unveiling what was kept in oblivion, could offer a way out of the Hegelian circle, Blanchot shows how the return to the Heideggerian origin also leads to wandering, the immobility of a perpetual repetition. Insofar as that which evades meaning is also that which threatens it with collapse from within, for Blanchot the origin can only be that which is missing, not what makes the beginning possible. But toward what other movement does Blanchot lead us?

Blanchot's conversation with Hegel and Heidegger on the subject of history allows us to describe his objective in greater detail. Blanchot is not concerned with producing movement (since movement could create immobility) but rather with *immobility as a source of movement*. In fact, time conceived as spirit (i.e., in an active form), as revelation or as the unveiling of meaning, describes an immobile movement. In contrast, immobility (namely, the passivity of time) could paradoxically break the vicious circle of a movement that, by turning upon itself, leads to wandering (and hence to immobility). Indeed, the immobility that is discovered in wandering is precisely that which forbids the return to the self. Therefore, if this immobility is a passive ordeal, one in which the self no longer has power and can no longer be an "I," it is from this immobility that we must begin to think of a movement that does not return to the same (and that immobilizes in this return), and thus, to think "another history." In this regard, it must be noted that the immobility in question here is not the opposite of movement, but rather that which *prevents movement*. It is that which breaks with its structure; namely, with what structures it into immobility. Put differently, the immobility in question is that of a "passivity more passive than any passivity," of a passivity that is not the nonactive, but one that resists activity. However, this passivity, which fails movement, frees from the perpetual return of the same entailed in this movement that comes from the self and returns to itself. Insofar as passivity is not voluntary, it does not belong to the order of the "I can"—it is not simply a nonmovement—and it leads beyond the order of the subject whose circular nature of activity paradoxically ended up making movement sterile. But if the way out of the vicious circle proceeds from immobility and passivity, how can we think of this passivity in terms of movement?

For Blanchot, the answer to this question takes different "forms." The ordeal of passivity is precisely that of the writer, for whom the problem of the beginning comes from an aporia and not from a possible (to write one must be a writer, but to be a writer one must write); it is the ordeal of fatigue that slows down time and prevents one from bringing a task to term; it is the ordeal of words that expose to the void of meaning that which constitutes them and thus suspends our immanence to the world. This test of passivity (which is rather a trial, an ordeal) casts a shadow on the language that the human being uses to define themself and on which they make possible the community, knowledge, the world, law, time. Furthermore, since the test of passivity touches on different areas of existence, in Blanchot's work it affects writing and speech in different ways: the story that no longer follows a thread of narrative, but instead a repetitive wandering or circling (of a time that does not come to term); the conversation that becomes infinite due to constant interruption (returns by diverting); and fragmentary writing, where the lack of unity gives place to infinite ramifications. As to Heidegger's difference, for whom poetry was the opening onto the origin, for Blanchot, the voices that allow us to detour are multiple.[17] Rather than referring to the pure sphere of poetry, these voices are part of our daily life: they are part of the passing of time, of its useless dimension. But they also challenge the question of writing and of language; that is to say, the future of the human being (for whom the dialectic, we have seen, also depends on language). The question is thus to identify how passivity is at stake in these different "forms" and how these different "forms" can give place to a mobility of the immobile.

The response to these questions holds on to what prevents them, since what we call "forms" here (i.e., the content) are not forms. If we take the example of *The Infinite Conversation* (*L'entretien infini*), we will first notice that the word *entretien*, which can be translated as "having a talk" or a chat but which also means "taking care of" or "having something last" (*faire durer*), in contrast to the conversation, does not assume that we're talking *about* something. To talk or, rather, to chat, is above all to occupy one's time with someone or oneself. "The infinite chat" is less a literary form than it is a relationship between language and time.[18] In *The Infinite Conversation*, time is occupied without doing anything specific; thus being occupied without purpose, one occupies time endlessly. But if "having a talk" is not the dialogue or the conversation that supposes a point of convergence or a common theme of conversation, it still seems structured as a dialogue in which different interlocutors would intervene. However, if the form seems to be present, such is not the case of the content. The so-called interlocutors in *The Infinite Conversation* do not speak to each other, no more than they embody common or opposite views. Through "them," a same idea repeats, but it is pushed to its limits in a way that—as when we "beat around the bush" in reality, in this test of limits—thought repeats, but this repetition never happens as the same. In the immobility of the chat in which one does nothing with one's time but rather squanders it by engaging in idle words, *something moves, a movement occurs*. Albeit insignificant and without location, the movement of this non-time has nonetheless rendered the thought an other.

We can describe this paradox of the movement of immobility by observing Blanchot's fragmentary writing. In *The Writing of the Disaster*, for example, that which could constitute a unit, through the fragment, is in fact not a unit. The "fragment," which is often illegible as such (i.e., not reducible to a meaningful content), causes one to think, however, about what escapes thought. Rather than constituting a "piece"—a unit of meaning or part of a reflection—the fragment delivers an "absent meaning" by which it is unidentified. As Leslie Hill has shown in *Maurice Blanchot and Fragmentary Writing* (2012), the fragment is not finished: it opens upon the fragmentary as an infinite space. But since this infinite space is produced in the reiteration of an insufficiency of meaning, this infinite is not thinkable as a continuous line: it fragments in turn in the scansion of *another time*, a time that is no longer linear or synthetic, or even ecstatic, since nothing more allows an imagining of the unit. Here we see, once again, how mobility passes through a test (an ordeal) of immobility. As a repudiation of meaning, the fragment immobilizes. The reading (of a fragment) cannot be a synthetic work that ensures the recovery of meaning. Yet this immobility is also how eternity passes through the reader and is thus historicized. Therefore, if with Blanchot, to read does not consist in re-creating history, reading, through passivity, rather consists in the crumbling of eternity. Hence the invitation or injunction that is found in one of the final fragments of *The Writing of the Disaster*: "Let us share eternity to make it transitory" (1995b, 146). While the fragment immobilizes, enclosing the reader in eternity, the very act of reading is that through which eternity will have passed and through which it will be historicized. *Here, "the other history" is the history of the other, of that which objects to history;* but it also requires that the one through which history occurs (namely, the reader) be another; that is to say, no longer there as a subject but tested by immobility.

"The Void of a Non-Place"

Through this movement (of the immobile), we find without a doubt the answers to the questions we have raised. The fact that for Blanchot the apocalypse is not only to come, but that it has also always already occurred, does not mean that he accepts the idea of the end of history and the sterility it implies. On the contrary, this shadow apocalypse that has to do with language and literature releases the need for a new responsibility before history. It means writing an "other history" that is in fact the history of history's other (of what is excluded from history), and that only occurs through this immobility that separates me from myself, delivers me to the other—as if the solemn tone of the second part of *The Last Man* situated us at *the end of time of which we would have to make history and whose history would not depend on a subject of history*. In this way, it would consist, for Blanchot, of *thinking of time from its end and not as a path toward the end*. But does this mean that, far from abandoning oneself to the imagery of the apocalypse that repeats from one age to the next, and also far from a prophetic writing directed to a future for which one can hope, Blanchot would write in the *language* of the apocalypse; that is, in the language of the end? In this sense, would Blanchot go a step further than Saint John? Would *The Work of Fire* be part of this language that, far from prophesying the end, would deliver us entirely from it? If such were the case, the time of the end would not even be in the order of a timeline: it would have happened as what had always already prevented time. There would be nothing more to say, no more books to write.

This is not what Blanchot calls "the other history." For Blanchot, eternity becomes historicized (becomes "transient") in what makes the present impossible. So nothing comes to term; no end is revealed. In response to the question posed by Blanchot in *The Writing of the Disaster*, "And what about the *other* history, if its characteristic trait is not to be a history," we should answer that it would be nothing, since "nothing of the present ever happens" (1995b, 138). The "other history" consists in disavowing all by nothing, but since this nothing is never present, we can never attest to the truth of this "other history." This, Blanchot writes, "would be a feigned history." This pretense is not a lie, indeed, but simply a withholding from the realm of truth as well as from belief (we believe what we consider to be the truth).[19] However, we still must ask if this affirmation of the ephemeral, of the transient, this historicity that no longer finds its anchor point in time but rather in eternity (an absence of time), does not pose a similar problem to the inertia before which we are placed by the end of history, conceived as a sterile event. In fact, can we simply disavow time and with it the duration in the name of the ephemeral, of that which never settles in time? This is certainly to deny the immobility of the end, but it can also lead to disavow the world (I will discuss this point more extensively in chapter five). Moreover, is it not by virtue of time that the ephemeral can occur? Is the duration not the test of what occurs?

By the "other history" and the responsibility for which it calls, Blanchot finds, undoubtedly, a solution to the problem perceived by Anders: that of an end of the world that arrives without judgment and that Anders also calls an "apocalypse without kingdom" (2006, 88). However, for Blanchot, this has nothing to do with locating an instance of judgment (and for that a meaning for history, a truth to be revealed), but with a redefinition of our responsibility. The "other history" calls on us to respond to what is subtracted from the kingdom, to that which from the beginning, and in virtue of the beginning, "protests against revelation." But this ethical issue could imply a political problem: having to evade all kingdoms, this responsibility toward the "absent meaning" (Blanchot 1995b, 41) could make us forget as well that history is also comprised of our being together; that is to say, of a multiplicity of histories. The "other history" cannot uniquely be a history of nothing and as nothing (the "void of a non-place"). Instead, it has to be a history with others for whom the problem of time not only concerns the eternal, but also the needs of the transient and the needs of the world.

Nota Bene: The World of the End of the World

In "Apocalypse et consolation" (2014), Michaël Foessel shows how the imminence of the end can leave a space for new metaphysical theories (as when the imminence of the "end of human being" leads to the anonymous affirmation of being or for all sorts of vitalist theories), or to a thought of the world as something that remains to be accomplished. On this note, Foessel evokes the film *Melancholia* by Lars Von Trier where, facing the imminent end of the world (an asteroid is about to collide with the earth), a woman and a child (her nephew) decide to build a shed: meaning, they decide to construct a still-possible world at the final moment of its impossibility. For Michaël Foessel, "this scene is comforting because it makes an event seconds before all events become impossible" (2014, 74), which is to say that "the time that is left," the "time of the end," is not only the time of eternity, but also a *time in common*. As I address in the following chapter, we can ask if this common is not what Blanchot's "other history" ultimately ignores. Let us note, however, that the responsibility toward the other of history that Blanchot convenes is not a way to give in to these new figures of metaphysics. For Blanchot, the end can neither be proven nor exceeded.[20]

Chapter 5

The Deconstruction of Christianity in Nancy and Blanchot

Conceived as inherent to the fall rather than as an original condition, the thought of innocence is double-edged. It can be apocalyptic in a sense near to what Anders conceived as the contemporary modality of the Apocalypse; namely, that innocence signifies the impossibility of assuming the position of a subject and hence a responsibility before the other and before history. In this sense, innocence is the name of what postmodernity has discovered to be the "incondition" of the subject, as its inability to act as a subject. In this frame, innocence refers to our being trapped into muteness and immobility. It names the end of responsibility and of history. However, within this very frame, innocence also accounts for another relation to responsibility and history. Because it takes place as a failure of the subject (because innocence takes place as a fall and not as an original condition from which one falls), one still has to respond to this failure. More precisely, one has to respond to this failure while falling, while being taken out of one's condition as a subject. Hence, innocence requires thinking of a responsibility that is beneath the human. It names the demand of a responsibility that befalls not on the subject but on a failed subject, and a responsibility to respond not necessarily to human subjects who are subject to the law (under the law's protection) but to what the law excludes. In this way, thought of as a failure of the subject and not as an original condition, innocence gives rise to a new thought of responsibility, which also promises a new—or another—history. Innocence gives voice to that which is excluded from history. As we have demonstrated, by requiring a new relation to language where what speaks is its inherent muteness and not its transcendent meaning, innocence demands making transient the immobile or the eternal. Within this framework, the apocalypse of innocence makes apocalypse itself historical.

By thinking of innocence as an unending fall, Blanchot brings about new perspectives on biblical notions, such as *law*, *grace*, and *apocalypse*. Or, rather, he unfolds another history of these notions, as if they were the double or the shadow of themselves: law being a void rather than a limit; grace being the love of death rather than its rescuing; innocence being a wandering out of a proper place and nature rather than a paradisiacal state; apocalypse being the end of the end rather than the end of time and of the world. In this reversal, these notions lead not to the abandonment of all ethics but to its renewal; namely, to an ethics that is no longer grounded on a subject, but located in the human condition of failure. Hence, innocence calls for a response to what, within the human, is not properly human. Thought in this way, can these notions still be considered as part of the Christian tradition? Do they not unfold, on the contrary, the other of this tradition, an otherness that belongs to it and that opens to its deconstruction? If this is the case, what would be not the ethical, but the political consequences of this deconstructing innocence?

I address these questions through the lens of Jean-Luc Nancy's last works on Blanchot, and in particular *The Disavowed Community*, where Blanchot's political thought is in fact approached through its relation to Christianity.

The Context

Nineteen years after the appearance of Blanchot's *The Unavowable Community* (1983), Jean-Luc Nancy published a critical reading of Blanchot's text entitled *The Disavowed Community*, published in its original version in 2014.[1] At first glance, Nancy's book seems incomprehensible (at least for the community of Blanchot's readers). In fact, the title of the book suggests that for Nancy, rather than contributing to the thought of community, Blanchot actually denies it. That is indeed what Nancy's title suggests: that Blanchot's *Unavowable Community* would disavow the issue of community. Moreover, Nancy's close reading of *The Unavowable Community* questions Blanchot's true political intentions. For Nancy, an ambiguity dwells in Blanchot's two-part book: one where the topic of the law is central, and the other focused on the topic of the heart. According to Nancy, who deals with a Christian matrix of hermeneutics (both Blanchot's and his own),[2] these topics refer to the Judaic and Christian tradition, respectively, and divide Blanchot's thought between an aspiration toward justice, which would nourish a left-wing thought, and an aspiration toward solitude, which Nancy associates with an aristocratic, right-wing thought. Divided into two irreconcilable parts, *The Unavowable Community* would secretly hide a right-wing thought concealed behind a very peculiar way of combining Christian topics.

Evidently, Nancy's book has been like the fall of a bomb for Blanchot's readers and for whoever pays attention to the way a writer such as Blanchot contributed to a new opening of the field of political thought after the Second World War. Despite the fact that Blanchot had indeed committed his writing to right-wing ideas and ideologies in the years he worked as a journalist before and during the war,[3] Blanchot's reflections on and relation to writing also open the field to what he himself called his "conversion"[4]—a conversion that is not merely personal, since it transformed the possibility of political thought and militancy in general. Between the periods before and after the war, Blanchot indeed underwent a change in his ideas, visions, and interests. Educated as a Catholic,[5] he had met Levinas and had developed a certain interest in Judaism.[6] A fervent defender of nationalistic ideas during the 1930s and '40s after the war,[7] he launched a radical critique of any politics based on identitarian claims.[8]

What matters in this so-called conversion is not the change, but what produced it. Ideas, strong convictions, don't change so easily. If they do, then we're not really facing a case of conversion with implications for the whole of existence, but rather a mere change of opinion. What brings Blanchot to relate otherwise to politics, to thought and to action (or militancy) are, as previously suggested and as Blanchot makes plain in his letter to Laporte,[9] his reflections on writing and his own relation to writing. In his letter to Laporte, Blanchot distinguishes a "writing of the day" and a "writing of the night."[10] In fact, alongside his activity as a professional journalist, Blanchot dedicates himself to literary writing. While the journalistic writing is correlated to the world (it speaks about its immediate changes) and belongs henceforth to the realm of the day, literary writing suspends the world. In this sense, it belongs to the realm of the night. What characterizes a text as literary is indeed the fact that it is not correlated to an object. Rather, within the "literary space," one relates to words as words and to stories as stories. What characterizes literature as a space is precisely the fact that although a book requires a material condition that correlates it to an object, it is an object that allows one to make a step out of the world. Hence, literature not only entails a change of focus but also a change of behavior.

While journalistic writing has a form of power over its object precisely because it has an object, by contrast, literature entails experiencing a form of non-power because it suspends our relation to objects. An example of this is the political text titled "Refusing the Established Order" (2010). In this text, Blanchot defines writing explicitly as a search for a non-power: "Writing is, at the limit, that which cannot be effected, thus always in search of a non-power, refusing mastery, order, and the established order above all, preferring silence to the speech of absolute truth, thereby contesting things and contesting them incessantly" (117). Blanchot's so-called conversion is hence guided by this change in relation to power that literature entails and that brings about a change of focus. What I can dominate is also what I can describe and reduce to knowledge. By contrast, a relation that suspends power is a relation to the unknown. Blanchot's conversion stems from this change of attitude and aspiration that literature entails.

If it is so evident that Blanchot has indeed been subject to a conversion that, in a way, he not only theorized but "practiced" (and this combination of theory and practice indeed allows us to speak of a conversion), why did Nancy, in his 2014 *The Disavowed Community*, put in question the evidence of such a change of focus? Moreover, why would it matter *for political thought in general* to cast a shadow on Blanchot's conversion? Isn't *The Unavowable Community*'s two-part structure and eventual ambivalence between Judaism and Christianity a mere *detail* in Blanchot's thought, as well as in the possibilities of political thought in general? Moreover, is the association between law/Judaism/left-wing on the one hand and between heart/Christianity/right-wing so evident? Isn't this division influenced by a Christian or, more precisely, a Hegelian conception of Judaism?[11] Finally, does this division into two parts not open to another reading of Judaism and Christianity that would simply give birth to new political possibilities?

Nancy's text has been the occasion of numerous commentaries[12] that mainly focus on the question of community in Blanchot's thought and on its relation to literature. For many commentators, Nancy's critiques of Blanchot are based on an odd (or maybe perverse) confusion between literature and myth that drives Nancy to see in Blanchot an aspiration to a new founding and metaphysics of the true, while literature is, on the contrary, what prevents any possible foundation. Whereas myths act as a founding rationality, literature belongs to the realm of fiction. It pretends neither to explain reality nor to determine it. In this sense, while myth can be an ideological weapon in the political field, literature has a critical dimension.

Indeed, Nancy's critique of Blanchot had to be addressed in these responses.[13] They recall the historical importance that literature holds within political thought. However, these commentaries neglect to highlight one important point of Nancy's critique: his idea—no less odd than his assimilation of literature to myth—that in the second part of *The Unavowable Community* dwells a hidden but apparent Christianity that would draw the line of a secret, unavowable, aristocratic, and hence nondemocratic politics, which would end up denying community as well as the promise of justice contained in Blanchot's conversion.[14] This idea is no less surprising than Nancy's analysis of the recurrence of the myth in the second part of *The Unavowable Community*. Indeed, Blanchot cannot be identified as a *strictly* Christian thinker. Moreover, pointing to the sacrificial figures of this small part of this small book seems too weak of an argument to disavow Blanchot's contributions to political thought. However, the point I wish to make is not whether Nancy's analysis is right or wrong. Rather, I wish to address the following question: How and why does Christianity matter in Nancy's apprehension of Blanchot's political thought? After all, can we not claim that there is an obvious Christian component in Nancy's own thinking? Along this same line, isn't it in the wake of Blanchot that Nancy unfolded his thought of a "deconstruction of Christianity"? Moreover, is Christian thought necessarily right-wing? More generally, what does a reflection on Christianity bring to the issues addressed in the field of political thought today?

Regarding these issues, my claim is twofold. On the one hand, I believe that Nancy's critical reading of *The Unavowable Community* does not aim *principally* at disavowing Blanchot's contribution to the thinking of community. Rather, his critiques constitute worries that Nancy addresses to himself and to a lack of political critical tools that would more characterize our time than be restricted to Blanchot's thought and writings. On the other hand, and correlatively, Nancy's worries in relation to Blanchot's use of Christian figures do not entail a critique of the relation between Christianity and politics *in general*. Rather, what Nancy would point out in Blanchot is both a hidden and an *undeconstructed* use of Christian figures. By contrast, what interests Nancy, concerning Christianity, is that Christianity deconstructs itself and hence opens to new historical and political perspectives.

Taking into account these two claims, my purpose in this chapter is not to ask whether Nancy's reading of Blanchot is right or wrong, but how their respective relations to Christianity open to the problem of the political. I will show in particular that both thinkers assume the idea that deconstruction is inherent to Christianity. However, whereas for both thinkers the point of departure of this deconstruction is finitude, a slight difference in their very analysis of finitude will open onto two very different political paths. To sum up, what will interest me in this chapter is not so much the pertinence of Nancy's critique and reading of Blanchot, but the relevance of a Christian reading of Blanchot to address contemporary political issues.

Finitude

As is known, for Nancy, the deconstruction of Christianity is not meant as a form of opposition to Christianity. It leads toward neither a destruction nor an overcoming, nor is it thought of as a secularization. "To deconstruct Christianity," writes Nancy, consists of "grasping in it (in it as it gets out of itself), from it, the excedent itself, the movement of a deconstruction" (2008a, 11, translation modified). In other words, Christianity contains the very principle of its deconstruction. For this reason, to deconstruct is not to destroy but to open: to connect with what disconnects Christianity from itself and which opens it to its to-come (*à venir*).[15]

If we consider both Nancy and Blanchot's gestures vis-à-vis Christianity, one can observe that both (although by different paths) find within Christianity the principle of its deconstruction, and that both find in finitude the guiding principle of such a deconstruction. If we think of Blanchot, who does not speak explicitly of a "deconstruction of Christianity," one sees that the topic of death places us on the path of this deconstruction in a twofold manner. In fact, the way Blanchot thinks (and deconstructs) the possibility of death relates to the Christian topic of eternity. As we have seen, Blanchot puts into question the possibility of thinking of the end in the sense of a termination, of something limited. The fact that Blanchot refers to the infinitive verb "to die" (*mourir*) rather than the substantive "death" (*mort*) entails that time is not made of a succession of ending moments, but of an unending end. Hence, the "to die" occurring as the "impossibility to end" is the time of an eternity. Yet rather than being a plain eternity, an eternal present, it is the eternity of that which doesn't come to presence. The "to die" is the impossibility of time conceived as what occurs within limits and that hence makes possible a chronology. It is an eternity of absence. It drives the Christian eternity in what Blanchot calls the eternity of absence or the immortality of the "to die." In this way, we can see that the difference between the substantive (death) and the infinitive (to die) leads to a thinking otherwise of Christian notions such as immortality and eternity: "To die according to the lightness of dying and not by the anticipated heaviness of death—the dead weight of the dead thing—would be to die in relation to some immortality" (Blanchot 1993, 110). It is therefore finitude that impels us toward a thinking anew of these Christian notions. Indeed, *eternity in Blanchot is not a time made pure of finitude, but the time of finitude*. It is the time of an infinitive that implies a new conception of life's temporality and of the infinity that occurs with death. In fact, this slip into an infinity within finitude can be observed not only in the infinitive "to die" as the "to come" of the end, but also as the experience of death as, for instance, what occurs with the death of the other. Paradoxically, while finitude makes it impossible to conceive time within limits (to conceive a secular time), death confronts not a finite absence, but an absence that is infinite. The death of a friend or of a relative does not give birth to a finite mourning that would be overcome within time. Because death is irreducible, because death is always the death of the irreplaceable, of the one whose singularity cannot be measured; because, as the Derrida of *The Work of Mourning* would say, death occurs as the end of the world (2001, 115), it confronts an endless absence. Mourning is therefore the ordeal of an infinite pain that (Christianly!) makes it impossible to think of redemption within time. Hence, there is immortality only within finitude, as Blanchot writes in *The Step Not Beyond*: "To die," as previously quoted, "would be to die in relation to some immortality" (1993, 110). Yet for this very reason, because the only infinity is the infinity of finitude, there is no way out of finitude. There is no redemption.

Second, this eternity of absence that destitutes the possibility of time also makes unthinkable the frontier between a here on Earth (a here below) and a here beyond—between the secular time of finite life and the time of eternal life. For Blanchot, as for Nancy, finitude is infinite, and its infinity prevents thinking of the beyond in terms of an opposition with the here below. For this reason, Blanchot could say with Nancy that "all the weight—the enormous weight—of religious representation cannot change the fact that the 'other world' or the 'other kingdom' never was a second world, or even a world-behind-the-worlds, but the other of the world (*of every world: of all consistency tied up in beings and in communication*), the other than any world" (Nancy 2008a, 10). In other words, while thinking of death, which is at the heart of the theology of salvation, under the aegis of the infinite finitude, *Christianity empties itself of any metaphysical content*. The topics of the beyond and of eternity no longer belong to another world. They can be thought of—as Nancy does, echoing Blanchot—in terms of "Outside"; namely, not another world, but the very emptiness of this world.[16] In this way, we can see how Nancy and Blanchot meet in their shared gesture of the deconstruction of Christianity and how Blanchot's meditation on the difference between "death" and "to die" has nourished Nancy's reflection on Christianity. The first volume of *The Deconstruction of Christianity* and Nancy's *Noli me tangere* unfold the different ramifications of this deconstruction, made possible by the topic of finitude. It is, for instance, because death is not reducible to an end that we can think of a resurrection of death and not of the dead (*les morts*), as Nancy suggests in a reflection explicitly inspired by Blanchot.[17] Just as in Blanchot's description of death, for Nancy the absence that death represents does not have an end: it gives birth to an endless absence that constitutes, within finitude, an experience of eternity.

Finitude is the common thread of Nancy and Blanchot's gesture toward Christianity. Blanchot and Nancy's deconstruction of Christianity can be assumed to be a new way of thinking about Christianity and finitude. However, this does not mean that Nancy and Blanchot adopt exactly the same point of view on Christianity. Although Nancy and Blanchot both conceive of finitude as the operator of the deconstruction of Christianity, they differ in their analysis of death. According to Nancy, Blanchot thinks of death not as what happens to us, but as what separates the "I" from others. In *The Disavowed Community*, Nancy writes, in lines that don't immediately appear to coincide with Blanchot's thought: "If death is understood as separation from others rather than from self, the 'impossible' is understood as that which excludes itself and excludes everyone from all relation (sometimes to the point of being the general exclusion of any exclusion)" (2016, 74, translation modified). For Nancy, Blanchot's analysis of death makes the subject impossible, for, as Blanchot says, one cannot be contemporary to their death, or present to their absence. Although Blanchot clearly describes this impossibility as a relation, a "rapport," Nancy insinuates that this "rapport," this community that would appear in place of death, is in reality withdrawn, repudiated, disavowed, as the title of his book, *The Disavowed Community*, suggests. In fact, how can there be a relation or a community there where the "I" is absent?

It must be underscored that Blanchot's thinking of death—or, more precisely, Blanchot's conception of the "to die," of its impossibility—does indeed open to a *rapport*, to an Outside. In fact, the first part of *The Unavowable Community* is focused on the (Christian) problem of sharing death. If death, because of its impossibility, can be lived only in the modality of the relation (*rapport*), it is the very heart of community.[18] However, Nancy's argument is that in making impossible the subject—this "Outside" to which the effaced "I" is related—death rejects it in an "essential solitude" that would be, at least according to Nancy, Blanchot's last (or real) words on community. In this way, thought of under the aegis of death, the topic of finitude appears to mark a significant difference between Nancy and Blanchot. For the latter, death that *could* appear as the very issue of the question of community is in reality its denial. Paradoxically, Nancy meets with Blanchot (or vice versa) on the topic of infinite finitude, and departs from him on the topic of death. Finitude is the common thread in the deconstruction of Christianity—as well as of a particular Christianity in Nancy and Blanchot—but it is also a point of divergence on the question of community. It is therefore—I wish merely to suggest—a point of political divergence.

World

Interestingly, finitude is Nancy's and Blanchot's common thread of their deconstruction of Christianity as well as of their relation to Christianity. However, it is also the point of their divergence within their relation to Christianity. This divergence has decisive political consequences. Whereas death constitutes a major difference in their thinking of community and of Christianity, we shall also see that the difference in Blanchot's and Nancy's Christianity is the problem of the world. In fact, in Blanchot, finitude coincides with the impossibility of the present, and therefore of a here below: therefore of a world (conceived largely but precisely not as the planet or the biosphere, but, in a more Heideggerian sense, as the opening of possibilities). In Nancy, we also find the idea that death is irreducible to a present moment. Yet, for Nancy finitude is the problem of the limit conceived as affection; therefore, it does not coincide with a *sole destitution* of the present. While he insists on the priority of the relation toward separation, the impossibility of the present is not closed to possibilities (*possibles*), *and therefore to the world*. On the contrary, not only *through* finitude—"something is common" (2016, 74), writes Nancy[19] (and Blanchot would agree)—but in this priority given to the relation, the impossibility of the present also becomes "the infinitesimal suspension of time where gazes—voices, silence—are exchanged, and bodies touch" (2016, 72). In other words, Blanchot's deconstruction of Christianity is a wordless gesture. It affirms the impossibility of the here below and of the present. In this way, it is a gesture that thinks of the relation as impossible rather than as prior, constitutive, as is the case for Nancy. It is thus a gesture that seems to adhere to the end of the world. By contrast, Nancy insists on the priority of the *cum*. By doing so, he thinks the impossibility of the present contains the event of the very gap or interval of the *cum*, and therefore, of the world. Although only furtively evoked, the question of the world is Nancy's central argument against Blanchot's surreptitious Christianity in *The Disavowed Community*. "In this suspension," writes Nancy, "something appears—one might say a world—and doesn't disappear" (2016, 72). In this sense, Blanchot's Christianity would be apocalyptic. Without being directed to another world, and, as shown in the previous chapter, though it deconstructs the idea of a limit that makes possible any apocalypse or revelation, the notion of infinite finitude that he evokes relates to an impossible world—to a disavowed community, as Nancy would say. Nancy's Christianity, for its part, has to do with the priority of the relation. It thus contributes to the advent of the world. It is bound to the "meaning of the world" (*le sens du monde*), to adoring the world—namely, to greeting what constitutes the opening of sense. Located in the place of an infinite finitude, these conceptions of Christianity open along a twofold path: the path of the disaster or of the adoration, and the path of the apocalypse or of the belief in this world.[20]

That being said, can we really believe in the world? Rather, does Nancy's consideration of the sense of the world implicate, if not an unavowed metaphysics of the world implicit in his deconstruction of Christianity, at least an excessive trust in the world, in its possibility (*possible*) or in the world conceived as the possibilities opened by the advent of the "*cum*"? In fact, when Nancy writes, for instance, in *Adoration*, "The world is simply the presence of all those who are present" (2012, 46), does the simplicity of "the presence" and of "those who are present" not entail an implicit metaphysics of presence?

Before this certainty—if not of the "sense of the world," then at least of the necessity to think the meaning as coming from the world and as *a* world, as the "in common" (*en commun*) that opens to the world—should we not think that the "in common" that constitutes the "sense of the world," rather than opening to the meaning of the world, is what is fragile beyond everything? Moreover, are there not situations—of solitude, of pain, of violence—that testify to a loss of a world? Shouldn't we, in any case, confront seriously the end of the world?

"Nothing Is What It Is": Disaster and the Adoration of Nothingness

That Nancy is the philosopher of the world certainly does not mean that he ignores the event or the advent of the end of the world. In *The Sense of the World*, Nancy states explicitly that we are at the end, where he writes: "We are at the end, but the end of sense means that we cannot think this end" (1997, 6). This means that "it is the end of the world, but we don't know in what sense" (6.). For Nancy, the "being with" constitutes the world as the opening of meaning. Yet this meaning is not the one of theologies, nor does it belong to a metaphysical principle. This meaning is not a principle exterior to the world that would found it and orient it. On the contrary, what the deconstruction of Christianity discovers and discloses is concomitant with this absence of core, of foundation, of principle, and therefore of meaning, of *sens*. Thus, on the one hand, for Nancy this meaning (*sens*) is nothing other than the touch (*la touche*), "the referring (the relation, the address, the reception—the sensibility, the sentiment)" (2012, 12)—namely, it is this spacing of the common that makes the world.[21] On the other hand, the sense, which is deprived of sense (of a "sense of the sense"),[22] is concomitant with the end of the world conceived as an oriented and meaningful (full of sense) totality. Therefore, to speak of the "sense of the world" doesn't necessarily entail a metaphysical principle. On the contrary, the sense of the world is this absence of a (metaphysical) guarantee[23] by which the existents are opened to one another, and therefore make a world happen (*font monde*). It is thus because it is the "end of the world" that we are exposed to the meaning of the world. "The end of the world" is the principle of the opening of the world: the world is always at its end. It is the challenge—the ordeal—of the limit. Out of this challenge, by which the world is experienced or felt (*éprouvé*) in its finitude, we are in the realm of what Nancy calls the "unworld" (*l'immonde*, which means in French "the squalid," as if the squalid were what does not happen as a world); namely, of what is closed to the world's condition of possibility: the challenge or testing of the limit as the challenge of the being-toward. The end of the world therefore gives us the world as infinite finitude.

Nancy is the philosopher of the world, but we cannot say that his trust in the world depends on a metaphysical principle. The belief in the world includes and even presupposes the end of the world. With this in mind, can we really oppose Nancy and Blanchot, considering the latter as an apocalyptic thinker and the former as the philosopher of the world?

In a way, one would have to turn in this direction. It is remarkable that for Nancy, the deconstruction of Christianity opens onto the world and not onto *another* world. In fact, while for Blanchot the topic of the infinite finitude (the impossibility of the end) deprives us of the world precisely where it deprives us of anything beyond the world, Nancy thinks the outside of the world as what opens the world. Thus, this deconstructed Christianity, far from conducting us beyond the world, constitutes the thread of what Nancy calls the "in the middle of the world" (*au milieu du monde*). The monotheist's God, far from being the principle of the *mundus*, of the world as a signifying totality, is the principle of the deconstruction of the world understood as *mundus*. It entails a shift in the meaning from *mundus* to *Welt* to "in between the world"—to the world opened as "being with." "God," writes Nancy in *Adoration*, "is nothing but . . . this *with* itself" (2012, 40).

By moving in this direction, one discovers that the problem is not Nancy's trust in the world but rather Blanchot's trust in the end of the world. Indeed, Nancy argues that the world is fragile, that its meaning depends only on the abyss of its end. And he argues this point beyond the *temptation* of substantializing the non-sense, and therefore beyond the temptation of *believing* in the end of the world. For if an adoration of the world can be the exact contrary of an idolization, by way of contrast, it is always possible to adore the disaster. This happens when the end of the world is taken as the negation of *all* meaning; when it is a way of hypostatizing the "nothingness" of meaning.

At this point, the divergence between Blanchot and Nancy (the divergence within belief) is now located in their understanding not of finitude but of nothingness. In play here are two different gestures toward Heidegger.[24] In this respect, we can observe that an identical sentence appears in *Adoration*, the second volume of Nancy's deconstruction of Christianity, and also in *The Writing of the Disaster*, which could be considered as the second volume of Blanchot's deconstruction of Christianity: "Nothing is what there is."[25] In its two iterations, this sentence could constitute two different folds of Heidegger's thought. In fact, when Nancy states in *Adoration* that "nothing is what there is," he shows that the opening of the thought, the surprise that provokes thinking, is not the alternative between being and nonbeing (which would lead us to choose between one ontology and another, between an onto-theology and a hypostatized nihilism), but the fact that being (*l'être*) is immediately—immemorially—plural. The "nothing" of being, the nothing that being *is*, the nothingness that is produced with being, does not enclose us in a sterile alternative, in a dualism. Rather, it is productive of being*s*. Being, in being nothing, is that through which all things only *are* in relation to others. But this being-in-relation of being does not mean that the sum of discrete beings forms a totality. On the contrary, being, in being nothing, exposes us to the "infinite of a sense" (2012, 13). Thus, the statement that "nothing is what there is" does not reduce sense to nihilism. Instead, it leads to the surprise of "being singular plural," to the "the gift of this: that there are some things, things, all beings (*étants*)" (14). By contrast, when Blanchot writes "nothing is what there is," what writing produces immediately is not the surprise of a world ("that there are some things, things, all beings [*étants*]"), but its collapse. Unlike Nancy, who focuses his reading of the ontological difference on the primacy of Heidegger's *Mitsein*, Blanchot's thought is not a displacement within Heidegger, but an opposition. In play for Blanchot is the idea that the nothingness of being prevents any relation, any world, any possible understanding. "Nothing is what there is" is not exactly Blanchot's last word on the end (since there is no end). It is rather his way of thinking of the impossibility of a whole, of everything, including of the being-with that makes it possible to think of the world as the exposure to the "infinity of a *sense.*" This nothingness is what appears only in a deferred way (and thus as impossible) within fragmentary writing. It is true that nothingness, in Blanchot, can be thought as the midst of the relation (*le milieu du rapport*) (nothingness being also the experience of the Other). Yet it is not "in the midst of the world" (*au milieu du monde*), as Nancy calls it. Within fragmentary writing, nothingness is produced as that which prevents meaning from realizing itself. It leads to a "collapse of every language" (Blanchot 1992, 97), and in the "collapse of every language"[26] there is no more world to be constructed.

While Nancy's belief in the world includes (and presupposes) the acknowledgment of the end of the world, Blanchot's thought runs the risk of idolizing nothingness in a rejection of the world. But is this view fair? If Blanchot's writing prevents meaning from realizing itself, should we conclude that Blanchot is hypostatizing nothingness? In this case, one would really be facing an apocalypse (a *revelation* of nothingness!). Or, rather than revealing nothingness as the completed end of any world, does Blanchot seek a way to give voice to the end of the world *within* a world that, however fragile, should be said and thought within what has put it into question?

Consolation

To answer this question, I would like to return to a question I have already answered: the question of trust in this world. A new point of convergence can be found between Blanchot and Nancy precisely at the point of their most radical divergence.

The essay titled "Consolation, Desolation," included in the first volume of Nancy's deconstruction of Christianity, answers a question analogous to the one we addressed about Nancy's trust in the world. It is the question that Derrida takes up in *On Touching—Jean-Luc Nancy*. For Derrida, resurrection in Nancy, even conceived as *anastasis* (literally, "lifting body"), would still belong to a kind of confidence or faith (the word for "trust" in French, *confiance*, entails the idea of faith: *fiance*). Resurrection would have a consoling effect that would be unable to assume the abyss that death constitutes: it would be unable to assume the end of the world that happens with each loss. Thus, for Derrida, quoted by Nancy, the *anastasis* "continues to console, were this with the rigor of a certain cruelty. It postulates both the existence of some God and that the end of *one* world might not be the end of *the* world" (Nancy 2008a, 98). Understood in this way, the topic of an infinite finitude would contain a kind of overcoming of finitude, within finitude itself.

Interestingly, Nancy answers this question not by adjoining it to the way he elaborates the topic of resurrection, and not by arguing that what is endless, infinite, is finitude's ordeal. Rather, Nancy unfolds his argument in a twofold manner. First, he focuses on the topic of death's salutation—of the salute addressed to the deceased—which should remain without salvation. He argues that there is salutation only in desolation; namely, in an ordeal that is without consolation. The deceased being unique, Nancy explains, his disappearance desolates in that it is an abandonment to "total isolation" (2008a, 99). The uniqueness of the dead is an abandonment to the "end of the world." In this sense, the one who is saluted is not the one who remains or comes back, the one who maintains the world intact, but the one who devastates, who desolates. The second step of Nancy's argument consists in saying that if the one who is saluted is the one who devastates, then "the salute stands and addresses at the precise point where there remains nothing to be said" (102). In other words, the effect of death is that language emerges on the edge of absolute loss—a topic also addressed by Blanchot in *The Writing of the Disaster*, where he writes that the origin of speech is a loss of speech.[27] Thus, Nancy's understanding of resurrection does not lead to consolation understood as an overcoming of finitude. Rather, it amounts to saying that what makes us speak, and therefore live with one another in common, is loss, finitude. Moreover, and more importantly, his understanding of resurrection also amounts to saying that the experience of loss—of loss without consolation—always happens *within* a world. Albeit death is without consolation, loss is nevertheless located *within* consolation;[28] namely, in what Nancy calls the "restoration of a possible": within a world. Indeed, one is not consoled by resurrection. However, since the experience of loss is the very origin of speech and therefore of community, it holds us, in a way, to consolation within the realm of possibility—which is to say, within the world. It calls us back to the world, although without guaranteeing that world. As Nancy writes, insofar as "the salute . . . proclaims something—more precisely someone . . . whatever it might want and whatever it might claim, it cannot fail to console others and itself" (2008a, 100).

Infinite finitude, resurrection, and consolation can be thought of in line with the impossibility of redeeming loss, with the end of the world. Yet we wouldn't speak of loss if we didn't belong to a world, albeit to a "ruined world" ("*monde abîmé*"; 100) that is nonetheless still a world in its loss. We belong to consolation without being able to be consoled. Consolation keeps us open to the abyss, just as it keeps us open to a speech whose origin is loss.

Can this surprising and perhaps Hegelian dialectic be associated with Blanchot's *Writing of the Disaster*? Is the latter not the very ordeal of a loss of consolation and, in this sense, rather than a gesture of deconstruction of Christianity, one that is anti-Christian?

I believe Blanchot's evocation of the loss that constitutes language responds precisely to the necessity of preventing any substantiation of nothingness. If it is true that fragmentary writing constitutes a "collapse of every language," writing in Blanchot is also what sets this collapse in motion. It is what prevents any stabilization into nothingness and of nothingness. It is, in this sense, what disavows nihilism. For this reason, as shown in the previous chapter, rather than consisting in the revelation of nothingness in its hypostasis, Blanchot's apocalypse searches for the historicization of nothingness.

What conclusions can we draw from these convergences and divergences between Blanchot and Nancy around this plot line constituted by "finitude," "Christianity," and "world"? Paradoxically, Blanchot and Nancy have both thought of the topic of finitude as what constitutes the principal guide for their deconstruction of Christianity, and therefore as what allows for a new understanding of it. Even if both include the event, in their thought, and in the advent of the end of the world, both assume that there is nothing to be saved. There is no being that can be separated from nonbeing; no life that can be separated from death; no finite time that can be separated from eternity; no infinity that can be separated from finitude. In Blanchot and Nancy, therefore, the end of the world will not determine conservative actions such as the preservation of life against the idea of an imminent destruction, or the adherence to an idea of goodness, of those who will be saved from hell. What differentiates Blanchot and Nancy is rather their understanding of the limit, which, for the former, prevents any world to be constituted and, for the latter, constitutes the opening, the adoration of the world.

But this divergence between Nancy and Blanchot should not be reduced to a mere opposition. On the one hand, the thinking of the world is not exempt from the thinking of the end of the world. I am not, here, thinking of the various catastrophisms that impede thought (for they only lead to fright). Rather, I'm alluding to the idea that thought cannot be grounded on a guarantee, and that what links us to one another in no way constitutes the guarantee of a meaningful world. In this sense, *the adoration cannot be separated from the disaster*. On the other hand, we must say that to think, to talk, and to write, despite the differences among these gestures, always already situate us in the common, in the world: we could say nothing of the disaster were we not in the world. The world is given to us by finitude, but not as something that is there, that is given. On the contrary, it is given to us as what is utterly irreducible in finitude; namely, the fact that absence is irreducible, that what relates us to one another does not constitute a secure link, a link that could maintain us in the security of a world. The world is, on the contrary, concomitant with the end of the world, an end which is uttered in each of our words, for words link us merely to the fragility of the world.

Politics

Recalling, once again, that finitude is the common thread of a deconstruction of Christianity for Nancy and Blanchot, of a way of thinking (from within it) of Christianity as opened to its "to come" (*à venir*), the deconstruction of Christianity thus overcomes the opposition between the secular and the religious. It reveals the trace of an atheism that inhabits religion and that permits a description of our time: our world is not the one founded and structured by Christian beliefs; rather, it happens *as a world* because of God's void. For Nancy (explicitly) and for Blanchot (more surreptitiously), this void is at the heart of the historicity of Christianity, constituting and opening it to its own overcoming.

Although we find in both Nancy and Blanchot a common gesture of deconstruction of Christianity, we have seen that they ultimately diverge on the question of community and of the world. It is now time to address the question of the political consequences of this divergence. In *The Disavowed Community*, Nancy does not believe that Blanchot's disavowal of community coincides with a disavowal of politics. On the contrary, for Nancy, such a disavowal coincides with a hidden and even unavowable politics; namely, a right-wing politics Nancy deems problematic not for being right-wing, but for being hidden, inexplicit, and inhabiting left-wing positions, as well as for being anti-democratic. If we consider Nancy's political worries expressed in the last two decades, the crucial political difficulty faced by our time—a time that is no longer based on truths but that is opened by the void of God, by a certain "asbentheism" or "dis-enclosure," following Nancy's neologism (2008a, 18)—is the lack of an articulation between the political (what opens to politics) and determined politics (what gives concrete forms to the political). By denying the importance of this articulation, either nothing is political and the world is abandoned to the fate of the market, or we believe everything is political and we therefore, without being aware of it, accept the totalitarian principle that there are no separate spheres, that everything *belongs* to one sole principle (Nancy 2008b, 1, 26). In other words, as suggested by Juan Manuel Garrido and myself in "Politique au-delà du politique. Le coeur ou la loi de l'exigence communautaire" (2015),[29] Nancy's primary concern in the political sphere is the confusion between the political and determined politics. This confusion abandons the political either to populism that fills the gap left by the political (where politics is reduced to the so-called *real politick*) or to new forms of totalitarianism that take advantage of the gap left by determined politics (where apolitical forces like the laws of the market rule the world). So, taking into consideration Nancy's general political concerns, what troubles Nancy in *The Disavowed Community* is not Blanchot's political position (e.g., as would be a "right-wing" one), but rather *its confusion* or its way of hiding itself, and the way this very confusion ends up contradicting what "our time" urgently requires: a democracy capable of resisting populism and the new totalitarianisms that globalization is giving birth to. In this sense, the stakes of *The Disavowed Community* are not limited to studies of Blanchot. Rather, through this detailed reading of *The Unavowable Community*, Nancy addresses an issue that concerns our time. *The Disavowed Community* is a reading of Blanchot inasmuch as Blanchot's work comprises a major legacy in contemporary political thought. In a way, through Blanchot, Nancy converses with himself, with our time, and, more precisely, with the legacy that French post–World War II has bequeathed to us today. Let us therefore try to understand how Blanchot and Nancy's deconstruction of Christianity is decisive for his questioning of this legacy.

THE *UNAVOWABLE COMMUNITY*'S DIVISION BETWEEN THE LAW AND THE HEART

As previously stated, Nancy's *Disavowed Community* is not a book on Blanchot but a close reading of *The Unavowable Community*, which constitutes a peculiar response to Nancy's *Inoperative Community*. Indeed, Nancy states in *The Disavowed Community* that Blanchot's "little book," *The Unavowable Community*, left him in silence because of the enigmatic nature of the book.[30] Taking seriously this silence and this confession of incomprehension, we could argue that Nancy's 2014 text is not only a reading of *The Unavowable Community* but also of the long silence (Nancy's own silence) that took place between 1983 and 2014. Moreover, rather than suspecting that Nancy took advantage of Blanchot's death[31] in order to publish those diverse critiques of Blanchot in *The Disavowed Community*, we may consider that Nancy's work on the deconstruction of Christianity afforded him some philosophical and political clues with which to approach Blanchot's little but difficult book. For Nancy, 2014 would be a moment of philosophical lucidity regarding the problem of the political in general (or of the articulation between the political and determined politics), and regarding the political issues that concern Christianity's deconstruction. In fact, as observed in my and Garrido's article "Politique au-delà du politique," Nancy's reading takes as a point of departure *The Unavowable Community*'s division into two parts. What draws his attention is the fact that the first part of this little book would disclose a rather ethical point of view grounded in Judaic motives, whereas the second part would coincide with a political point of view based on a strange use of Christian figures. In this sense, and as has been analyzed at length in "Politique au-delà du politique," the first part of the book would affirm the priority of the Judaic law over the Christian topic of the heart, whereas the second part of the book would rather unfold a new conception of the Christian topic of the heart (Garrido and Messina 2015, 127). Indeed, in a Levinassian way, the first part of the book affirms the death of the other as what puts the "I" into question. By contrast, the second part of the book turns upon figures of sacrifice that seem to have the last word on the question of community. Read in this way, Blanchot's "little book" would be illegible precisely because it would be comprised of two heterodox languages: one that would refer to Judaic motives and one that would enigmatically use Christian figures—two languages that in 1989 were irreconcilable—unless thought of within a gesture of deconstruction. Moreover, as stated in "Politique au-delà du politique," this division into two parts makes plain the amphibology[32] that characterizes the problem of the articulation between the political and determined politics. However, in Blanchot's 1989 text, nothing is said of their articulation, which remains enigmatic: an enigma that, in 1989, enabled thinking anew of the political, opening to a thinking of community that was based not on any truth and that would henceforth resist any identitarian and nationalistic politics. But it is also an enigma that in 2014 begins to become problematic, since it can either correspond to an abandonment of a political point of view, properly speaking (where the political is articulated to a determined politics), or to a political appropriation of this void of concrete politics. Interestingly (and surprisingly), Nancy tends to think that albeit ambivalent, *The Unavowable Community* could indeed be plotting a political, Christian appropriation of the ethical; namely, a "preference for the heart over the law" (Garrido and Messina 2015, 127). For reasons that must be clarified, this preference for the heart over the law would also mean Blanchot's ascription to a right-wing politics (127).

Let us now turn to a discussion of Nancy's claim.

Reading Blanchot's Silence

As seen thus far, Nancy claims that it is *The Unavowable Community*'s structure and enigmatic end that is problematic. This structure opens, in fact, to an indetermination regarding the problem of the political. Worse, as we will see, this indetermination is not innocent since it hides or could hide unavowable topics that would confine Blanchot to the right wing. In brief, this indetermination would foment a new political semantic that we would not be aware of precisely because of the enigmatic character of Blanchot's little book. According to Nancy, and simplifying of course his complex argument, there where Blanchot's thought seems to be democratic, open to the Other and, in this sense, close to the Jewish tradition, it is in reality aristocratic and Christian.

In order to understand Nancy's difficult and surprising arguments, let's first focus on Nancy's hermeneutical matrix from which he is reading Blanchot's book in political terms.

As shown in "Politique au-delà du politique," Nancy poses three main arguments, which tend to assert that the first part of *The Unavowable*

Community is overcome by the second part—the law by the heart, or "Judaism" by "Christianity"—an overcoming in which Blanchot would secretly draw the lines of an unavowable, right-wing politics (which, as already said, would be problematic not necessarily because it is right-wing, but because it is brought about secretly, out of speech, in this sense mythically).

Nancy's first argument is related to Blanchot's reading of Duras's *The Malady of Death*. In Blanchot's reading, Duras's book affirms the impossibility of love. In this sense, for Blanchot "the second part of *The Unavowable Community* is ultimately a denial of community" (Garrido and Messina 2015, 127).[33] According to Nancy, "Blanchot's unavowable avowal comes down to disavowing the community" (2016, 58). The impossibility of love is an affirmation of solitude (Garrido and Messina 2015, 130; Nancy, 2016, 60). Hence, it secretly draws the lines of an aristocratic politics (58). In this first case, it is not the Christian topic of love and of the heart that gives birth to a right-wing politics, but *the way it is elaborated*; namely, thinking of *love as the heart of solitude and not of communion or of community*. In this sense, Nancy is not criticizing Blanchot for secretly bringing about Christian topics, but rather for their peculiar meaning and for their peculiar way of dissimulating their meaning. What is decisive in Nancy's reading is not the division (which is here simplified) between Judaism and Christianity, but this internal division within Christianity.

Nancy's second argument is related to *the way* literature is convoked in the second part of Blanchot's book. In fact, in this second part, the allusions to literature are at once evocative and mysterious. Rather than allowing arguments and points of view, they seem to form a chain of affirmed but mysterious truths. Hence (and surprisingly, for Nancy), in the second part of Blanchot's book, literature would be mythical, presenting "a truth (or a foundation) that is offered beyond all possible verification" (Nancy 2016, 64). Here, as shown in "Politique au-delà du politique," what leads Nancy to identify literature with myth is not the fact that it would present a founding truth. On the contrary, it presents itself as a mystery. Henceforth, Nancy sees in this second part of *The Unavowable Community* an "evasive mythography or mythopoesis" (2016, 64) that leads to an imposing silence.

Nancy's third argument regarding the idea that the second part of the book overcomes the first one is related to the content of the literary figures evoked in the second part. Nancy focuses his attention on the reference to Madame Edwarda, the eponymous prostitute of Bataille's narrative, and on the crime that occurs (or would occur, since the book is mysterious) in Duras's *The Malady of Death*. Interestingly, for Nancy the transgressive dimension of this second part of the book (through the question of the murder of the figure of the prostitute)—namely, the attraction toward a dimension out of law—would expose a "profoundly paulinian disposition" (2016, 65). As stated in "Politique au-delà du politique," whereas "Paul sees in Christ the possibility to overcome (namely to surpass and accomplish) Law within love . . . Blanchot sees in Madame Edwarda the annulation of law into transgression" (Garrido and Messina 2015, 130). This is indeed the most surprising aspect of Nancy's argument. Blanchot's Christianity would lie in these evocations of transgressive figures that, because they overcome law, would relate to Saint Paul's idea of the fulfillment and overcoming of the law through love (127). Indeed, Nancy locates Blanchot's attraction to Christianity, beyond his political conversion, and hence beyond Blanchot's awareness of "the issues concerning justice inherent in anti-Semitism" (Nancy 2016, 65). However, here again, what draws Nancy's attention is not the Christian dimension of Blanchot's thought directly but *the way it is elaborated*: evasively, through the use of feminine figures of sacrifice, where love is not only claimed as impossible but also mixed with murder. *This elaboration* of Christianity leads Nancy to see in the second part of *The Unavowable Community* a Christianity that "reinforces" an "aristocratic anarchism, which in turn subsume[s] his Christianity" (65).

Albeit surprising and disturbing, Nancy's hermeneutical gesture is indeed interesting and brilliant (in that it highlights new frames of understanding, new hermeneutical premises). In fact, by reading Blanchot through the very silence that provoked this little book, Nancy ends up reading Blanchot's silence, Blanchot's mysteries, and Blanchot's twists, and by doing so he shows that those silences produce a semantic—an unavowable semantic. Nancy shows—and this is hermeneutically extremely risky and interesting—that Blanchot's "aristocratic anarchism" is not to be found in his conception of the individual, who would be superior, but in Blanchot's way of denying community, *all the while seeming to affirm it*. As has been shown in "Politique au-delà du politique," at first reading, Blanchot should be read as a critique of aristocracy, since Blanchot speaks of what drives at the failure of the subject and puts its power or supremacy into question (Garrido and Messina 2015, 128). Indeed, as previously stated, Blanchot seeks a writing that implies the failure of power. Although Nancy doesn't refer to this aspect of Blanchot's thought, he is of course aware of it. However, his point is precisely that Blanchot's "aristocratic anarchism" lies *there where the "I" fails*, because for Nancy, in this failure, it is the "in-common" that is disavowed. In this failure, what is affirmed is an essential solitude, not a world.

In the same token, *at first reading*, Blanchot's thought is not only a critique of aristocracy (of its *cratos*), but it can also be correlated to democratic worries. As argued in "Politique au-delà du politique" (Garrido and Messina 2015, 128), one of Blanchot's most affirmative articles on the question of the *demos* is the short text "The Refusal" (1997), originally published in 1958, a few days after De Gaulle's return to power. In this text, Blanchot posits the refusal as two correlated exigencies: the exigency to refuse the language of the political authorities, and hence the refusal to speak *any language*. Through this refusal, what is ultimately affirmed are "the ones who cannot speak" (1997, 112). Here, and as in "Politique au-delà du politique" (128), it is important to highlight that Blanchot is indeed not saying that we should *talk* for the ones "who cannot speak," but rather that what should be affirmed is the collapse of language, its failure. Hence, here we would have to bring language through which one is constituted as a subject of politics, to innocence, as the *incondition* of the ones who are structurally deprived of law. In these twofold stakes of the refusal, we see that Blanchot's conception of writing indeed not only has a political dimension, but also that it is clearly correlated to a radical idea of the people in that it aims at giving voice to the ones excluded from language, and henceforth from power. As said in "Politique au-delà du politique," in the measure to which in this text "Blanchot doesn't limit the duty to refuse to the ones who do not possess speech, but indeed to the ones who cannot speak," he could be opening the horizon to a conception of democracy "freed from this humanistic dimension where only the ones who speak would be represented" (Garrido and Messina 2015, 128).

Within the radicality of Blanchot's 1958 short text could lie a political problem. As asked in "Politique au-delà du politique," "Is there still a politic there where the refusal requires the effacement of the self and of language?" (Garrido and Messina 2015, 129). In fact, democracy can take place only if a plurality of speech is possible. By contrast, Blanchot's proposal to *refuse all language* makes discussion, negotiation, *and henceforth democracy* impossible. Although Nancy doesn't refer to "The Refusal" in his book, he is indeed critical of the way *The Unavowable Community* refers to May 68 and to its passion not for the people but for its disappearance (Nancy 2015, 33), to the point of affirming its "absence."[34] As suggested in "Politique au-delà du politique": "If there is a people only in what is refused to language, and in the name of the ones who are deprived of it," Blanchot's idea of people ends up closer to a sort of mystic or silent Other than to the plural and concrete dimension of the others (129). Hence, here again Nancy's point relates not to Blanchot's thesis but to his writing, his silent writing and his writing silence—to what Blanchot would call the "white writing" (Blanchot 1993, 430); namely, the effacement that dwells within language. There where Blanchot seems to relate to the people in the radicality of the exclusion and destitution of language, Blanchot is in reality denying the people. There where Blanchot relates to the radicality of otherness (that which fails language), he denies the *others* in their concreteness and plurality (Garrido and Messina 2015, 129).[35] As Nancy states, Blanchot's social "I" is asocial (Nancy 2015, 33). Blanchot's relation to the Other denies the others. In other words, *what is problematic in Blanchot's political thought is not what is said, but what fails the realm of language*, what drives the very language (and hence the world) to its collapse. It is in this sense that, according to Nancy, an aristocratic unheard (and probably unconscious) right-wing politics inhabits this apparently left-wing democratic thought.[36]

BLANCHOT'S BILINGUALISM

Considered as a gesture of political hermeneutic, Nancy's book and analysis seem to me crucial and extremely useful to think of *our time*, including our time as a legacy of postwar thinking, which includes Blanchot's work. Now, taking a step back from *our time* and returning to Blanchot's writing in the peculiar context that gave it birth, three issues must be addressed: (1) Is the second part of *The Unavowable Community* as Christian as Nancy states? Or, rather, does Nancy read Blanchot's book "Christianly"? (2) Is *The Unavowable Community* enigmatic, or is it ambivalent? Does it hide a secret, or does it play with the meaning? (3) If, as I argued, Nancy is not only reading *The Unavowable Community* but the silence that leaves this enigmatic book, and more precisely a silence maintained throughout various decades, is this silence absolute, or should it be placed in context? Does it mean by itself as if it were sacred, or is it produced by peculiar semantics and political contexts?

Regarding the first question, Nancy's hermeneutical gesture could be put into question by his own implicit hermeneutical matrix or habits. Indeed, as previously mentioned, this assimilation between law and Judaism and between love and Christianity is not evident. Rather, it reveals an already Christian reading of what would be a hidden Christianity in Blanchot's text. The proposal to overcome law by love, which is a central issue in Saint Paul's Epistles, is made on the basis of a confusion between what Paul calls the Thora of death (law) and what could be called the "Thora of life" (the commandment).[37] On Nancy's part, this Christian division means that only the second part of *The Unavowable Community* would have a political stake, while the first part would be merely ethical. It means, moreover, that the second part of the book, the (so-called) Christian part, effectively overcomes the first, the (so-called) Judaic part, as if—contrary to what Nancy himself allows to be thought[38]—the "Judeo-Christian" could hold meaning only through Christianity's synthetical understanding of Judaism.

Second, and in line with this first observation, we could also remark that the idea that Blanchot's book is enigmatic and that the second part of the book (somehow) overcomes the first (in several occasions, Nancy leaves the question open) seems framed in a precisely Christian idea of overcoming. In order to put into question this idea of a synthesis or an overcoming, it is important to observe that these two-part structures are frequent in Blanchot's writing. Many of Blanchot's narratives (e.g., *The Last Man*) are divided into two.[39] The book *Friendship* contains (almost in the "middle") a text without title, which begins to evoke Mallarmé's idea of "division" as an essential structure of language:[40] "By means of a violent division, Mallarmé separated language into two forms almost without relation: the one, raw language, the other, essential language" (Blanchot 1997, 148). In Mallarmé's way, for Blanchot language serves as a means to name and hence to possess, but language is also open to the unfounded dimension of meaning in general, to the "unworking." Hence, "The writer is en route to a speech that is never already given: speaking, waiting to speak" (148). This means that language's division posits not *two meanings* or two systems of meanings (as could be Judaism and Christianity), but that the second part is the void echo of the first, which undoes the first but also opens it to its "to come." As written in "Politique au-delà du politique," " 'The community of lovers' is not another version of the 'negative community' (namely, the first part of *The Unavowable Community*) but what opens it to a foreign language, to a language to come" (131). Hence, the second part is related to the impossibility of enclosing the first part in a unified meaning; it makes plural the meaning of the first. In this sense, it certainly doesn't overcome the first. Indeed, *Blanchot is rather ambivalent than enigmatic*. Here, however, "ambivalent" doesn't mean oscillating between two meanings, but *playing with the impossibility that is inherent to one sole meaning in general*. Following this idea, the question is therefore: does Blanchot use literary figures in order to affirm (secretly) a secret and unavowable Christianism that entails unavowable political consequences? Or is this second part of

Blanchot's book literary; namely, more prone to play with the meaning, and hence with law, than to overcome it?[41]

Regarding the third question, although I strongly believe we cannot make a politics out of the defection of language and of the self, two arguments could nuance not only this point (which is indeed crucial to me) but also Blanchot's way of merging with silence. First, in Blanchot there is not a pure effacement of the "I."[42] Rather, in Blanchot the "I" is echoed by its impossibility. It is in this sense, as stated in the introduction to this book, that the subject is concomitant to innocence, and not preceded by it. If the "I" is not merely absolved by its effacement, community might not be completely disavowed. Second, the refusal to negotiate with the adversary, and hence Blanchot's refusal to talk and write (which is made plain by a way of talking and of writing), has to be placed in context. Blanchot's relation to De Gaulle's speech in 1958 takes place in a context of the violence of nationalistic discourses that was recent and that opens the space of their new semantics.[43] To advocate silence for silence, or the defection of language for the sake of silence, is indeed dangerous (because then there are no more limits and anything can happen), yet not so risky for the one who keeps silence. However, to introduce silent ways of using speech in determined political contexts might, on the contrary, open to a plural relation with speech. In fact, in Blanchot's "By Means of a Violent Division," he calls "bilingualism" a way of writing that makes plural *our relation to language, and not its meaning*. Hence, *in Blanchot, silence has to be understood not as a content of language (as an enigma: something that is kept secret), but as a plural relation to language*.

For sure, and following this idea that it is necessary to contextualize Blanchot's silence, as many commentators of Blanchot's politics have observed, this notion of "refusal" by which Blanchot makes plain his "conversion" and even prepares the ground for a left-wing militancy was already at stake in Blanchot's writings in the 1930s; namely, in Blanchot's right-wing "writing of the day." In fact, as Leslie Hill has noted in his important article "La pensée politique" (2003), what is common to Blanchot *before and after* his "conversion" is precisely his refusal of politics thought of as a space of negotiation. Although Blanchot moves from one extreme to another (Balibar 2014),[44] what Blanchot will never cease to affirm is the excess that is inseparable from law—an excess that, as Hill remarks, is twofold. It is the force *and* the weakness of the law. In this context, the issue is thus: Does Blanchot's idea of refusal maintain him in a (secret or unavowed) right-wing position? In this sense, rather than a conversion, Blanchot's political views would rather be the fruit of a new elaboration of the same demand. Or, on the contrary, does Blanchot's conversion allow for a new approach to the refusal? In this case, Blanchot's refusal(s) would need to be understood in contexts that are hermeneutically different. After all, in the 1930s, the refusal still belonged to a "writing of the day," while in the late 1940s, to refuse was inseparable from a conception of writing where all that belonged to the realm of the day was suspended. Inspired by Leslie Hill, we could say that in the 1930s, the refusal would rather affirm the force of the law, while in the late 1940s, the refusal would respond to law's weakness. Hence, although Blanchot maintains himself in a position of refusal, in going from one extreme to another, the right- and left-wing extremes, he radically modifies what is at stake in the refusal.

This being said, it seems to me that what really matters in this confrontation between Nancy's and Blanchot's relation to politics is that this relation is inseparable from their relation to language. Indeed, Nancy's insistence in criticizing Blanchot's mystery is that the destruction of speech destroys the possibility of the others. It cannot affirm a people because it negates its condition of possibility. Hence, Blanchot's radical democracy ends up preventing its own democratic aim. Blanchot's radicality and exigency for what fails speech has authoritarian effects rather than democratic dimensions: "Blanchot's anti-authoritarian gesture becomes authoritarian" (Garrido and Messina 2015, 132). However, Blanchot's passion for the silence of speech (the "white writing") leads us to think that the relation to speech defines the relation to others. Regarding this point, the difference between an enigmatic speech and the ambivalence of speech is crucial. But in any case, we can (and must) accept the premise (central in Nancy's thinking) that in order to be a people, there has to be a world. My relation to others needs a world, needs the "in common." The "people" cannot be affirmed by its pure absence. It needs a political frame in order to be heard, and, in many cases, in order to be rescued.

Atheism and Politics

In an important article entitled "The Aggrieved Community," Kevin Hart argues that "Nancy's claim that Blanchot's political 'conversion' is 'internal to Christianity' is hard to justify, in part because he makes Christianity into such a vast and fuzzy set, one that includes atheism, that it is difficult to see what would not be internal to it" (2019b, 38). This claim is important since, in fact, Nancy's conception of Christianity is inseparable from its deconstruction and embraces our whole conception of the West. Moreover, as Hart remarks, it should not be forgotten that Blanchot's writing indeed responds to an unheard exigency of atheism that relates Blanchot to Nietzsche and, hence, not necessarily to Christianity. However, Nancy's observation highlights not only the way Christianity merges with atheism (because for Nancy, Christianity contains the principle of its deconstruction), but also that Nietzsche's atheism stems precisely from an intimate relation to Christianity.[45] Nancy's point of departure is that there is no opposition between Christianity and atheism. This does not save Nancy from being imprecise when he happens to speak of Blanchot's relation to Christianity—although what interests Nancy is not Christian theology but Christianity as a principle of understanding the West, and hence, among many other topics, understanding globalization, the problem of secularization and its political consequences, and our relation to death and time. Nancy's point of departure allows us to understand that what is at stake when he points to Blanchot's relation to Christianity is not whether Blanchot is or is not a Catholic thinker, but how Blanchot's atheism stems from—according to Nancy, not to me—an undeconstructed Christianity. According to Nancy, within Blanchot's atheism dwell Christian motives that have a founding dimension. For this reason, they play in the political realm the same role as a founding myth.

In my view, within Blanchot's atheism dwells another way of thinking about the deconstruction of Christianity. Blanchot affords a sort of second chance to Christianity. He thinks of law not as what should be overcome, but as what is driven to play its own game and to deal with its inherent contingency or absence of foundation. He thinks of grace not as what *saves* from law's ordeal, but as what puts it at stake otherwise. What Blanchot calls the "detour of grace" is a way of turning law's ordeal upside down. Set in play within the contingency that inhabits it, law is not merely a power of limitation and a threat of death; it calls for an affirmation of finitude and for a relation to what law, as a power of limitation, excludes. Thought in this way, grace is no longer individual. The detour of grace is the detour toward the ones who are excluded by the realm of law and hence unprotected. Blanchot thinks of innocence not as what has been lost by original sin, as a condition that would be anterior to the fall, but as an interminable fall that makes impossible the constitution of a subject and then a secure subjection to law. The fall of innocence is this double-edged (in)condition that questions the Judeo-Christian legacy that founds the possibility of responsibility (namely, the idea of a subjection to law guaranteed by the possibility of the subject) and that calls for a way to think of responsibility anew. The fall of innocence entails a response that is not settled on a subject founded on self and that hence requires a "writing outside of language." He thinks of apocalypse not as a revelation, not as the moment of truth and of the last judgment, but as the exigency to give heed to what history excludes. In Blanchot, apocalypse is not the time of the end nor the end of times. It responds to the exigency of "another history" where what is made transient, contingent, or historical is the eternal; namely, that which cannot end.

To give Christianity a second chance does not mean that Blanchot is surreptitiously reaffirming Christianity. Neither does it mean that Blanchot's conversion is merely inherent to Catholicism, as Nancy claims. This point of view is limited. It entails that Blanchot's thought is framed by an alternative where Christianity exists only as opposed to Judaism. However, to give Christianity a second chance means to open Christian notions to chance; namely, to what is contingent and does not obey a determined law. This necessarily transforms our relation to Christianity, and hence the opposition within which Nancy works between Christianity and Judaism. In this context, the two parts of *The Unavowable Community* do not necessarily mean an oscillation between Judaism and Christianity, between the law and the heart, or between ethics and politics (if ever there could be such a strict separation between law and the heart). Indeed, Blanchot's point of departure is that there is a call, that there is otherness (irreducible to an "I"), and, as Hart claims, that there is dissymmetry (Hart 2019b, 32). We are therefore not in the Christian idea that we are all one in the body of Christ. Blanchot's thought does not strictly hold to the "Judaic" idea of a subjectivity bound to law. He is indeed close to the Paulinian idea of questioning the authority of law—although, it must be recalled that law in a Judaic view is not as authoritarian or mortal as in Paul's view. But Blanchot is also inspired by an otherness that does call to respond, albeit this otherness is at play in the transgression of law, precisely, in writing as what puts law into play. So, whereas Blanchot's conception of writing offers Christianity a second chance, it could extend to Judaism a second chance as well. It could at least offer a second chance to the hermeneutical frame from which a Judeo-Christian tradition (a hyphen) has been defined. Contrary to what many commentators of Blanchot affirm, there is indeed an important and singular re-elaboration of Christian topics in Blanchot's work. But contrary to what Nancy claims, this does not entail an oscillation between Judaism and Christianity, thought of in terms of an opposition between law and the heart, or between ethics and politics. On the contrary, while affording Christianity a second chance, Blanchot proposes a new elaboration of this opposition as well as of ethics. The fall of innocence coincides with an ethics of transgression, where transgression entails deactivating the authority of law, while neither suppressing nor confirming it. The fall of innocence is law as a failure, as what gives itself as impossible. It is this failure (*faille*) that summons (*il faut*), but without properly binding because this failure fails the limit and fails the subject.

Blanchot's peculiar way of putting the deconstruction of Christianity at stake opens to a new thinking of ethics. However, in addressing the question of Christianity's deconstruction in the wake of Nancy's reading of Blanchot's political (and secret) use of Christian figures, Blanchot's political thought can indeed be put into question. Whereas in Nancy the deconstruction of Christianity opens to the world, in Blanchot we are closer to a gesture of deconstruction that is apocalyptic. Blanchot's ideas of death and of solitude take place as the defection of the world. In this context, the people appears as evanescent. This evanescence ultimately affirms the people only *as absent* and hence cannot be articulated to a thought of democracy.

In a way, what separates the two thinkers is what Nancy calls "Absentheism"(2008a, 18)[46] and what Blanchot calls "A-theism" (1993, 457).[47] For Nancy, "Absentheism" is this lack of meaning that is also what opens to the world thought of as the in-common. Deeply, in Nancy, this lack is not a mere lack that signifies negativity. Rather, it is the meaning (*sens*) as what can never be substantialized, as the in-common that opens onto a world each time unique, but urgently to be made. It is the meaning as an opening (and not a direction). Atheism in Blanchot is the "absent meaning" (1995b, 41) that calls for a "writing outside of language"; namely, a writing that responds to what is withdrawn from meaning and from the world—without, however, relying on a meaning and a world. Blanchot's writing is a writing of the fragmentary, of that which can never be one, united, fixed.[48] In this regard, Blanchot's writing goes farther than Nancy's in thinking Christianity's inherent atheism and, in general, in assuming the consequences of the death of God. However, this radicality runs the risk of losing the world. In this radicality there is indeed a risk of "ultratheology,"[49] as Nancy states in *The Disavowed Community* (2016, 40). There is the risk that this "writing outside of language," this writing for "the ones who cannot talk," not in order to speak in place of them but in order to "refuse all language," ends up overly silencing language and speech, without which, as shown in "Politique au-delà du politique," there can be no negotiation, no democracy, nor any politics. Instead, there is the risk that this silence of writing—to which Blanchot dedicates his whole life—resembles, without being identical to, the silence of God.

Conclusion

The Innocence of the Stone

In *The Phenomenology of Spirit*, Hegel, for whom there is nothing outside consciousness except what comes from consciousness (and what produces it), affirms that innocence cannot be. If everything begins with and through consciousness, then there is no possible experience of innocence. If the only possible experience is spiritual, then the spirituality or the lack of consciousness characterizing innocence corresponds to nothing real. Innocence is a myth, or it is nothing more than the innocence of a stone, of the element in the maximal expression of its insensibility. Only the stone is innocent, Hegel says. Not even children, who are always already in cognitive processes, are innocent.

Hegel is right to say that innocence is nothing real (it being understood that, for Hegel, the real is the spiritual: it is reality insofar as it takes form, meaning insofar as it becomes comprehensible). Nevertheless, if indeed nothingness (of meaning) is what consciousness negates so as to constitute itself as such, it is also that which resists the process of absolutization. Absolute knowledge, which coincides with consciousness's process of totalization as the experience of its own process, necessarily confronts its specter: that which negates and returns, not in the form of something real, something spiritual, but rather as that which questions the totality of the process; that is to say, being as a process of self-determination. Specters are not myths, inventions of self-conscious subjects. They are the latter's shadow. They are what manage to question the solidity of the real. They are nothing external to the real: they are its lack of anchorage. If Hegel is right to say that innocence is not, what he did not manage to think is that this negating nonbeing *questions* being. Nonbeing is the nonbeing of the being that comes to feel itself a stranger in its own home. Innocence is the specter of being. Innocence is being's impossibility.

By saying that only a stone is innocent, Hegel accounts for the fact that the world we shape is a spiritual world: a world of meaning. The world is not given naturally; it is the product of our tasks. It is a human world, a world transformed by the hand of humanity. The human, in turn, is not given either. The human carries out their task such that each human is an image of the world. When Hegel says that we cannot extract ourselves from the eras in which we live, he signals the fact that the eras of the world are historical products. Eras are produced by humans and make humans human. If Hegel's thought is profoundly Christian insofar as it conceives reality as a product of spirit and spirit as that which reveals itself through history, Hegel's Christianity is nevertheless profoundly worldly. It does not admit the idea of creatureliness; namely, the idea of beings whose existence is related and owed to something that exceeds them. To be in the image of the world is not the same as to be in the image of God. In the first case, beings are immanent to their world. That which mobilizes them to act is a state of the world in its entirety. In the second case, beings cannot reflect upon themselves and attempt to understand themselves without referring to an authority that escapes their power of understanding. To be in the image of God is not to be the cause of oneself. It is to advance toward the unknown. The creature is, in a certain way, the complete opposite of filiation. In filiation, we track the cause of an existence. The creature entails the trace of something that exceeds it, but it cannot move back to its cause. The creature is alone and strives toward the outside. The child of an era is immanent to the era; the child of an era has no exteriority.

Albert Camus's *The Stranger* gives this Hegelian scene a twist. Meursault, the central character of this story, is no doubt a product of his era, but his consciousness does not appear to conform. When his mother dies, Meursault seems indifferent, a stranger not only to the customs with which we say good-bye to the dead but also to the proper feelings that we suppose in human beings confronted with death (feelings that shift, incidentally, and that are therefore historical products). Moreover, in his apparent apathy, Meursault comes to commit a murder, but he does so without a determinate reason and therefore without being able to take responsibility for such an act as a subject. Curiously, Meursault is not a product of his era: he is a stranger. He is not an *étranger* insofar as he comes from another country, insofar as he is a foreigner, but rather insofar as he does not conform to any world or custom. Now, Meursault's apathy is also his hypersensibility.

It is in a fulgurating instant, while the sun shines and exacerbates his sensibility, that Meursault fires the first shot with his gun. In this case, the intensity of the light and heat are not the *causes* of the murder; rather, they cause the instantaneity. More precisely, they do not give rise to *an act* (as is the case of a murder that already has a predetermined meaning): the sun's light and heat only free an instant that is heterogeneous to the order of meaning. This instant is the reverse of a *form* of the world, of an era understood as a conglomerate of meaning from which our actions can be understood and from which we constitute ourselves as responsible subjects. If the "murder" coincides with a moment of hypersensibility, it is because Meursault's apathy describes a new passion, a pure passion: a passion pure of meaning, of direction, of reason, even of feelings. Meursault does not suffer *for humanity* as, for instance, Christ does. In fact, Meursault does not suffer: he feels. And his feeling is not sentimental. A sentimental feeling is already a form; it is in itself a world and correlates to a world. By contrast, Meursault explains to his lawyer that his "nature was such that [his] physical needs often got in the way of [his] feelings" (Camus 1989, 65). With a monotonous tone, he tells his lawyer that, the day his mother was buried, he was very tired and wanted to sleep such that he "wasn't really aware of what was going on" (65). Paradoxically, if Meursault is apathetic, it is because his physicality, his sensibility, makes him a stranger to customs, to the world. Similarly, in *The Stranger*, we are not immanent to the era. We are, as Levinas would say, "flashes" (1998, 8).

For Hegel, law evolves. This implies that individual interests are overcome in universal interests. Similarly, thanks to law, we become free. While the individual is no longer stuck on their particular interests, they do not need a law to limit them. For the same reason, for Hegel, the death penalty redeems and thus liberates the individual from their particularity. In contrast to this perspective, during his trial, Meursault does not reach the universal because he does not even reach the particular. He observes his lawyer reconstruct the reasons for his story in a comedy in which he speaks in the first person, acting as if he were Meursault, whereas Meursault, by contrast, could never say "I" precisely because, rather than reasons for his actions, there was a "flash." Yet, whereas Meursault is a stranger to his own judgment and sees no reason for which he should defend himself against the accusations, his apathy is no doubt a point of view on the law. While his lawyer and his judges fight among themselves over the *reason* for his actions, thus reconstructing a scene *with* or *without* premeditation, Meursault sees only contingency:

> Because, after all, there really was something ridiculously out of proportion between the verdict such certainty was based on and the imperturbable march of events from the moment the verdict was announced. The fact that the sentence had been read at eight o'clock at night and not at five o'clock, the fact that it could have been an entirely different one, the fact that it had been decided by men who change their underwear, the fact that it had been handed down in the name of some vague notion called the French (or German, or Chinese) people—all of it seemed to detract from the seriousness of the decision. I was forced to admit, however, that from the moment it had been passed its consequences became as real and as serious as the wall against which I pressed the length of my body. (Camus 1989, 109–10)

Meursault's apathy, his way of excluding himself from both the particular and the universal, shows that there is a parallel between the contingency of the "murder" (the act of firing shots) and the necessity of the verdict. Like the "murder," the sentence is of the order of a "flash." It occurs because, within a determined context, elements unite that could have been otherwise. In this way, we can draw a chiasmus: the law, which is necessary, is also random, whereas the "murder," which was random, gives rise to necessity. We look for an explanation for it, a causality, whereas it occurred precisely as an exception. With Meursault, the law's necessity is reflected in its contingency, and his death sentence does not free him from the particular; it delivers him to the elements. As Meursault says, "I opened myself to the gentle indifference of the world" (122).

In Hegel's world, stones are, in a way, invisible. They do not count. If they are innocent, and if innocence is nothing, then stones are nothing, nothing worth thinking of. Stones are given in the world if they pass through a process of spiritualization: if they shape our habits, or if they coincide with an artistic project. Beyond this, the stone is insensible. It cannot give rise to a cognitive process. Hence, it is not. By contrast, when the priest visits Meursault in prison, he tells him that, if he entrusts himself to God like a child, God will forgive his act and he will no longer be alone in the prison. He will be able to see the image of God in the stone. But Meursault grows angry. He says: "I had been looking at the stones in these walls for months. There wasn't anything or anyone in the world I knew better" (119). Meursault thus sees only the stone. Moreover, Meursault is perhaps the only one who sees the stone—and who sees it as such, without projecting the image of God upon it.

Hegelian idealism, the idea that the real is the spiritual, develops the logic of a Christianity without innocence, without a fall, without original sin. For Hegel, we lose nothing: everything begins with consciousness, with a process of self-overcoming oriented toward absolute knowledge. Yet, not only does every subject experience a form of irreducible loss that prevents precisely this dominion and this totalization; spirit does not advance without its apathetic shadow, without that pure passion that is Meursault and in which murder and guilt coincide with innocence, the without why, the without cause. We manage to face the stone's innocence when reasons no longer sustain the world. Does this redeem us? Does it guarantee us happiness?

To be redeemed, one must take responsibility as a subject—and this is what Meursault cannot do. In order to be happy, the "indifference of the world"—that is, the stone's insensibility—would have to be able to open itself gently. But indifference (the neutral, as Blanchot calls it) is not gentle. It is a trial without end and without redemption. Perhaps this indifference of the world, this irreducible face-to-face with the stone, also takes place as the end of the world (the end of the meaning that fully sustains it), albeit as a silent cry, a language that is no longer the language that seeks to transmit meaning and that calls us to respond beyond all the security and homogeneity of the world. The important point is not that only the stone is innocent, but rather that there is a moment in history when history no longer progresses, when failure does not redeem us, a moment in which we are alone with the stone. At that moment, the stone's innocence is not merely a nothing of meaning. It is the (impossible?) opening of time from which we expect nothing more. For that very reason, perhaps, it is an infernal closure. But it is also what resists the order, the law, and its claim to say everything. It is perhaps the only witness of randomness, of flashes, of that which occurs beyond a cause, beyond a law.

Notes

Notes to the Introduction

1. In *Finitude and Guilt*, Ricoeur sheds a positive light on the mythical status of Adam and Eve's innocence. In fact, whereas Adam and Eve's innocence and fall cannot be understood in historical terms as if they were facts that could be established scientifically, for Ricoeur, "'the story of the fall has the greatness of myth'—that is to say has more meaning than a true story" (1967, 236). In fact, whereas history establishes facts, myth requires an act of speculation. It indeed doesn't speak of a remoted moment. It rather entails a reflection on the human condition.

2. This idea has been developed by Levinas in *Totality and Infinity*, where he shows that because the unfolding of history provides general narratives of human being, these are not made free by history. On the contrary, history's narrative being general and hence anonymous, it finally sounds like destiny (Levinas 1991, 275). This point has also been highlighted by Gabriela Basterra (2005) in *Seductions of Fate*, in particular when she points to a "necessary fate" (14–35).

3. The association between language and law has been made explicit in Jacques Lacan's (2006) thought and, in general, for structuralist thinkers. In fact, if language is constitutive of the subject, it is also inaccessible to it. For this reason, it is the Other. As law, it is transcendent as well as constitutive and irreducible. The association between law and language is also at the heart of Blanchot's *The Infinite Conversation*, where language stands as the order of meaning that gives to reality its shape, and hence as law.

4. Chapter three of this book, "Innocence," establishes a difference between not being and being nothing.

5. In the section on "The History of the Moral Sensations" in *Human, All Too Human*, Nietzsche unfolds the opposite thesis. For Nietzsche, because there is a genealogy of morals, the human being's history is opened to innocence. The moral phenomenon is in fact only an *effect* of pleasure and egoism; there is hence a humanity beyond morality that allows for the idea of a "becoming innocent." Hence, Nietzsche can imagine a human being "wise, innocent (conscious of his innocence)"

(1996, 59). However, this consciousness of innocence cannot be understood in terms of a self-consciousness that supposes an active and constitutive ego.

6. In his analysis of the concept of responsibility, Derrida highlights in *The Gift of Death* the aporia of the decision. On the one hand, a decision, in order to be such, has to be based on a certain knowledge. On the other hand, a decision is not a mere calculation; it happens as a rupture. Hence, a decision also entails a relation to what is not known: "Such, in fact, is the paradoxical condition of every decision: it cannot be deduced from a form of knowledge of which it would simply be the effect, conclusion or explication. It structurally breaches knowledge and is thus destined to non-manifestation; a decision is, in the end, always secret" (Derrida 2017, 77).

7. As we know, in *The Critique of Judgment* (1965), Kant defines genius as the capacity to produce a rule (and not merely to apply it). This productive aspect of aesthetics is particularly important for Arendt, in particular in her thinking of judgment and in her analysis of Eichmann. In a way, whereas Eichmann merely obeyed the Nazi party's rules, what he lacked was the imagination to produce his own rule, and hence his own critical judgment. On this matter, in her article "Gramáticas de la escucha: aproximaciones filosóficas a la construcción de la memoria histórica" (Acosta López 2019), María del Rosario Acosta López has marvelously shown, through her reading of Arendt, that this productive judgment is a weapon that allows us to move from the "paralysis" to which politics binds us (Acosta López 2019, 76).

8. This point crosses Fynsk's approach of the "infant" in *Infant Figures: The Death of the Infans and Other Scenes of Origin*. For Fynsk, the infans (which does not coincide with the legal figure of childhood but rather with a silence that haunts language) has a "'quasi-transcendental' character" (2000, 52). It is indeed interesting to observe that in order to expose this "quasi-transcendental" dimension of the infans, Fynsk's thought is addressed in the form of a dialogue in which the reader is convoked and where the frontiers that could allow the identification of speakers and readers are blurred. This way of exposing the infans' thought responds to the problem of how to think of the transcendental when we acknowledge the fact that it cannot be an object of thought. By convoking the reader, Fynsk invites to a form of exposition where what it is exposed is the very subject of the speech (and its trembling) rather than an object of speech.

9. The relation between revolution and innocence has been made in an explicit way by Blanchot in his only text that alludes to Benjamin: "A Rupture in Time: Revolution" (2010), first published in 1968 in the journal *Comité*. For Blanchot, here following Benjamin, revolution consists of an interruption of historical time, a rupture that is necessarily innocent since in this interruption nothing happens (nothing but the interruption!). In fact, Blanchot writes: "The only mode of presence of revolution is its real possibility. Then there is a state of arrest and suspension. In this suspension, society undoes itself, entirely. The law collapses. Transgression occurs: for a moment there is innocence; interrupted history" (2010,

100). Now, if revolution consists of an interruption and if this interruption is a way of experiencing innocence, how can we think of revolution and of innocence in a context such as ours, namely, in a context that doesn't unfold historically and that is itself continuously interrupted? This is, in a way, the issue raised recently by Eric Alliez in "1968–2018 or 'From the Revolution Impossible' to the Impossibility of Revolution? Variations on the object petits" (2018). On Blanchot's text "A Rupture in Time: Revolution," see also Hill's commentary in *Blanchot: Extreme Contemporary* (1997)

10. Let's recall that in *The 18th Brumaire of Napoleon Bonaparte*, Marx calls for an idea of revolution whose very language breaks with any past grammar: "The social revolution of the nineteenth century cannot derive its poetry from the past, but only from the future. It cannot begin with itself, before it has shed all superstitious belief in the past. Earlier revolutions needed to remember previous moments in world history in order to numb themselves with regard to their own content. The revolution of the nineteenth century must let the dead bury the dead in order to arrive at its own content. There, the phrase exceeded the content. Here, the content exceeds the phrase" (Marx 1963, 18).

11. Interestingly, in *Beyond the Verse*, Levinas defines the "revolutionary essence" by that which exceeds any prediction. Hence, he analyzes a Talmudic verse in light of Marx's idea of revolution: "'No eye hath not seen' oddly calls to mind the strange passage where Marx accepts socialist society to bring about changes in the human condition, frustrating any prediction by virtue of their actual revolutionary essence" (Levinas 1994, 2017). On the idea of revolution as a complete renewal, see Levinas's text "Judaism and Revolution" (1977) and my commentary of the *possibility* of such renewal in *L'anarchie de la paix. Levinas et la philosophie politique* (Messina 2018), in the chapter "Préparer la révolution dans le déchirement de la conscience: Levinas face à Marx."

12. Innocence is indeed a key topic both in environmental and biopolitical studies. In her book on *Nietzsche's Animal Philosophy*, Vanessa Lemm claims, for instance, that as soon as humans put aside their humanity in order to recover their animality, they also recover their innocence. Lemm explains, in fact, Nietzsche's idea that "everything is innocent" by assimilating humans with animals, and animals with innocence (Lemm 2009, 66, 67). However, environmental studies have also raised critical questions on this association of plants and animals with innocence. Such is the case of Michael Marder in *Plant Thinking* (2013). In the latter, rather than overcoming the knowledge of humans by the innocence of animals or plant, Marder sees a form of thinking and freedom at stake in life (and in particular in plants). Another interesting perspective on the relation between innocence and environment and life is unfolded by Natalia Cecire in "Environmental Innocence and Slow Violence" (2015). In this article, Cecire defines "environmental innocence" as the juridical problem of who can be held responsible for the destruction of the environment when this destruction occurs so slowly. She then analyzes the

aesthetic resources that make possible the staging and accounting for the destruction. Interestingly, when violence occurs in an invisible manner, children, or innocent figures, might be the ones who can witness "innocent destructions" (Cecire 2015).

13. I borrow this expression from Levinas's thought in which "incondition" names the fact that the human condition is not guaranteed (Levinas 2006, 66).

14. In her book, *A Theology of Failure: Žižek Against Christian Innocence* (2019), Marika Rose claims that failure is inherent to Christianity, which thus can neither return to innocence nor be "innocented." However, it is different to think of innocence as outside or previous to the fall, and to think of innocence as concomitant with the fall, *as a fall.* If innocence is a failure, then we cannot be against it because we cannot master it.

15. I would like to thank Cheryl Emerson for highlighting the semantical, conceptual, and oracular proximity between awareness and whereness.

16. It would be interesting to confront Hegel's interpretation of the fall with the topic of the *imago dei*. God in fact creates the first human being in his own image (Genesis 1:27); however, once Adam and Eve eat the prohibited fruit, once their eyes become open, this resemblance or this being in God's image becomes an abyss. As Kevin Hart (2021) remarks, the resemblance cannot be an anthropologic projection, nor can it be merely symmetrical. If we think of Saint Augustine's *Confessions*, God is sought and loved in his unknown dimension. What is extraordinary and moving in Saint Augustine's *Confessions* is that his love *and* writing entail a limited experience of his very human condition. Now, one issue that could be addressed is whether Hegel's dialectical understanding of the human being becoming spiritual is not an anthropological one. In fact, in Hegel, the divinization of the human being relies on its capacity to objectify and to reflect upon itself. This absolutization means that the human being coincides perfectly with themselves, with their image. In this progression toward Absolute Knowledge, doesn't the human being betray the *imago dei*? Don't they become a mere idol to themself? Or, on the contrary, isn't it this perfect resemblance that allows one to see oneself as unknown? On this point, Kevin Hart (2021) suggests that the fall coincides with the propension to create idols. This idea could be understood thus: opened to the unknown, Adam's and Eve's eyes search the knowable. Instead of living their resemblance to God, they create idols. On this topic, see Kevin Hart's *L'image vulnerable*: "Ce ne serait pas parce que l'*imago* peut être perdu dans cette vie, mais parce que nos relations avec Dieu sont en permanence menacées par notre propension, en tant que créature déchues, à commettre l'idolâtrie. Et l'idolâtrie n'est pas seulement la fabrication d'autre dieux . . . mais la méconnaissance de Dieu qui est le fruit des limites de nos cœurs" (2021, 38). (*"It would not be because the* imago *can be lost in this life, but because our relations with God are perpetually menaced by our propension, as fallen creatures, to commit idolatry. And this idolatry is not only the fabrication of other gods . . . but the misrecognition of God which is the fruit of our limited hearts."* Translated by Cheryl Emerson and myself.)

17. In the first session of the seminar *Life Death*, Derrida explains that because life cannot be explained in its mere opposition to death—in other words, because death has always already contaminated life—he will not write "life death" with an "and" in between (Derrida 2020, 21). Following this line, we could also reflect on the absence of the hyphen in the final title given to the seminar. In fact, the question of how to think of the difference between life and death is a void.

18. The differences between Blanchot and Levinas have been highlighted by Alain Toumayan in his important book, *Encountering the Other: The Art Work and the Problem of Difference in Blanchot and Levinas* (2004). However, it is interesting to read in these evident and explicit differences an unheard and more concealed proximity, as Micheal Fagenblat does in "Back to the Other Levinas: Reflections Prompted by Alain P. Toymayan's *Encountering the Other: The Art Work and the Problem of Difference in Blanchot and Levinas*" (2005). In fact, whereas it is common to observe Blanchot and Levinas diverge on the topic of the "il y a" and of the neuter, which Levinas apparently refuses and which Blanchot would claim, it is also true, as Fagenblat observes, that Levinas's description of the encounter with the Other is always on the verge of the "il y a" and that Blanchot's conception of the neuter does not amount to a mere atheism, but rather to a reformulation of the relation between theism and atheism. Following Fagenblat, Blanchot and Levinas indeed meet not on ethical questions, but rather on ethics' fragility and on what blurs the frontier between theism and atheism. In the same token, but taking a different path, in "Levinas, Blanchot and Art," Kevin Hart (2019a) observes that although Blanchot differentiates his thought from that of Levinas, in his last writings he affirms not only an indefectible friendship with Levinas, but also a strong proximity of thought. To my mind, these readings indicate that what exists between Levinas and Blanchot is not a game of identity or opposition, but a friendship of thought there where the frontiers are blurred, and there where what has to be thought is not the identity of the same but the difference of the neuter. This topic of friendship between Levinas and Blanchot has been remarkably staged by Danielle Cohen-Levinas in "Entre eux. Maurice Blanchot et Emmanuel Levinas . . . Là où ils sont se rendre à l'impossible." In this article, Cohen-Levinas (2009) shows that the neuter is indeed the space of friendship and does not constitute a topic of opposition between Blanchot and Levinas.

19. In his very early text, "Reflections on the Philosophy of Hitlerism," Levinas argues that Hitlerism is the fruit of the Western dissociation from the body. However, rather than defending a conception of the body grounded on force and expansion, as in the case of what he calls "Philosophy of Hitlerism," Levinas thinks it is in its passivity that the body is tied to the soul, as in the experience of pain: "And in the impasse of physical pain, is it not the case that the sick man experiences the indivisible simplicity of his being when he turns over in his bed of suffering to find a position that gives him peace?" (1990, 68). Regarding the question of suffering in Levinas and its political stakes, see my article, "Souffrance éthique et

souffrance tragique. L'élaboration lévinasienne de la critique Nietzschéenne de la compassion" (Messina 2016).

20. Unlike Levinas, for Blanchot, suffering is an anonymous experience that instead of individualizing a subject reveals its emptiness. Hence, in the chapter titled "The Indestructible" in *The Infinite Conversation*, Blanchot writes: "In affliction—and in our society affliction is always first the loss of social status—the one who suffers at the hands of men is radically altered. Having fallen not only below the individual, but also below every class and every real collective relation, the person no longer exists in his or her personal identity. In this sense the one afflicted is already outside the world, a being without horizon" (1993, 131).

21. In two homonymous articles titled "Disastrous Responsibility," Ann Smock (1984) and Arthur Cools (2011) highlight the idea that in Blanchot, responsibility is without a base but not annulled. However, I prefer to speak of a "disastered" ethics in order to focus on the idea that disaster in Blanchot is not only a disgrace but also the shining of a lack (in French "dés-astre" entails the absence of "aster," namely of "stars") and thus, if not the beginning of a new language, at least the hearing of an unheard meaning of the words.

22. This rapid association between Judaism and Law is not proper to Judaism nor to Levinas. Rather than speaking of Law, Levinas speaks of the face as expressing the fifth commandment, "you shall not kill." Interestingly, Levinas's phenomenological approach to the commandment shows that this last one transcends the subject only in the measure in which its transcendence is located in the immanence of the face. Indeed, in Levinas, the "face" (*visage*), which commands, transcends in the measure in which it is naked, in the measure in which it disturbs the usual way of looking. Hence, in Levinas, subjectivity is not the correlate of the transcendence of Law but rather of the disturbance of the face. This is why Levinas speaks of anarchy rather than of Law. On this point, see also note 30.

23. On the topic of the "last man," see chapter three of this book.

24. As Hill remarkably says in "From Deconstruction to Disaster (Derrida, Blanchot, Hegel)": "In transcribing Hegel's text, Blanchot, however, partly rewrites it, first by changing the original German syntax and word order, second by omitting the second part of the sentence, and finally by translating 'Nichttun' twice over, once, literally, as 'le non-faire,' and once, in standard philosophical idiom, as 'l'absence d'opération,' thus forcing a reader to stumble, and tread twice, so to speak, once on the left and once on the right, on the self-same step—a step that, interrupting and redoubling itself, cannot do other than re-mark itself as an abyssal symptom. Approximate or inaccurate quotations of this kind are a not uncommon feature in Blanchot's later texts, and it is often hard to tell whether they are simply errors, caused by Blanchot's sometimes crabbed handwriting or by his habit of citing from memory, or whether they are consciously intended as improvement of the original wording" (2016, 194).

25. In *Literature and the Right to Death*, Blanchot quotes Hegel: "Adam's first act, which made him master of the animals, was to give them names, that is, he annihilated them in their existence (as existing creatures)" (Blanchot 1995, 323).

26. Albeit Blanchot's literature relates to the silence of things, namely, to "their existence before the world exists" (328), literature doesn't properly *reach* this silence; otherwise, the collapse of language and hence of human being would be a matter of fact, a reachable end. On the contrary, what interests Blanchot is to inscribe silence *within* language: "If we were to become as mute as a stone, as passive as the corpse enclosed behind that stone, its decision to lose the capacity for speech would still be legible on the stone and would be enough to wake that bogus corpse" (329). In this passage, the image of the stone recalls Hegel's idea that only a stone is innocent. Whereas innocence does not exist and cannot be reached, one can relate to it through language's silence. On the question of literature's relation to things, I would like to thank Amanda Olivares, whose rigorous reading of *Literature and the Right to Death* raised new issues to be addressed and allowed me to avoid an empirical understanding of the question of the "thing."

27. The idea that Blanchot's writing relates to Adam's silence finds an echo in Pierre Madaule's idea that the principal character of Blanchot's *Thomas the Obscure* is double of Adam (Madaule 2009, 43). In "La vengeance d'Adam," Madaule observes that in *Thomas the Obscure*, Thomas is compared to Adam. However, this comparison is possible not in that Thomas would have originary characteristics, as if he had not been stained by history. On the contrary, for Madaule, it is death, the impossibility to die, and hence to *be* a man (a human being), that in ultimate instance allows Thomas to be a double of Adam. Hence, this presence of Adam in Blanchot's writing is not a mere repetition of the Saint History. It is rather, as suggests Madaule, a "Counter-Saint History" ("contre-Histoire Sainte") (43). As I will put it throughout this book, it is the impossibility of such a History, and the history of this impossibility.

28. In *Blanchot and the Literature of the Outside*, William S. Allen makes an interesting point on the relation between the figure of the "last man" and the topic of the "end of history." Since the "end of history" relates to the end as an impossible limit and hence as an impossible overcoming, the "last man" "becomes a vector of the dissembling of meaning as it goes even further towards the limit of its own impossibility" (2018, 48).

29. As will be argued throughout this book, albeit Blanchot has often been associated with the Jewish tradition, it is also important to highlight his relation with the Christian tradition. The question is not whether Blanchot's thought is closer to Judaism than to Christianity, but how his relation to writing entails a new reading of both of these traditions. Hence, we can just as well say, with Nancy (2014), that Christianity is a key topic in Blanchot's writings and, with Fynsk (2013) or Hammerschlag (2010), that Judaism is the major experience of writing. However,

the point is not to say that Blanchot's thoughts stick to both traditions, as if they were synthesizable, but rather that Blanchot's relation to Judaism or to Christianity is inseparable from the way the question of writing opens to new ways of reading that escape the hermeneutical frames through which these traditions might have been synthesized.

30. It is important to outline that this idea of the Judaic conception of subjectivity as subjected to law is precisely Christian and derives from Saint Paul's association between the law and death; for instance, in the Roman Epistles. Now, if we think of law as the Thora, this latter means an orientation rather than a limit. It is inseparable from the hermeneutic condition of the subject who receives the law in the moment in which he interprets it, and hence gives it *life*. The association between death and the law misses the law's hermeneutical dimension. The association between Judaism and the law confuses the commandment with a mere prohibition that limits. However, the commandment doesn't limit; it opens the subject.

31. It is interesting to observe that it is in the journal *Lignes* that Blanchot's political views appear and are discussed in a clearer way, first in 1998 when the relation between writing and politics is made explicit and when writing becomes a practical dimension of communism, as well as the renewal of its meaning; and then in 2014 when this new point of view on communism is discussed and criticized (see *Lignes* no. 33 and *Lignes* no. 43). Now, whereas Lars Iyer (2004) explicitly relates writing with communism, showing that communism entails the experience of the unworking, namely of a radical dispossession, we can ask, in line with Bremondy's (2014) analysis, whether this unworking dimension of communism is not confined to a certain aristocratic understanding *and* practice. In fact, following Allen (2018), we can say that Blanchot's writing is by itself a practice; hence, not only an interpretation of the world. However, the question is whether the "unworking" leads also to its transformation or only to its mere defection (this point will be developed in chapter four, "Apocalypse," and in the closing chapter of the book). The discussion on the political aspect of Blanchot's writing will also be developed at length in the closing chapter.

Notes to Chapter 1

1. In French, "future" can be said as "future" or "*avenir*." Taking this second use of the word, Derrida speaks of the future as the "*à venir*"; namely, the "to come." The idea is to think of the future in terms of an imminence that disturbs the present, rather than what can be securely posited from the present.

2. The problem of the decision in Blanchot and Derrida has been remarkably analyzed by Leslie Hill in *Radical Indecision: Barthes, Blanchot, Derrida, and the Future of Criticism* (2010). Whereas one could think that since for Blanchot and Derrida the decision is impossible, then one is bound and stuck to indecisiveness. However, as Hill remarks: "Indecision . . . is not indecisiveness." In fact, the indecision that

structures Blanchot and Derrida's thought frees that which exceeds the possible, the calculation or knowledge. In this sense, the impossible is not a negation of the possible but an affirmation of what exceeds possibility. Hence, affirming indecision can be a responsible act. As Hill states: "To decide, then, is to be responsive to the undecidable: to answer to it and for it" (170).

3. With regard to the double-bind and thus the relationship between possible and impossible, the difference between Blanchot and Derrida is both small and decisive. For Derrida, as with Blanchot, the secret or silence that haunts the law is not external to the language from which we receive the law. In *Force of Law*, Derrida writes: "Here a silence is walled up in the violent structure of the founding act. Walled up, walled in because silence is not exterior to language" (1992, 14). However, while Derrida reflects on this silence from the domain of the known, which is determined by the law, Blanchot thinks of this silence within the question of literature, where language extracts itself from the world and therefore from the order of the known. Thus, in Blanchot's work, the silence or the impossible can no longer be defined from the known or the possible without immediately experiencing their collapse, their impossibility.

4. This question has been addressed by Christopher Langlois in "Literature Outside the Law: Blanchot's *The Infinite Conversation*" (2018). As Langlois puts it very clearly, the Outside is not pure of the violence of law. On the contrary, "This place where no Self comes into being and where there is no hope of crossing the distance that frames it is the site of an originary experience of writing that guarantees only violence and terror without end (an experience of the impossibility of experience" (101). Whereas Langlois sees literature as a force of dislocation "that must double as the force of its own sovereign exception" (103), the question will be whether literature's play with the law stems from a force or from a weakness, and whether its fight can still be thought of in terms of sovereignty. On the question of the "force," it is important to ask—as does Rodolphe Gasché in *Deconstruction, its Force, its Violence*—whether force is merely opposed to form, or if it is concomitant with it. In his reading of Derrida's essay "Force and Signification," Gasché defines force as that which breaks the economy of meaning and relaunches it infinitely: "The force of the written is to relaunch infinitely any signified that would seek to arrest the movement of indefinite referral into the signifying process, into the economy of signification" (2016, 24). Following this analysis, we can say that there is a force within writing's weakness. On the relation between law and literature in Blanchot, see Thurschwell's important article "Law and Literature and the Right to Death" (Thurschwell 2007).

5. *The Most High* is published before *Aminabad*, but I will define it as Blanchot's last novel in order to insist on the fact that writing progresses through its interruption.

6. This coincidence between law and life meets Agamben's description of the "impossibility of distinguishing law from life" in *Homo Sacer* (1998, 53). In fact, for Agamben, it is the vacuity of law that enables it to invade life. As we will see,

it is precisely this vacuity of law that is staged in *The Most High*. In fact, Agamben writes: "For life under a law that is in force without signifying resembles life in the state of exception, in which the most innocent gesture or the smallest forgetfulness can have most extreme consequences" (52).

7. "All you had to do was walk by: the passerby fulfilled a duty. Wasn't it extraordinary? I had gone out for a few minutes with Louise, I wanted to take a walk—and what was I doing? I was making the law circulate, I was contributing to the application of a public decree. This should invigorate me, I thought, and help me live. And still, I felt very uncomfortable. Knowing that everyone was grateful for my glance and that even those on the other side of the barrier, those condemned to isolation and destruction by this glance, were grateful—what could I do? I couldn't stand it; it bored a hole in my sight. In other words I really tolerated it, in spite of everything; for this hole changed nothing, I didn't even go away. I continued to look according to the rules, also absorbed by the rules, became an honorable feeling of sadness provoked by the spectacle of common misfortunes" (Blanchot 1996, 80).

8. This idea that passion could be due to law's void has been unfolded in another way by Levinas in his article on Blanchot's *The Madness of the Day*. There, Levinas focuses his attention on the double meaning of the genitive in *La folie du jour* (*The Madness of the Day*). For Levinas, whereas the "day" stands as the law (where everything is ordered and seen), "madness" can be a passion for the day and a passion provoked for the day. See Levinas, "Exercices sur 'la folie du jour'" (1975, 58).

9. At the beginning of the novel, Sorge comments on his isolation in terms of a criminal offense: "But if there's no answer, if I raise my voice and realize that I'm speaking all alone, I suddenly almost start trembling—it's worse than anything. It's an insult, a real offense. I feel as if I've committed a crime, I've lived outside the common good. And besides, am I alive? Life is elsewhere, amid these thousands of people packed together, who live like that, who get along, who have attained law and liberty" (Blanchot 1996, 27).

10. The topic of the illness in *The Most High* has been remarkably analyzed by Ann Smock (1976) in her important (and early) article "Où est la loi?" and by John Gregg in *Blanchot and the Literature of Transgression* (1994). Although Gregg is right to see in disease a moment of disruption that escapes control by the law, it is also important to highlight that disease, precisely because it entails an exception, embodies law's sovereignty (which lies in its exceptionality). Gregg states in fact that "the epidemic disrupts the delicate balance that enables the State to have control as it converts one into the other in a continual process of appropriation" (1994, 90). However, Smock sees in disease (and in weakness in general) the shining of the ambivalence of the law *and* the ambivalence of resistance: "The law is the deafening silence of the cry against it. Does that mean that it has silenced the cry, or been silenced by it? The state is the visibility of pain, humiliation, sickness, dying. Does that mean that it is itself dying, or that it has revealed and thus conquered death? It has itself accomplished the obliteration of its own boundary. Does that mean that

it has contained revolution, that the obliteration is without effect, or that always spilling outside itself, it defers indefinitely its own inscription?" (Smock 1976, 103). On the topic of law in *The Most High*, see also "Maurice Blanchot: The Thought from the Outside" (Foucault, 1987).

11. In a similar way (but for other reasons), Leslie Hill states that "what constitutes the force of law is its weakness" (2003, 35–37). Yet, Hill does recognize that the force of law is "grounded" in its void (its absence of ground); in this context, the weakness of the law has rather an ethical meaning (in a Levinassian sense). Hill analyzes the very end of *The Most High*, where Jeanne is about to kill Sorge and weakens in front of this possibility (a gun she holds in her hand. The weakness of the law is then described by Hill as that "infinite relation to the other of any law" that "constitutes Law"; namely, the ethical encounter. While this is very important, this way of describing the weakness of the law in ethical terms seems too rigid compared to the way the meaning of law in Blanchot is constantly escaping. Although present in both *The Most High* and in Blanchot's work in general, the ethical (the relation to the Other) is either too weak or too forceful to have this status of being one side of the law (its weakness). Following *The Writing of the Disaster*, we can say that when *properly* ethical, ethics (the relation to the Other) relies on a conception of subjectivity that, at least in Blanchot's view, doesn't break thoroughly enough with the idea of a subject and therefore acts like a force. But for Blanchot, this *properly* ethical is improper, and therefore nonethical. For Blanchot, in front of the Other, the "I" shifts out of itself. It is made Other than itself; namely, anonymous. It is not, therefore, as in the Levinassian view, the One (unique) who can subjectively respond for the Other. In this encounter, the ethical subject risks turning irresponsible. In Blanchot, ethics is therefore weakened in its force; but in its weakness, it is no longer ethical. Although these considerations belong to Blanchot's late writings, we already find in *The Most High* such slips from the ethical to a void of ethics. For instance, while ill, Sorge is constantly concerned by what is happening behind the wall of his room, by the others, but this concern is also self-destructive; it is Sorge's way of being brought out of law in the very moment he could mold it. Regarding Blanchot's relation to Levinas and its critique of the concept of subjectivity, see the introduction to this book.

12. The fact that Christianity aspires to the overcoming of the law doesn't mean that Christians live without law. The Church has, of course, a code of Canonical Law. This can be explained by the fact that we have not yet reached the *parousia*. We belong to Adam's generation, not to the second Adam. Our flesh is indeed vulnerable. Yet the question addressed in this book is if the law, once overcome, doesn't still transcend, precisely for the void that haunts it.

13. On this subject, see Lorenzo Fabbri, "Chronotopologies of the Exceptions: Derrida and Agamben Before the Camps" (2009, 93).

14. In fact, in *Homo Sacer*, Agamben states: "The fundamental categorial pair of Western politics is not that of friend/enemy but that of bare life/political existence, *zoë/bios*, exclusion/inclusion" (8). He adds: "When its borders begin to

be blurred, the bare life that dwelt there frees itself in the city and becomes both subject and object of the conflicts of the political order, the one place for both the organization of State power and emancipation from it. . . . Democracy presents itself from the beginning as *a vindication and liberation of* zoë, and that it is constantly trying to transform its own bare life and to find, so to speak, the bios of the *zoë*" (9, my emphasis). Hence, what is at stake in Agamben's political thought on law is the freeing of life, understood also as the overcoming of the difference between *bios* and *zoë*. There is therefore a teleology at stake in Agamben's thought: "Until a completely new politics—that is, a politics no longer founded on the exception of bare life—is at hand, every theory and every praxis will remain imprisoned and immobile, and the 'beautiful day of life' will be given citizenship only either through blood and death or in the perfect senselessness to which the society of the spectacle condemns it" (11). This teleology, not so different (at least in its logic) from Hegel's dialectic, aims at the liberation of life from law, overcoming the difference between *zoë* and *bios*; namely, between "bare existence" and "political life." Hence, although this overcoming is not a regression to "natural life in the *oikos*" (188), it indeed aims at a "form of life" that is pure of the formality of the law: "This biopolitical body that is bare life must itself instead be transformed into the site for the constitution and installation of a form of life that is wholly exhausted in bare life and a *bios* that is only its own *zoë*" (11). On the difference between "*bios*" and "*zoë*," see Derrida's critique in *The Beast and the Sovereign* (2009, 325–26). Although several scholars affirm that Derrida is wrong to see that Agamben's thought works with a clear opposition between "*bios*" and "*zoë*" (Meyer 2014, 152), it cannot be denied that life defines in Agamben's thought the horizon of a teleology. Moreover, as will be argued, this teleology is based on Saint Paul's idea not of a natural idea of life, but of a pure life free from law's morality or formality. Hence, the problem is not whether Agamben would or would not rely on the distinction between *bios* and *zoë*, but rather that life is indeed the horizon of a renewal that pretends to be independent from law.

15. See note 6, this chapter.

16. This idea is developed further in the next chapter, "Grace."

17. This idea is developed further in the next chapter, "Grace."

18. On this subject, see *L'anarchie de la paix: Levinas et la philosophie politique* (Messina 2018, chapter 4).

19. This point can be contrasted with Iyer's beautiful analysis on the question of inspiration in Blanchot and Levinas. As Iyer puts it, in Levinas, inspiration is a matter of breathing, while in Blanchot, it is rather a matter of asphyxiation: "Blanchot points not to the respiration of language but its asphyxiation, not to Levinassian saying, but to a smothering, not to the wisdom of love of *Otherwise than Being*, but to the madness of a foreword that unravels every word in advance" (2003, 57). This difference between inspiration and asphyxiation corresponds to what Blanchot calls the "dying" (*mourir*); namely, the fact that life has always already been

contaminated by death. On this point, see also Lacoue-Labarthe's (2015) idea of "transcendental dying," which is not, as would be the case of an inspiration, life's condition of possibility, but rather "life's condition of impossibility" (177). In this sense, life is an experience of its intrinsic insecurity.

20. On the idea that there would be a life *pure* of language and of the law, Agamben is ambivalent. In *Homo Sacer*, Agamben speaks rather of a "form" of life rather than of a "pure life" (188). Moreover, faithful to Heidegger, Agamben does think human existence is rooted in language. However, what Agamben calls a "form of life" is unclear. Whereas he distinguishes it from the idea of a natural life, he still seems to believe that it can overcome the duality (by itself problematic) between *bios* and *zoë*, between a good life and a bare life: "Just as the biopolitical body of the West cannot be simply given back to its natural life in the oikos, so it cannot be overcome in a passage to a new body—a technical body or a wholly political or glorious body—in which a new economy of pleasures and vital functions would once and for all resolve the interlacement of *zoë* and *bios* that seems to define the political destiny of the West. This biopolitical body that is bare life must itself instead be transformed into the site for the constitution and installation of a form of life that is wholly exhausted in bare life and a *bios* that is only its own *zoë*" (1998, 188). On the other hand, whereas his idea of a "form of life" is unclear, his theory of language is problematic. Undoubtedly, Agamben does not think that the impurity of language can be overcome in the naturality of the voice. However, he thinks the language of the generality can be overcome in a language of the singularity. As Thomas Carl Wall says in *Radical Passivity: Levinas, Blanchot, and Agamben* (1999), Agamben's proposal is not to think "pure being" but "pure being in language" (131). It is a matter of saying the very difference between the generality of names and the singularity of things. However, how can this difference be grasped in its purity? Doesn't this gesture resemble Heidegger's proposal to overcome metaphysics; namely, to reach the metaphysical difference? It is this theoretic contradiction that leads us to think that Agamben's idea of a "form of life" amounts to aspiring to free life from the impurity of law and language. As Lorenzo Chiesa and Frank Ruda put it in an extremely interesting article, Agamben's "political discourse—the critique of the form of law—is founded upon a vitalistic ontology" (2011, 168). This "vitalistic ontology" derives from the idea that the event of language happens as a force of life, as the title of their article—"The Event of Language as Force of Life"—suggests.

21. The contamination between life and death is at the heart of Blanchot's *The Step Not Beyond* and of Derrida's writings on Blanchot published in *Parages* (2011), as well as of Derrida's seminar *Life Death* (2020). The question of the contamination between life and death in Blanchot will be further examined in chapter two of this book.

22. In 1995, when *Homo Sacer* was first published, Agamben was of course acquainted with Nancy's and Blanchot's work on community; namely, with Nancy's *The Inoperative Community* (Nancy 1991) and with Blanchot's *The Unavowable*

Community (Blanchot 1990). It is interesting to observe that Agamben does quote Nancy in "Form of Law." However, whereas he recognizes the importance of Nancy's conception of being as abandonment that hence is not reducible to a law, he argues that in Nancy such abandonment exceeds law but is never freed from it (1998, 51). Regarding Agamben's explicit relation to Blanchot's reflection on community, one would have to reflect on their respective conceptions of language and writing. In this respect, Aaron Hillyer's *The Disappearance of Literature* is interesting since it seeks to analyze the problem of community in Blanchot and Agamben precisely, in relation to their respective conceptions of literature. However, whereas for Hillyer Agamben finds in literature a way out from language, and hence from law and from the logic of guilt (Hillyer 2015, 36–37), Blanchot's idea of a "writing out of language" (e.g., as developed in *The Infinite Conversation*) doesn't precisely lead to the idea that *there is a way out* from language. As for Derrida, writing is for Blanchot the movement of a differing. It is the ordeal of the Outside but doesn't reach it. Similarly to what Leslie Hill states in "From Deconstruction to Disaster (Derrida, Blanchot, Hegel)" (2016, 197), we can say that Blanchot's idea of a "writing out of language" is still a law. Hence, there is no community that would be redeemed from the violence of the law.

23. This question is further developed in chapter five of this book, titled "The Deconstruction of Christianity in Blanchot and Nancy."

24. In this sense, contrary to what Lorenzo Fabbri states in "Chronotopologies of the Exceptions: Derrida and Agamben Before the Camps" (2009), it is not certain that Agamben's proposed reversal of the law through life opens up ethical perspectives, by "the creation of dwelling places in which living beings could experience new perspectives of life in common" (93). Indeed, there can be no "living in common" if life is thought of independently of finitude, and therefore—in the last instance—of the law, which derives precisely from this shared finitude.

25. See chapter two of this book, "Grace."

26. This argument is further developed in chapter two of this book, "Grace."

27. On the "neuter," see Nancy's remarkable article titled "The Neutral, Neutralization, of the Neutral" (2018), where Nancy argues that, whereas the neuter is nothing that can be named as being part of language (otherwise it would have a determined signification; it would not be neutral), it is neither out of language, such as, for instance, the name of God. Being neither part of language's significations, nor out of language, Nancy argues that literature is an exposition of the neuter in that it exposes language's void.

28. The hypothesis that Blanchot's writing engages a kind of freedom is at the heart of Christopher Fynsk's reading of *The Madness of the Day*. In "Writing and Sovereignty," Fynsk (2010) remarkably shows that Blanchot's narrative of the impossibility of the narrative not only puts at stake law in its unicity and power of unity, but also in the multiplicity of its ordeals. Indeed, the writing's specific combat puts at stake law's sovereignty. Hence, albeit Blanchot's conception of writ-

ing is not meant to overcome law, neither does writing submit to it. This is why, with all the precautions it requires, Fynsk can speak of *The Madness of the Day* as announcing a "freedom" (192).

29. This is what Derrida highlighted very well in *Parages*. In "The Law of Genre," in particular, Derrida shows how this narrative questions the limits that make it possible as a narrative, and still narrates the absence of narrative. Hence, while Derrida describes *The Madness of the Day* as making impossible the very law that makes possible its production as a narrative, it also narrates this very impossibility: "All is *récit* and nothing is; the exit out of the *récit* remains *within* the *récit* in a non-inclusive mode, and this structure is itself related so remotely to a dialectical structure that it even inscribes dialectics in the *récit*'s ellipse. All is *récit*, nothing is: and we shall not know whether the relationship between these two propositions—the strange conjunction of the *récit* and the *récit*-less—belongs to the order of the *récit* itself" (2011, 237).

30. See in particular "A Turning," where Hill distinguishes the fragment understood in a romantic way as a unity of meaning and the fragmentary understood as the division of what cannot be united. Whereas the fragment is a unity and hence belongs to a present of time, the fragmentary breaks with the idea of presence. This is why for Hill "the Romantic fragment is not yet the fragmentary, the fragmentary is still to come" (2012, 31). See also "Le tournant du fragmentaire: prolégomènes" (Hill 2007).

31. In the English translation of *The Infinite Conversation*, "*l'entre-dire*" has been translated either as "speech" (226) or as "speaking" (221), or as "speaking between" (260). It's important to observe that "*entre-dire*" is a play on the word "*inter-dit*," which means prohibition (interdiction). By using the word "entre-dire," Blanchot shows that speech is inherently divided: it enacts the law and transgresses it; it posits it and takes it away. The identification between "entre-dire" and "inter-dit" leads us to think that the same happens with the law: it has the power to prohibit (interdire), but this prohibition is always already transgressed.

32. The word "*entretien*" in French can be translated as "interview" or as "entertainment." It is, in fact, more an encounter (as in a job interview) than a proper conversation, but it is also a way of occupying time, or of dealing with its void. Moreover, in *The Infinite Conversation*, there is nothing such as a totalizing dialogue or meaningful conversation. The voices that take place might be the voice of the One that constantly diverges from itself. It would henceforth be the voice of the One's impossibility. And rather than gathering around a unique point of view, there are voices that diverge from themselves, that experience a form of distraction.

33. On this topic, see Serge Margel's very interesting article titled "De Blanchot à Blanchot: Les pouvoirs de l'écriture et le droit à la mort" (2019) where writing is associated with the interruption or the break (*coupure*) and where the break is described in its very tension with language and hence with the law. In this article, Margel interprets writing as a force inseparable from language, hence from the

force of a form. This inseparability between force and form promises writing to its interruption or effacement. Indeed, writing drives law to play its own game, to play with its inherent void. For this reason, maybe what Margel calls the indifference of writing, its "power of effacement" (2019, 90) could be its non-indifference to law's indifference or neutrality. To make law play its own game is in fact a way of putting a stake law's indifference, to make law play a singular game.

Notes to Chapter 2

1. The fragment of *The Step Not Beyond* in question reads: "But isn't grace always the gift made by someone, gift unique and from the Unique?" (1992, 25). Note that the signification of the Greek "Karisma" (grace) determines the idea of grace as a gift. God's grace is the fact that God freely gives himself to humanity through his son, Jesus Christ. Grace or Karisma, then, is this very gift or favor.

2. See Romans 8:4, "In order that the righteous requirement of the law might be fully met in us, who do not live according to the flesh but according to the spirit."

3. This idea pertains to what Bernard Bourgeois, in *Hegel à Francfort: Judaïsme, Christianisme, Hegelianisme* (1970), says about the relation between love and law in Hegel's conception of Christianity: "Telle est l'unité vivante de l'amour, qui rend la loi entièrement *superflue*, car l'amour *ne s'oppose pas* à la loi, auquel cas il se contredirait, mais il est comme tel l'*absence*, le non-être de la loi" ("Such is the living unity of love, which makes the law entirely superfluous, for love does not oppose the law, in which case it would be contradicted, but rather is as such the absence, the non-being of the law") (Bourgeois 2000, 21). Grace saves from death and overcomes law in that love allows for its accomplishment, which makes the transcendence of law superfluous.

4. See note 1, this chapter.

5. Marx's words in *The Eighteenth Brumaire of Louis Bonaparte*, "The social revolution of the nineteenth century cannot draw its poetry from the past, but only from the future" (Marx, *Collected Works*, volume 11, 106), could certainly be related to Saint Paul's idea of grace. In fact, grace not only saves from death and, in this sense, from a certain mortality of the past and the injustices sedimented in it. Grace also "overflows" in that it exceeds the formality of law. In this sense, in grace, "the content goes beyond the words."

6. From *Thus Spoke Zarathustra*: "What is great about human beings is that they are a bridge and not a purpose" (Nietzsche 2006, 7).

7. On the relation between the content of Paul's preaching (grace) and the specificity of Paul's speech, Giorgio Agamben has suggested in *The Time That Remains: A Commentary on the Letter to the Romans* that Paul's speech amounts to neither a denotative structure in which speech is separated from reality nor a

performative structure in which speech is at the same time an action. For Agamben, Paul's speech has an effect on his interlocutor because it does not amount to signification. In Paul's speech, what would speak, what would be addressed, what would act as grace is a remainder of meaning: "The word of faith manifests itself as the effective experience of a pure power [*potenza*] of saying that, as such, does not coincide with any denotative proposition, or with the performative value of a speech act. Rather, it exists as an absolute nearness of the word. One therefore understands why, for Paul, messianic power finds its *telos* in weakness. The act itself of a pure potentiality of saying, a word that always remains close to itself, cannot be a signifying word that utters true opinions on the state of things, or a juridical performative that posits itself as fact. . . . 'Messianic and weak' is therefore that potentiality of saying, which, in dwelling near the word not only exceeds all that is said, but also exceeds the act of saying itself, the performative power of language" (Agamben 2005b, 137).

8. According to Barth (1956, 225), "the man under grace is engaged unconditionally in a conflict. This conflict is a war of life and death, a war in which there can be no armistice, no agreement—and no peace."

9. See note 3, this chapter.

10. In the last volume of *Homo Sacer*, and more precisely in his synthetical article "For a Theory of Destituting Power," Agamben sketches the political stakes of Paul's overcoming of law (and directly relate it to his own—Agamben's—theory). For Agamben, Paul's "Katargese" (1 Cor 14:25) is the deactivating of any power. What is at stake with grace would thus be a political understanding of anarchy where law would not be overcome in another law, but suspended in its very power (Agamben 2017, 1274). Two questions can be raised: Is this "theory of destituting power" not the supreme affirmation of power? In fact, whereas it is not law in its ambivalence but in its anomy that is affirmed, no constituted political instances can limit law nor interpret it. Hence, we run the risk of being abandoned to a mere anonymous anomy. Second, Agamben translates "Katargese" by the word that Blanchot often uses: "inoperative" or "unworking" (in Italian, *inoperante*). Does this sketch a possible political affinity (on a theoric level) between Blanchot and Agamben? Or does Blanchot's rewriting of the Christian notion of grace thought of in Blanchot not as a "gift" but as a "detour" entail other political stakes? This is one of the issues this book will address, in particular in chapter five where the consequences of Blanchot's relation to Christianity are discussed.

11. In his letter to the Romans, Paul establishes a contrast between the figure of Adam and the figure of Jesus Christ. Adam is innocent, to be sure, but his innocence doesn't prevent him from sinning. By contrast, Jesus Christ saves from sinfulness through his death: "For if, by the trespass of the one man, death reigned through that one man, how much more will those who receive God's abundant provision of grace and of the gift of righteousness reign in life through the one man, Jesus Christ!" (Romans 5:17). However, it is interesting to observe, as Barth

does, that the figures of Adam and Christ, even if symmetrically opposed, are correlated. For Barth, in fact, Christ is not separated from Adam; he is the secret of Adam. As he writes in *Christ and Adam: Man and Humanity in Romans 5*: "Here the new point is that the *special* anthropology of Jesus Christ—the one man for all men, all men in the one man—constitutes the secret of 'Adam' also" (Barth 1956, 14). This means that Christ does not coincide with a mere historical moment: he is always already present in Adam. Thus: "Because of it, even in that past we were not completely forsaken and lost" (15).

12. On the relation between silence and sinfulness, see chapter three of this book, "Innocence."

13. It is interesting to observe that the death that correlates to transgression is not the interruption of life, but rather another modality of sensibility. Eve, however, reminds the serpent that "God did say, 'You must not eat fruit from the tree that is in the middle of the garden, and you must not touch it, or you will die'" (Genesis 3:3). This death is made concrete by the fact that once Eve and Adam ate the forbidden fruit, their eyes opened, and they saw themselves naked: "Then the eyes of both of them were opened, and they realized they were naked; so they sewed fig leaves together and made coverings for themselves" (Genesis 3:7). Now, this eye-opening consequence was what the serpent objected to, in his words to Eve. For the serpent, there is a difference between dying and opening one's eyes (Genesis 3:4–5). However, one might wonder whether this opening is not precisely death as an exposition to the Outside, whereas being naked stands here, as Levinas would say, not as an absence of clothes, but rather as the rupture of the immanence of forms. What Eve and Adam experience as death after their transgression is the very fragility of existence; namely, finitude.

14. On Blanchot's deconstruction of this boundary and the role of Literature therein, see "Living On: Borderlines" in Derrida (2010) as well as the seminar *Life Death* (2020). It's important to observe that the deconstruction of the boundary that separates life from death doesn't mean a confusion or identity between the two. What Derrida highlights in *Life Death* is that their difference cannot be understood in terms of dialectical opposition. As Derrida makes plain, the issue is not to leave behind this logic but to expose its internal impossibility; namely, to go toward another way of dwelling in such a logic, "toward another topos": "So that, by saying, with the blank of a pause or the invisible mark of a beyond, 'life death,' I am neither opposing nor identifying life and death (neither and [et] nor is [est]), I am neutralizing, as it were, both opposition and identification, in order to gesture *not toward another logic*, an opposite logic of life and death, *but toward another topos*, if you will, a topos from which it would be possible to read, at the very least, the entire program of the and and of the is, of the positionality and presence of being, both of these being effects of 'life death.' How to think position and presence as effects? That presupposes, obviously, another thinking of effect" (Derrida 2020, 6, my emphasis).

15. On this point, see the thirteenth book of Saint Augustine's *The City of God*, where Augustine stems the impossibility to locate death and to think of death as an event. As Augustine states, death cannot be located in the living being, since it is living, and it cannot be located whence the living being has ceased to live, since in this moment there is no more being. In this sense, death is more than another "topos," as Derrida would say (see note 14, this chapter); it's a destruction of the logic. It's rather atopic. On this topic, see the introduction of this book, where Blanchot's *The Step Not Beyond* is read as a commentary on this thirteenth book of Saint Augustine's *The City of God*.

16. In "Living On," Derrida suggests that the duration entailed in the verb "to survive" is rather the one of the "to die" than the one referring to a temporality that would be proper to life. In the survival, death's condemnation has already started, but as an interrupted temporality or as a temporality of interruption. This explains the double meaning that can be given to Blanchot's *L'arrêt de mort*, which means "death sentence" but which could also mean (adding an article, as in *l'arrêt de la mort*): the interruption of death. In this game of meaning, Derrida analyzes the homonymy that can be found between the words "arrêt" that means "sentence"—as in the "death sentence"—or "interruption," and "arête" that means a very thin limit, an "angle of instability." "To survive" is to put at stake the death sentence as a continuous limit. See "Living On" in Derrida (2010, 142–43).

17. In *The Step Not Beyond*, for instance, Blanchot speaks of "the fragile fall that abolishes time in time" (1992, 14).

18. In his beautiful book *The Dark Gaze*, Kevin Hart gives an interpretation of what Blanchot calls "the nearnest of the Eternal in the Bible," which is a quotation from a Blanchot article titled, according to Isaïe's verses, "Paix, paix au lointain et au proche" (Blanchot 1985). For Hart, Blanchot's idea of eternity is not correlated to a form of atemporality that could be an object of contemplation. It derives from Blanchot's dialogue with Levinas and would rather be the "time of the Other" (Hart 2004, 183). However, albeit I do agree that eternity in Blanchot should be thought in terms of "trace" (183)—namely, as what appears only in the form of its absence—the idea of finitude of time in Blanchot puts certain limits to the association between Blanchot and Levinas, and to the latter's idea of ethics.

19. This point was highlighted very early by Derrida in his long article "Pas" ("Pace"), as well as by Lacoue-Labarthe in *Ending and Unending Agony* (2015) and by Nancy in the first volume of *The Deconstruction of Christianity* (2008a). The "to die" being the temporality of death as the impossibility of coming to term, the "perpetuity of dying" relates to a "death of eternity," to use Blanchot's words in *The Step Not Beyond* (1992, 30). However, it is important to highlight a determining difference between Nancy and Derrida on this point. While for Nancy eternity is the correlate of finitude that allows one to think eternity within a secular or worldly frame, for Derrida such "infinite finitude" in Blanchot makes time impossible, and hence also makes impossible a world thought of in secular terms. This point,

which I will further develop in the closing chapter of this book, has important consequences regarding how one is to understand Blanchot. Associating eternity to presence, Nancy's reading of Blanchot is in fact Christian. By contrast, for Derrida, the impossibility of dying in the present is also the impossibility of the present. This distances Derrida from a *merely* Christian reading of Blanchot.

20. For important and justified reasons, many of Blanchot's commentators associate Blanchot with Judaic thought, highlighting his proximity to Levinas. This is the case for Christopher Fynsk, for instance, who sees in Blanchot's writing an ethical exigency grounded on a "firm . . . opening to Judaism" (Fynsk 2013, 12). Recently, Eric Hoppenot (2015) has focused his attention on the use of biblical topics in Blanchot's writings. Drawing support from Blanchot's indirect references to Judaism and from his political texts, Hoppenot emphasizes Blanchot's unconditional support of Israel. However, it is important to highlight the fact that although Blanchot's thought does include an affirmation of an exigency of justice that is inherent to Judaism, his approach to both Christianity and Judaism has to be understood through the way literature questions our relation to the Book and through the way writing in Blanchot entails a reflection on "the absence of the Book" (Blanchot 1993, 422). Blanchot's thought does not *reproduce* biblical topics. He thinks those topics anew through the perspectives of reading onto which the question of writing opens. In this sense, Blanchot's proximity to Levinas's thought cannot be denied. However, because Blanchot's starting point for this subject is the question of writing, he is certainly critical of Levinas's idea of subjectivity and ethics. In this sense, Blanchot's thought cannot be *circumscribed* to Judaism or to Christianity. Rather, his thought entails a way of tackling, criticizing, and relating in a new way to these traditions through perspectives opened by the question of writing. This point will be developed in chapter five of this book.

21. The question of the relation between Judaism and Christianity is addressed by Jean-Luc Nancy in "Le Judeo-Chrétien" (2003b), after and in dialogue with Lyotard, who had developed his views in *The Hyphen: Between Judaism and Christianity* (*Un trait d'union*, 1999). Both Nancy and Lyotard take for their starting point an interrogation of the hyphen that brings together Judaism and Christianity. For Lyotard, this hyphen can only be a void. Against Paul, for Lyotard, there is no unity in these traditions because Judaism is constitutively heterogeneous to any possible synthesis. In "Le Judeo-Chrétien," Nancy argues that Christianity cannot assume this unifying role because Christianity deconstructs itself and is therefore constitutively opened to what exceeds it. In line with Nancy's argument, what is argued all along in this book is that Blanchot's peculiar gesture of deconstruction coincides neither with a unification nor with a clear separation of the Judeo-Christian, but with their common renewal in that which makes impossible Christianity as such.

22. See Nietzsche, *Thus Spoke Zarathustra*, "On Old and New Tablets" (2006).

23. In "On Old and New Tablets," Nietzsche writes: " 'Thou shalt not rob! Thou shalt not kill!'—such words where once held holy; before them one bent the knee, bowed the head and removed one's shoes. / But I ask you: where in

the world have there ever been better robbers and killers than such holy words?" (2006, 161).

24. "Enjoyment and innocence, you see, are the most bashful things: both do not want to be sought. One should *have* them—but one should sooner *seek* guilt and suffering!" (Nietzsche 2006, 160).

25. After the passage quoted in note 24 of this chapter, Nietzsche continues: "Is there not in all life itself—robbing and killing? And for such words to have been called holy, was *truth* itself not—killed? / Or was it a sermon of death that pronounced holy what contradicted and contravened all life?—Yes my brothers, break, break me the old tablets!" (2006, 162).

26. In his recent book, *Nietzsche and the Dyonisian: A Compulsion to Ethics* (2018), Peter Murray sketches a different interpretation of what is at stake with Zarathustra's active prophecy of the New Tablets. For Murray, the New Tablets create a new humanity defined by its love for life. As Murray writes: "The revaluation of past values requires the creative willing of a future based in the affirmative sense one has of life as the grounding for an interpretation" (247). Hence, like in Paul, Nietzsche's idea of New Tablets responds to the necessity to overcome the mortality of the Old Tablets; their way of making us act *against life*. Albeit Paul and Nietzsche do not share the same idea of life, following Murray's argument, there would be at least an identity of structure between Paul's and Nietzsche's proposals to overcome (or fulfill) law. However, this argument should be problematized. First, if it's life (in a sense that it is not gifted from God) that enables an overcoming of the Old Tablets, are we still in the realm of the human? Second, if the New Tablets aim at overcoming the gravity and sinfulness contained in the Old Tablets, what would make this overcoming possible? If the problem of the Old Tablets is that they are written and hence bury life and contradict its impulse, then to the extent in which the New Tablets will still be written, they will still entail a gravity. The problem is hence: How can a new law, a new humanity, derive from life without overcoming what characterizes humanity; namely language and writing? By delving into the difference between what Blanchot calls "the white writing" and "the black writing," the last part of this chapter aims at showing how Blanchot finds a positive issue to this problem.

27. To speak of "movement" in Blanchot can only be done by putting the word "movement" into quotes. As previously stated, the "to die" in Blanchot is passive, inert. However, this inertia stems from a passivity that is so excessive that it has as a consequence a resistance to action. Hence, this passivity gives birth, in a way, to a movement. On the idea of a movement of the immobile, see chapter four of this book, "Apocalypse."

28. See, for instance, the twelfth part, entitled "The Break: Writing Outside Language," of chapter 12 ("Atheism and Writing: Humanism and the Cry") of the second part of *The Infinite Conversation*.

29. On the notion of the Book as an institution where meaning is inscribed and History constituted, and the "Absence of the Book" as what entails this history's

failure, see John McKeane's (2013) interesting article titled "Change in the Archive: Blanchot's *L'entretien infini*," where Blanchot's different writings are analyzed as performing the "absence of the book."

30. In "The Absence of the Book," from *The Infinite Conversation*, Blanchot distinguishes writing as a trace and writing as logos: "There are two kinds of writing, one white, the other black: one that renders invisible the invisibility of a colorless flame; the other that is made accessible in the form of letters, characters, and articulations by the power of the black fire. Between the two there is the oral, which, however, is not independent, it being always involved with the second kind of writing inasmuch as it is this black fire itself, the measured obscurity that limits and delimits all light and makes all light visible" (Blanchot 1993, 430). Although different, these two writings are obviously inseparable. The association of writing with a flame and with fire is frequent in Blanchot's work (one thinks of his major and early book, *The Part of the Fire*, and of the allusions to fire in *The Last Man*). I will propose an interpretation of this reference to the fire in chapter four, where I relate the topic of the fire to the topic of the Apocalypse.

31. In *The Dark Gaze*, Kevin Hart associates Blanchot's notion of the "white writing" to the Kabbalistic tradition. In fact, in *Shekalim*, we can read, "It was written with letters of black fire upon a background of white fire" (*Shekalim*, 13b, quoted by Hart in 2004, 176). Although this reference is fundamental, in my view, the dialectic that is at stake in "The Absence of the Book" between the "black writing" and the "white writing" is not merely inherent to the Jewish tradition. The idea of the book at work in this chapter is correlated to Hegel's idea of History and of end. Hence, those references belonging to the Jewish tradition are also read in a Hegelian optic, which is also Christian. Moreover, this is how we can understand the idea of "Unity" at work in this chapter, whereas, as Kevin Hart observes, *Elohim* is essentially plural (2004, 177). On the Judaic frame of "The Absence of the Book," see also Goerges Préli's important and early book, *La force du dehors* (1977).

32. On this relation, Blanchot's interpretation of the Mosaic topic of the broken Tablets is particularly interesting. In fact, the topic of the broken Tablets connects law with its necessary interpretation. Broken, the Tablets do not make sense by themselves. It is henceforth the responsibility of human beings to give, each time, a new meaning to law. However, Blanchot sees in this rupture a way of legalizing the exteriority of writing. In the case of the broken Tablets, the rupture correlates to an idea of unity. By the "exteriority of writing," Blanchot is thinking of the previous rupture with the One. Hence, the rupture of the Tablets makes the exteriority of writing part of this history of the Book: "In other words, the breaking of the first tablets is not a break with a first state of unitary harmony; on the contrary, what the break inaugurates is the substitution of a limited exteriority (where the possibility of a limit announces itself) for an exteriority without limitation—the substitution of a lack for an absence, a break for a gap, an infraction for the pure-impure fraction of the fragmentary: that which, on the hither side of

the sacred separation, presses in the scission of the neutral (the scission that is the neutral). To put it yet another way, it is necessary to break with the first exteriority so that with the second (where the logos is law and the law logos), language, henceforth regularly divided, in a reciprocal bond of mastery with itself and grammatically constructed, might engage us in the relations of mediation and immediation that guarantee discourse, and then with the dialectic, where the law in its turn will dissolve" (Blanchot 1993, 432). This approach to the topic of the broken Tablets is crucial for understanding Blanchot's relation to Judaism and Christianity. Contrary to what Eric Hoppenot proposes in *Maurice Blanchot et la tradition juive* (2015), the clue to Blanchot's use of biblical topics in his work cannot be given merely by the question of intertextuality since intertextuality always presupposes a meaning at work (and hence the submission to law). If Blanchot gives so few elements for understanding that which grounds his use of biblical topics, it is because they stem from the question of writing in general, which maintains a double relation to law and to meaning: legitimate and illegitimate.

33. These two writings, which threaten language with collapse, are described in relation to the difference between "death" and the "to die" in *The Step Not Beyond*: "Where is the event of death? Where is the obscurity of dying? Like two speeches never pronounced that, boringly repetitive and frightening, would resonate only at the moment—at each moment—of the collapse of every language" (Blanchot 1992, 97).

34. Blanchot's thought of a "writing outside language" (*écriture hors langage*) is not one that would break with logos understood as what is proper to the Human in favor of some apology of nature or animality. Such an opposition between the human and animality belongs to the very logos we inevitably speak. Blanchot's "writing outside language" refers to what fails language and, hence, any constitution of essence (be it human or animal). Whence Blanchot's passion for what is underground, for what is beneath in the sense of what fails to qualify, for what is wordless and that, in *The Infinite Conversation*, he calls "vermin": "What is speech if not the very site where the vermin, this people of the underworld that men of all times have rejected by calling them lemures, restlessly move about: something very abject and very deceptive, which is to say, once again, the desolation of hell. This would be a speech in which the vermin disappear, but precisely because it is this very disappearance that defines vermin, just as it defines speech, or at least a certain, strange speech" (Blanchot 1993, 182).

35. In *The City of God*, Augustine observes that death is twofold—it's both the consequence of sin and the path toward sanctity or redemption: "Thus, by the ineffable mercy of God, the penalty of sin is transformed into the panoply of virtue and the punishment of the sinner into the testing of a saint. In the case of the first parents, death was incurred by sinning; now sainthood is attained by dying" (1952, 304).

36. The question of the "love of death" and of Blanchot's conception of grace is crucial to understanding Blanchot's position regarding the death penalty. As is

known, in the seminar on the death penalty, as well as in the conference "Maurice Blanchot est mort,, held in 2006 just after Blanchot's death, Derrida affirms that Blanchot's position on the question of the death penalty is ambivalent (Derrida 2014, 111–13; Bident/Vilar 2003, 595–624). Taking into consideration Blanchot's apological pages on terror, his assimilation of the figure of the writer with that of the revolutionary and the freedom that conveys his terror, taking moreover into account the fact that this article is—according to Derrida, who is wrong on this date—published one hundred years after the Declaration of Human Rights and hence after the valorization of life's inviolability, Derrida asserts that one could read Blanchot's important article, "Literature and the Right to Death," "as the counterpoint, but in the name of literature itself, to the inviolable right to life and as the Hegelian-Mallarmean obverse of Hugo's abolitionism" (Derrida 2014, 111). Derrida's argument is mainly based on the fact that Blanchot doesn't take a stand against the death penalty. However, Blanchot's positions regarding the death penalty obviously stem from his position regarding sovereignty and from his considerations on death. The death penalty is the power of the sovereign. It is neither a crime nor the freedom that—at least abstractly—conveys terror. Now, Blanchot's reflection on writing puts into question this sovereign power. Moreover, the death penalty, such as reflected by Hegel, for instance, is meant to humanize the criminal through death. Whereas by transgressing the law the criminal forfeits dignity, death, according to Hegel, allows the overcoming of an animal condition in favor of the human. This idea that death dignifies is precisely the one that Blanchot rejects when he speaks of a "love of death." Again, in Blanchot the "love of death" entails death's impossibility. It refers to what cannot be overcome, to what never reaches human dignity—hence, to what remains outside of law.

37. The relations between Nancy and Blanchot concerning the idea of a "deconstruction of Christianity" will be analyzed in chapter five.

38. This will be analyzed in chapter four.

39. On this point, see David Banon, *La lecture infinite* (1987), which was an important reading for Blanchot.

Notes to Chapter 3

1. This idea has been developed by Ann Smock in *What Is There to Say?* (2003). In her reading of Billy Budd's incapacity to speak, Smock explicitly argues that innocence is a "speech defect" (2003, 58).

2. As with all of Blanchot's writings, it is difficult to define the genre to which they belong. As Derrida shows in "La loi du genre" in *Parages* (2011, 217–51), Blanchot's writing consists in transgressing the law as what institutes the frontiers of "genre." However, it's also important to observe, as Michael Holland has done, that this transgression of "genre" does not merely lead to indifference, as if all writing meant the same. Each of Blanchot's writings come back to the anterior writing,

composing a new way of approaching the problem of the relation between writing and time (see Holland 2010, 263–65). In addition, we can also observe that each of Blanchot's *kinds* of writing deal with a peculiar philosophical problem that only a determined kind of writing can address. Hence, although impossible to strictly define, what characterizes Blanchot's writing is that it constantly differentiates itself. It is each time unique.

3. In "As Though with a New Beginning," Caroline Sheaffer-Jones closely analyzes the possible affinities between Nietzsche's idea of the "last man" and the way Blanchot stages this figure in *The Last Man*. For Sheaffer-Jones there are obvious affinities between Nietzsche's and Blanchot's references to the "last man." Yet, if the figures cannot be identified, it is because what characterizes the "last man" is that it is by definition impossible to define what it announces, what could be the future of "man" (namely, of the human being). Hence, in Sheaffer-Jones, the question of the proximity between Blanchot and Nietzsche around this topic remains a question: "Is the future with us? Do we belong to the past? Do Blanchot's last man and Nietzsche's Superman join together?" (Sheaffer-Jones 2010, 255). In line with this argument, it is crucial to recall that not only have we no idea of what could be the "superman" or the future of man, but also that it is structurally impossible to locate its end, for, if there is an end, the human being is no longer there to witness it. What is at stake with the question of the "end of man" is henceforth broader than the mere question of what would be the future of human being. It entails the problem of being a witness and of "storytelling" such as Rodolphe Gasché defines it in *Storytelling: The Destruction of the Inalienable in the Age of the Holocaust* (2018). If the "end of man" could be attested for once and for all, then history's unending end would end, there would be no more need for stories, we would no longer be accountable for the past, and there would be no more future. Hence, in addition to what Caroline Sheaffer-Jones says of Nietzsche and Blanchot's figure of the "last man," it is important to add that human being can only unendingly end and that this impossibility to end is what makes it necessary to tell stories even at the end of history. This impossibility to end explains why most of Blanchot's tales are divided into two parts, as if, instead of ending, the book that contains stories could only repeat its impossibility. On this point and the division in two parts of Blanchot's *The Last Man*, see chapter five of this book, "Apocalypse."

4. On this topic, see Michael Holland's original interpretation of the role of Nietzsche *in between* Blanchot and Bataille in "Blanchot, Bataille et le '*dernier homme*'" (2015). For Holland, while Bataille and Nietzsche see in "the last man" a negative moment, Blanchot takes it as a "literary figure" and not as a mere "logical" determination (2015, 326). In this sense, it is a figure that cannot be simply overcome. In this way, we could say that "the last man" is not a negative figure but the figure of the negative; namely, its impossibility.

5. As previously explained in the introduction of this book, the word "incondition" is used by Levinas and points to the groundless dimension of the human condition.

6. The French word *angoisse* has been translated as either "anguish" or "anxiety." Since we will refer not only to Kierkegaard's *The Concept of Anxiety* (in French, *Le concept d'angoisse*) but also to Blanchot's interpretation of it, as well as to his own thought on "anguish" (also inspired by Heidegger's "*Angst*"), and since Blanchot's "*angoisse*" has been often translated as "dread," we will use "anguish," "anxiety," or "dread."

7. In *Fortunate Fallibility*, Jason Mahn discusses the idea that for Kierkegaard anxiety would be an *explanation* of the Fall. According to Mahn, taking anxiety as an explanation would lead again to a theodicy. Although this is a very important point, I believe that what matters in the relation between anxiety and innocence is not the fact that the Fall is explained and therefore justified, but that with his description of anxiety, Kierkegaard is giving a new view on the question of freedom. In this way, Kierkegaard escapes the aporetic explanations that consist in saying that either the Fall is explained by human freedom or was due to the concupiscence generated by the prohibition. In the first case, as Kierkegaard explains, the will to go against the law is impossible since the state of innocence consists precisely in ignoring the law (Good and Evil); in the second case, if the fall into guiltiness amounts to the prohibition, then one would have to guilt God, which is nonsensical. Rather than taking a position in a theological debate, which Kierkegaard says to be "ingenuous and stupid" (in *The Concept of Anxiety* [38–39], he says he does not "intend to repeat all the ingenious and stupid hypotheses with which thinkers and speculators have encumbered the beginning of history"), he displaces his focus onto the problem of freedom considered as a philosophical issue. See Mahn, *Fortunate Fallibility* (especially "Does Anxiety Explain Sin" and "Explaining Nothing"), 72–75. This question has also been explored by Ricoeur in *Finitude and Guilt* in which he argues that the difference between innocence and guilt amounts to the difference between a limit that orients and inspires and a limit that constrains. In fact, "authority becomes interdiction under the regime of fallen freedom"; moreover, "for an innocent freedom, this limitation would not be felt as an interdiction" (1967, 250). In innocence, the limit defined by the prohibited fruit would not be felt as a limit. Hence, in innocence, freedom is not limited, while in guilt, we are in the regime of a "finite freedom." This difference might then be articulated to Kierkegaard's explanation of innocence as an experience of angst. Angst is in fact the experience of an unlimited void; namely, to an unlimited freedom.

8. In a similar way, in his article titled "The Anxiety of Innocence in Blake and Kierkegaard," Matthew Schneider states that innocence is not a peaceful state and that "innocence by its very nature is more psychologically complex than experience because innocence already contains within it at least an intimation of its contrary"; namely, experience (2005, 358).

9. In the section titled "Immediate Religion or Nature Religion" of his *Lectures on the Philosophy of Religion, and Encyclopedia of Logic*, Hegel makes several arguments to discredit the idea of innocence and, in particular, the acceptance of

an original condition. One of those arguments is that if one considers innocence to be the unity of the spiritual with nature, this unity must be mediated and therefore can only exist in the element of consciousness. Moreover, for Hegel, the fact that innocence has been lost indicates that the original state can be considered not as an absolute state but as only contingent. It can therefore be understood only within a system and cannot be considered as original (Hegel 1995, 243). On Hegel's critique of the immediacy of innocence, see Kierkegaard's *The Concept of Anxiety* (1980, 35).

10. "Innocence is something that is canceled by a transcendence, precisely because innocence is *something* (whereas the most correct expression for immediacy is that which Hegel uses about pure being: it is nothing" (Kierkegaard 1980, 37).

11. As Kierkegaard says, "linguistic usage also says pregnantly: to be anxious about nothing" (1980, 43). In these same pages, Kierkegaard takes care to make a distinction between anxiety and fear, as will Heidegger in *Being and Time* (1996).

12. For an interpretation of the difference between a logical and an ethical conception of innocence, see Stewart 2003, 411–19.

13. See note 7, this chapter.

14. After asserting that Hegel does not deserve "immortal merit" (Kierkegaard 1980, 35) for having said that "immediacy must be annulled" because immediacy "at no time exists," Kierkegaard ironically plays with the idea that what mediacy reveals is not its opposite (immediacy), but its impossibility: "immediacy is not annulled by mediacy, but when mediacy appears, in the same moment, it has annulled immediacy" (37). In a way, Kierkegaard *repeats* Hegel's logic, but he does so ironically; that is to say, he displaces the accent from mediacy's being to immediacy's inexistence. A footnote made by the editor where Hegel's *Lectures on Philosophy of Religion* (1995) is quoted shows, in fact, that between Hegel and Kierkegaard, it is a question of accent. The footnote quotes Hegel's *Lectures on the Philosophy of Religion*: "But even if we take up an empirical, and external attitude, it will be found that there is nothing at all that is immediate, that there is nothing to which only the quality of immediate belongs to the exclusion of that of mediation; but that which is immediate is likewise mediated, and that immediacy itself is essentially mediated" (Hegel 2007a, 409).

15. In *Being and Time*, Heidegger writes, for instance, "*Angst* reveals in Da-sein its *being toward* its ownmost potentiality of being, that is, *being free for* the freedom of choosing and grasping itself. *Angst* brings Da-sein *before being free for* . . . (*proponesio in*), the authenticity of its being as possibility which it always already is" (1996, 176).

16. See note 7, this chapter.

17. This dis-appropriation is described, for instance, in *The Instant of My Death* (Blanchot 2000), where a narrator describes a young man at the point where he is about to be shot. Interestingly, among the very few works dedicated to Blanchot and Kierkegaard, most of them concentrate on the topic of death. It is for instance the case of Catherine B. Michaelsen in her very insightful article,

"Ways of Dying: The Double Death in Kierkegaard and Blanchot," where she claims that both Blanchot and Kierkegaard apprehend death as double (as possible and as impossible, as an end and as unending), and where she shows the consequences of the temporality of the question of faith (Michaelsen 2014, 278). For his part, in *Literature Suspends Death* (2011), Chris Danta analyzes the topic of Isaac's sacrifice in Kierkegaard and in Blanchot (especially in *When the Time Comes*). In both cases, what must be highlighted is that for Blanchot there is no such thing as an authentic instant of the decision that would be provided by the unicity of death. Hence, it might be problematic to speak of a "double death" in Blanchot. In Blanchot, death rather "occurs" as the impossibility of any unity and unicity (on these topics and on the question of Isaac's sacrifice, see also "L'hospitalité animale. Faim de l'histoire," Messina 2009).

18. On faith in Kierkegaard's *Fear and Trembling*, see Derrida's discussion in *The Gift of Death* (2008). For Derrida, faith is not a lack of knowledge but a suspension of knowledge. By contrast, the topic of non-knowledge in Blanchot cannot be related to faith but precisely fails both faith and knowledge (Derrida 2017, 80). In that sense, in Blanchot, innocence is an atheistic figure that fails belief in God (beyond knowledge) as well as in humankind (defined by its capacity to know). On Blanchot's relationship to atheism, see Stefanos Geroulanos, *An Atheism That Is Not Humanist Emerges in French Thought* (2010), where Blanchot's atheism does not consist in the negation of a transcendence in order to affirm an immanence. His atheism, rather, breaks with the certainties of humanism. It is interesting to observe that Geroulanos bases his argument on a subdued early text of Blanchot, "Du côté de Nietzsche," collected in *The Work of Fire* (1949) but first published in 1946. In taking this essay as a starting point, Geroulanos can remark that Blanchot's distance from humanism has different moments (Geroulanos 2010, 251–68). On this last point, see also Michael Holland's "Blanchot, le nihilisme et la 'mort de Dieu'" in *Avant dire* (2015) and his peculiar attention to the differences between the two publications.

19. See, for instance, *The Step Not Beyond*: "If I am in dread as in truth, it is a truth that already deceives me and that I, meanwhile, can leave behind only in deceiving myself" (1992, 62); or: "dread: the sureness that excludes the uncertainty of doubt, what decisiveness is left for doubt to exert itself" (91).

20. About Adam, Kierkegaard says: "In innocence, Adam as spirit was a dreaming spirit" (1980, 48).

21. For a lengthier discussion, see the introduction to this book (22).

22. See Blanchot's comment on Levinas's conception of responsibility: "Responsibility is innocent guilt, the blow always long since received which makes me all the more sensitive to all blows. It is the trauma of creation or of birth" (41). These words recall what Levinas says about innocence and guilt in *Otherwise than Being*: "The self, the persecuted one, is accused beyond his fault, before freedom, and thus in an unavowable innocence" (1998, 121). To a certain extent, this structure of an innocent guilt could also apply to Heidegger's conception of responsibility. In

The Gift of Death, for instance, Derrida shows how guilt structures responsibility in Heidegger as well as in Levinas. Although the formula of an "innocent guilt" comes from Levinas, the idea that subjectivity is structured and made possible by guilt without the subject's knowing is the condition of possibility of the subject's unicity, and therefore of unicity. As explained in the introduction to this book, what Blanchot's reading of Levinas dismisses is precisely his idea of subjectivity. On Blanchot's reading of Levinas in *Otherwise than Being*, see Arthur Cools's important book, *Langage et subjectivité: Vers une approche du différend entre Maurice Blanchot et Emmanuel Levinas* (2007).

23. See Smock's commentary: "Innocence is unbearable guilt. By which I mean the bearing of a guilt that is as impossible to assume as to evade—a responsibility irrevocably incurred in a past still to come but impossible to incur at any time that ever has been or will be present." For Smock, guilt, "unlike innocence, is testable" (2003, 62).

24. Let us recall that in *Otherwise than Being*, Levinas describes the birth of subjectivity throughout the paradox of an innocent guiltiness: "The self, the persecuted one, is accused beyond his fault, before freedom, and thus in an unavowable innocence" (1998, 121).

25. In *Finitude and Guilt*, Ricoeur thinks of innocence as our status as creatures; namely, as beings who are not fully masters of themselves: "The *imagon dei*—there we have both our being-created and our innocence; for the 'goodness' of the creation is nothing other than its status as 'creature'" (1967, 251).

26. The question of space in Blanchot's narratives has been analyzed with extreme subtlety by Michael Holland in "Space and Beyond" (2010). Holland shows, in fact, with a very careful reading of *The Last Man* and *Awaiting Oblivion*, that there are many experiences of space in Blanchot's narrative and that they stem from the way language is emptied of its content. The "void is a space of disorientation" (270), says Holland, and this void is reached—or, more precisely, approached—as the silence of language is approached. Hence, the "turbulent, vociferous space to which narrative belongs, the more it approaches silence" (269).

27. In *The Step Not Beyond*, Blanchot uses the expression "fall," precisely, to speak of a fall of time: "Time; time: the step beyond (*pas au-delà*) that is not accomplished in time would lead outside of time, without this outside being intemporal, but there where time would fall, fragile fall" (1992, 1; translation modified).

28. The inferno or hell is what lies under the earth and is therefore what is dark. It is interesting to observe that this darkness is by itself a condemnation, a space without issue. Without thinking of the different ways of representing hell, we can think of hell as the experience of pain: that which obliges one to oneself without issue and upon which no light can be shed because it is precisely that experience that exceeds light, comprehension, meaning.

29. As seen in chapter one of this book, in *The State of Exception*, Agamben describes this anomy not as liberation but as the space in which a *pure* violence is exercised. If law is a limit (an affirmation that would have to be deepened), its

exception (be it constitutive) gives birth to unlimited violence. See, for instance, Agamben (2005a, 59).

30. In addition to Arthur Cools and Alain Toumayan, Lars Iyer has deepened the problem of the relationship between Blanchot and Levinas. Iyer observes that the difference between Blanchot and Levinas deals with the problem of the Other that affects differently the "subject," and he shows that this difference in this affection is also what draws the line between literature and philosophy. Yet we can wonder if such a line does not still entail the idea of a law. Do the fragmentary writings that mostly put at stake the exposure of language outside of the law not put into question this line between literature and philosophy? Iyer does not hold to the contrary. Rather, he states beautifully that the fragmentary writings expose philosophy to an asphyxia; namely, to the reverse of the spirit's activity. We can add that by doing so, Blanchot reveals philosophy from out of what constituted its law; namely, life, activity. See, in particular, Iyer (2003, 58).

31. In *The Writing of the Disaster*, Blanchot speaks of a responsibility that is not based on an ethics and that could even make evident its limits: "just as, once declared responsible for dying (for all dying), I can no longer appeal to any ethics, any experience, any practice whatever—save that of some counter-living, which is to say an un-practice." It is precisely this "un-practice" (26) that we are trying to explain as an ethics of innocence.

32. "C'est le commencement de la chute, la loi tombe en tombant, et, par là, se sauve encore comme loi." I have modified the translation in order to conserve the biblical idea of "fall" (*chute*) and the fact that in this failure, what is rescued is the law.

33. On this topic, see Michael Holland's very interesting article titled "Comment trancher le 'noeud paradoxal'? Blanchot et Levinas" (2015), which in fact is not only about Blanchot and Levinas, but also about Blanchot, Bataille, and Kierkegaard. In this article, Holland argues that what is at the heart of the problem of ethics is language and that what distinguishes Blanchot from Levinas and Kierkegaard is that Blanchot does not provide a name for the impossible (as would be God) but relates, through literature, to language's failure.

34. On this anonymity, see my commentary on Blanchot's first words of *The Most High*: "I wasn't alone, I was anybody" (1996, 1) in chapter one of this book.

Notes to Chapter 4

1. On this topic, see Blanchot's comment in Feret's *L'apocalypse de saint Jean, vision chrétienne de l'histoire*, in his article from 1943 titled "*Une étude sur L'Apocalypse*" (Blanchot 2007).

2. See, for instance, Günther Anders, *Le temps de la fin* (2006).

3. It can be noted that Anders does not necessarily associate the apocalypse with nihilism. For Anders, in fact, to wish for the destruction of values assumes that we assign a worth value to the world, and especially that we do not doubt its destructive characteristic (2006, 93). However, we can understand nihilism in a vaster sense, not as the destruction of values but as an observation of the absence of foundations of values. In this way, the apocalypse reveals the absence.

4. Concerning the atomic bomb, Anders notes that it implies that there is not necessarily a will to evil on behalf of the executor: "As I press the button, I am absolved of good and evil. Neither do I have the need to hate. No, I am even incapable of it. Neither do I have the need to be mean. No, I am as well incapable of it. More specifically: I should not be capable of it" (2006, 52). This is why the destruction of the world happens for no reason: because it is caused by no one. This is why Anders is able to conclude, "If there is something that can symbolize the evil nature of our situation, it is this innocence" (53). On this subject, see also the following note.

5. This is what Anders calls the "law of innocence" that is characteristic of our contemporary apocalypse: things are done in virtue of the devices that allow us to act without knowing, and thus being immediately cleared of any responsibility for evil.

6. On this subject, see Michaël Foessel's *Après la fin du monde. Critique de la raison apocalyptique* (2012). In addition to highlighting the political pitfalls of different catastrophisms, this book shows that there is an "apocalyptic reason," which is to say that these catastrophisms are not purely irrational. Finding a solution to the inertia of catastrophisms (or rather, to their fervent defense of survival) does not return to affix a reason to unreason, but rather to shed light on the limits of such "rational" discourses.

7. On this subject, see Eric Hoppenot, "De l'*Apocalypse* à Amalek. Esquisse d'une réflexion sur la pensée du mal dans l'œuvre de Maurice Blanchot" (2012).

8. Let us recall that the Apocalypse of Saint John has to do with thinking of the time of reigning after different stages of resurrection and that it is not only the living, but also the dead who are judged. If there are several resurrections, it means that while judgment is condemnation for some, it is also regeneration for others. Those who are resurrected to be judged will either be condemned to eternal death or delivered from death—this is a deliverance that, as Saint Augustine explains, is the condition of a regenerated life. There are "two resurrections, the first of which is temporal and spiritual and allows no second death, while the other is not spiritual but corporeal and is to be at the end of time. This resurrection, through the last judgment, will send some into the second death, others into that life which knows no death" (1954, 264). The Final Judgment, which is supposed to pave the way to the Kingdom, may be an action that affects the mortality of the body and life, and could offer hints for reading the way in which Blanchot elaborates the theme

of the final judgment, specifically when he writes in *The Last Man:* "And the last judgment is perhaps this pure gift through which, in the end, each person always rids himself of his moment of repose" (2007, 60).

9. Thus Blanchot affirms that on one side, literature is "the presence of things before the world exists, their perseverance after the world has disappeared, the stubbornness of what remains when everything vanishes and the dumbfoundedness of what appears when nothing exists" (1995a, 328).

10. Emmanuel Lévinas, "La réalité et son ombre" ("Reality and its Shadow") (1989). Remember that the text "Literature and the Right to Death" was first published in the journal *Critique* in 1948, before being included in *The Work of Fire* in 1995.

11. Emmanuel Levinas, "Reality and its Shadow," in *The Levinas Reader*: "Art is the falling movement on the hither side of time, into fate. A novel is not, as Jean Pouillon thinks, a way of reproducing time; it has its own time, it is a unique way for time to temporalize" (1989, 139).

12. "The characters of a novel are beings that are shut up, prisoners. Their history is never finished, it still goes on, but makes no headway. A novel shuts beings up in a fate despite their freedom" (1989, 121).

13. Blanchot writes: "The language of literature is a search for this moment which precedes literature" (1995a, 327).

14. In "Literature and the Right to Death," Blanchot describes the transformation of the language that is no longer that which is erased to name the thing, but which becomes something formless: "Literature has certainly triumphed over the meaning of words, but what it has found in words considered apart from their meaning is meaning that has become thing" (1995a, 331).

15. Blanchot also writes in the same thematic horizon, "By turning itself into an inability to reveal anything, literature is attempting to become the revelation of what revelation destroys" (1995a, 328). Because literature works with the part of language that no longer means anything, with a language transformed into a thing, in it language is not the way (the fire) that makes meaning and revelation possible. But what transforms language into a thing is what it cannot reveal: its nothingness.

16. Blanchot's confrontation with Heidegger on the question of history is done as a detour in his confrontation of Hegel. If Blanchot distances himself from Heidegger in the moment in which he could have come closer, it is that for him, to recognize the nothingness of the being is also to recognize the need to step out of the history of the being. On this subject, Blanchot acknowledges that Heidegger named this requirement, but not that he truly weighed it. In fact, Blanchot notes that in Heidegger the "end of the history of being" happens with the advent of being (*Ereignis*) because this occurrence implies the end of the history of being *as withdrawal*. But for Blanchot, this end is doubtful since it would suppose a form of presence that would inscribe it again in the regime of being. On this, see *The Writing of the Disaster* (1995b, 101).

17. On this subject, we can think of Blanchot's *The Space of Literature* (1982), which shows that poetry is an experience of exile, which opens already a critical perspective on the relation that Heidegger establishes between poetry and origin. This difference has to do with the aforementioned problem concerning the "departure of the history of the being." For Blanchot, such a departure is impossible because being is impossible. Therefore, it is not a question of knowing which is the privileged path to access the origin, but rather to think about how the absence of departure crosses in different ways the distinct parts of experience and experiences of language.

18. As I stated in chapter one, the translations of *L'Entretien Infini* as "The Infinite Conversation" or "Unfinished Dialogue" fail to preserve the idea of the *entretien*, which contains neither the logos of the (Platonic) dialogue nor the idea of convergence that exists in the *con*versation. On the contrary, what can be heard in the word "*entre*tien" (which would be closer to *inter*view) is that which lasts as what is in *between* us.

19. "The *other* history would be a feigned history, which is not to say that it is a mere nothing, but that it is always calling forth the void of a nonplace, the gap that it is, and that separates it from itself. It is unbelievable because any belief in it would have to overlook it." (1995b, 138–39).

20. For a reading of the film *Melancholia* with regard to the problem of the end, see also the scene in two acts, *La fin des fins* by Federico Ferrari and Jean-Luc Nancy (2015). The two voices in dialogue have a mixed interpretation of the film. The voices split on the meaning of the imminence of the end. What sustains the conversation is the face of the child that, according to one of the voices, "closes his eyes with confidence" (2015, 38) before the imminence of the end, while the other voice would only like to believe in this confidence (40). The end is thus shared between the two without being identical. In its coming, it disorients meaning, in the sense that it cracks open an "us," a community, and therefore a world.

Notes to Chapter 5

1. The dialogue between Nancy and Blanchot is part of those contingent matters that happened to be part of the history. In fact, while Nany's *The Disavowed Community* (first published in 2014 and published in English in 2016) is focused on Blanchot's *The Unavowable Community* (1983), the latter is, in its turn, a response to Nancy's article "La communauté désoeuvrée," which had been published in *Alea* no. 4, also in 1983. As is known, this dialogue has inspired other works on the topic of community, such as Agamben's *The Coming Community* (1993) and Esposito's *Comunitas. The Origin and Destiny of Community* (2009).

2. It is in fact interesting to remark that while Nancy seems to detect in Blanchot the use of a certain unavowable Christianity, I detect this Christianity

recurring in Nancy himself, through a certain Christian hermeneutics. For instance, and I will come back to this topic, Nancy's reading of Blanchot's *The Unavowable Community* as divided into two parts, one referring to the law, and the other to the heart, is typically Christian, or, more precisely, it recalls Hegel's reading of Christianity as overcoming the Judaic law by Christian love.

3. Although Blanchot's commitment to the right wing was known and underlined in the first studies on Blanchot, it is interesting to observe that in the last decade, new questions about this commitment have been raised. In 2014, the same year as the publication of Nancy's *The Disavowed Community*, the forty-third issue of the journal *Lignes*—a journal that had published numerous articles not only on Blanchot but also on Blanchot as a left-wing writer and militant—published, for instance, an issue titled "Les politiques de Maurice Blanchot 1930–1993." The presentation of this issue clarifies that it is now time to "articulate and think the totality of [Blanchot's] political trajectory" and that "important work on Blanchot remained to be done and ought to be done by the ones who are generally considered to be his friends" (*Lignes* no. 43, 5–6, my translation). This point is particularly interesting: What seems to matter in 2014, in the numerous studies that shed new light on Blanchot's politics, is not Blanchot's political commitment *as belonging to the past* but as questioning *our time*, our thought, and our thought as at least partially constituted by the legacy that Blanchot's thought represents. Hence, what happened in the last decade in Blanchot's studies is that Blanchot's political engagement and writings are no longer divided into two, one belonging to the past and the other worth being studied. It is considered as a whole in that this totality interests the present time.

4. It is in a letter addressed to Laporte in 1984 that Blanchot speaks of a conversion (see Nancy 2011, 61). The question of Blanchot's conversion has been widely debated. For Mascolo, for instance, to speak of a conversion entails merging the political with the biographic or the psychologic (2011, 66–67). By the same token, Surya argues that a conversion is necessarily religious and would entail the action of grace (Surya 2015, 51). Each of these elements—the biographical and the religious—can be elaborated as being part of Blanchot's conversion. As Claire Nioche notes in "Maurice Blanchot, deserter le myth," *L'instant de ma mort*, where Blanchot relates the moment in which he was about to be shot in 1944 by the Nazi army, can be a clue to understanding Blanchot's conversion (Nioche 2013, 146). Moreover, in this letter, Blanchot *explains* his conversion (with its biographical and religious implications or dimensions) in relation to the way the question of writing frames his existence and thought. This is indeed an important element in understanding the question of the conversion in philosophical terms (which don't exclude its biographical and religious dimensions). Nioche, who prefers speaking of a transfer (which conserves the trace of the past) rather than of a conversion (2013, 142), emphasizes how the experience of writing in Blanchot entails the ordeal of a

depersonalization (143) that breaks not only theoretically put also practically with nationalistic thought.

5. As Blanchot's political conversion has been questioned in the last decade, Blanchot's relation to Catholicism before and after such a political "conversion" can also be problematized. While for many commentators, Blanchot's Catholicism belongs to the past and is mainly a question of family background (see, e.g., Bident 2018, chapter one), and while Blanchot's political conversion would also entail a sort of religious conversion from Catholicism to Judaism (see, e.g., Bident 2018, 27–28), Nancy has wondered recently if such a conversion was not to be understood rather as a conversion *within* Catholicism (Nancy 2011, 61). I will develop this idea of an internal conversion and its political consequences further on in this chapter. On Nancy's reading of Blanchot's Catholicism, see also Idoia Quintana and Michel Lisse's important article titled "Maurice Blanchot de 'constitution catholique'? A partir des lectures de Jean-Luc Nancy" (Hoppenot and Rabaté 2014, 336–42).

6. See note 5, this chapter.

7. The question of how to situate chronologically Blanchot's so-called conversion is indeed problematic. Does, as Bident argues, Blanchot's rupture with nationalistic thought date back to its so-called silence, namely to July 1937, the date when Blanchot stops signing the section "Free France" in the journal *L'Insurgé* (Bident 2018 79, quoted in Brémondy 2014, 79)? Or is it after the war that "Blanchot seems to have become another," as Brémondy argues (82)? If Blanchot's rupture with right-wing thought is indeed a conversion, then such a conversion cannot be precisely located in time. It entails a whole revolution of one's thought and existence and, consequently, of the very way the words are thought and used. Hence, when in 1968 Blanchot takes part in May 68 and declares himself a communist, what matters is not that Blanchot declares himself a communist, as Brémondy critically argues against Blanchot (Brémondy 2014, 84), but how Blanchot understands it, how he renews its meaning, and how the whole of his writing takes part in this new way of thinking about and of practicing such communism.

8. Blanchot's critique of nationalism has been highlighted and discussed by Anat Matar in "Maurice Blanchot: Modernism, Dissidence and the Privilege of Writing" (2018). In this article, Matar criticizes the fact that Blanchot's fervorous critique of nationalism does not apply in the case of the Zionist movement. In Blanchot's view, this absence of critique would amount to Israel's vulnerability and to the fact that Israel would incarnate the Judaic idea of writing as the ordeal of passivity. Hence, Blanchot's conception and demand of writing would be contradictory: it would give birth to Blanchot's conversion to an anti-nationalistic thought and engagement, but it would also ground its absence of critique before the violence of the Zionist movement (see Matar 2018, 76–78). This argument is important. However, it neglects an important question: Is it the same to defend nationalism and to pay attention to a nation's vulnerability? On Matar's reading

about Blanchot's position on the State of Israel, see Danielle Cohen-Levinas's article, "Au commencement était le 'il faut'" (Cohen-Levinas 2019, 103).

9. As explained in Nancy's book *Maurice Blanchot, passion politique* (2011), Roger Laporte had written Blanchot a letter asking him for some explanations about his past political engagement. Blanchot's answer would have been published in a volume of *Cahiers de l'Herne*, which had been, at that time, in preparation. However, it never came to fruition and was published only in 2011 in Nancy's *Maurice Blanchot, passion politique*.

10. In his provocative article "L'autre Blanchot," published in *Lignes* (2014), as well as in his book *L'autre Blanchot L'écriture du jour, l'écriture de la nuit* (2015), Surya claims not only that such a political transformation might merely be illusory, but that there might not be a true difference between what Blanchot calls a "writing of the day" and a "writing of the night" since, as Surya states, Blanchot ultimately never ceased merging the political with writing. However, this argument is insufficient to refute the idea that Blanchot undergoes a political transformation and that this transformation is grounded on a change in his relation to writing. In fact, *the "writing of the night" changes our relation to the realm of the days*. This distinction is hence also a deconstruction of the frontier between the night and the day. In this sense, Michael Holland is right to claim that Surya's argument is not based on a serious reading of Blanchot (Holland 2014, 158). But what highlighting Surya's bad faith about these writings most seriously entails is to end up associating Blanchot's silence in relation to his past political engagement to Heidegger's silence in relation to his engagement with the Nazi party during the 1930s (Surya 2015, 12). This assimilation is highly problematic. Indeed, in Heidegger, silence is an absence of words, a nonresponse. In Blanchot, literature is a relation to the silence of language. It entails the idea of a response that comes from the experience of silence that is bound by language. Hence, according to Holland, not only has Surya not even begun to read Blanchot, but he is missing the whole point about the political implications of literature, which entail an unending relation to silence that completely transforms the question of responsibility. Surya's reading is hence grounded not on a philosophical understanding of Blanchot's writing, nor on a serious political understanding of literature. As Holland observes, it is a simple moral approach that aims at condemning, but not at understanding (Holland 2014, 150).

11. See note 2, this chapter.

12. See in particular *Cahiers: Maurice Blanchot* no. 4, published in 2015–2016, which contains a dossier on Nancy's *The Disavowed Community*. Before the publication of *The Disavowed Community*, Christopher Fynsk had written a lengthy discussion of Nancy's views (the ones expressed in Nany's 2011 *Maurice Blanchot, passions politiques*) in *Last Steps: Maurice Blanchot's Exilic Writing* (Fynsk 2013, 270–80, in particular in his footnotes). Recently, Leslie Hill published an important systematic answer to Nancy's *The Disavowed Community* titled *Nancy, Blanchot: A Serious Controversy* (Hill 2018). Most of the commentaries on Nancy's

recent publications on Blanchot highlight a systematic "hermeneutical violence" at play in Nancy's reflections. This is, for instance, Danielle Cohen-Levinas's explicit formulation in "Note et contre-note sur *La communauté désavouée*" (2015), and it is also what Fynsk suggests when he remarks that Nancy's recent reflections on Blanchot's political thought systematically avoid focusing on Blanchot's work as a whole, while concentrating on only *The Unavowable Community*. Although I plainly agree with Fynsk's observation, I will argue in the last section of this chapter, "Politics," that Nancy's elision is indeed a voluntary "hermeneutical violence." It aims at focusing on the violence that stems from Blanchot's writing, *there where this writing pretends to deactivate violence or to be a gesture of non-power*. In this sense, as Cohen-Levinas writes, this "hermeneutical violence" "is not related to humour or to a form of resentment that would express itself all of the sudden. It is the very thought that is never still, never closed upon itself" ("n'est pas le fait d'une humeur, ou d'un ressentiment qui s'exprimerait subitement. Elle est le fait de la pensée elle-même qui ne s'autorise aucun repos, aucun repli") (2015, 110). In this sense, now following Hill's formula, if Nancy's "hermeneutical violence" consists in going "from unworking to disavowed" ("Du désoeuvrement au désavoeu," Hill 2015), it is not, as Hill suggests, because Nancy misses the meaning of Blanchot's idea of the unworking, which consists in suspending violence, but precisely because there is a violence in this very suspension.

  13. Leslie Hill addresses Nancy's critique of Blanchot remarkably in his recent publication (Hill 2018). He underlines in particular Nancy's own contradictions in associating literature with myth (Hill 3–4). In fact, in *The Disavowed Community*, Nancy not only associates Blanchot's use of literature with myth, but he also seems to forget the importance of the distinction he himself had made in *The Inoperative Community* between literature and myth (Nancy 1991, 66, quoted in Hill 2018, 3). However, although Nancy's assertions in *The Disavowed Community* are indeed surprising, the context in which they are formulated might be relevant to understand their political importance. First, after *The Inoperative Community*, Nancy begins to have a different concept of the myth. In "Fin du colloque" (Nancy 2003), for instance, he conceives the myth not as the disposition of a certain kind of founding rationality and word, but in relation to the origin of language, as the opening of a mouth and not as a constituting rationality (633–34). Second, in *The Disavowed Community*, it is the mystery associated with Blanchot's reading of some literary texts that motivates Nancy's assimilation between literature and myth. Henceforth, this assimilation is not general but contextual, and it aims at opening a path to what would be "Unavowable," and in this sense also unsayable, in Blanchot's *The Unavowable Community*.

  14. In *Nancy, Blanchot: A Serious Controversy*, Hill does mention the topic of Christianity and, again, the problematic place it occupies in his own thought. In the chapter titled "Shared Legacies," Hill observes, for instance, that both Nancy and Blanchot share a Christian legacy. Moreover, he highlights that Nancy never

completely abandoned this legacy, along with the importance of Christianity in the elaboration of the concept of community. In this sense, rather than considering Blanchot's Christianity as problematic, one would instead have to focus on Nancy's. Hill also highlights the Judaic orientation of Blanchot's thought, which would distinguish it from Nancy's. In the following pages, I will propose that what matters in Nancy's argument and in its political stakes is not the place of Christianity in Blanchot's thought, but its *peculiar and silent* use of Christian figures.

15. It is interesting to note that although Nancy uses the term *deconstruction* in Derrida's wake, in Nancy deconstruction is not a method nor a way of relating to texts or ideas that would allow us to relate to them as constructed. In fact, the point of departure of Nancy's deconstruction of Christianity might not be Christianity in itself, as if something as such could be delimited, but our relation to Christianity, the way it constitutes our multiple frames of existence and of comprehension. In 1998, when Nancy first evoked the formula "Deconstruction of Christianity," he first remarks that the deconstructive issue is not in what measure Christianity constitutes us as subject ever since Christianity existed, but how Christianity constitutes our relation to history; namely, to what exceeds and precedes Christianity. Hence, what interests Nancy is not Christianity as an object but as an always already desconstructive frame, existential and hermeneutic, that cannot be located in one corpus of text, because, according to Nancy, what characterizes Christianity is that it always already exceeds itself (1998, 503–19).

16. Nancy writes: "Christianity can be summed up, as Nietzsche for one, knew well, in the precept of living in this world as outside of it—in the sense that this 'outside' is not, [or] not an entity" (2008a, 10).

17. See, for instance, "Blanchot's Resurrection" in *Dis-Enclosure*.

18. In *Nancy, Blanchot: A Serious Controversy*, Leslie Hill argues interestingly that the main difference between Nancy's and Blanchot's conception of death is rooted in their differing relations to Heidegger. While for Heidegger, death is the "possibility of the impossibility," it still opens to a world. By contrast, closer to Levinas, for Blanchot death is impossible (Hill 2018, 78–79). It hence deprives of a world (for a discussion on Nancy's trust in the world, see the following section of this chapter, "World").

19. More precisely, Nancy writes: "There is something common to us in its escaping" (2016, 74).

20. I'm here using those terminologies we find in Blanchot's and Nancy's work in their caricatured meanings rather than in their conceptual meanings. Out of this caricatured meaning, what Blanchot and Nancy call, respectively, "disaster" (as in *The Writing of the Disaster*) and "adoration" (as in *Adoration: The Deconstruction of Christianity II*) cannot be simply opposed. Yet, it is interesting to remark that, digging into their meanings, even these terms, *disaster* and *adoration*, do come to occupy a certain opposition between the "end of the world" and the "sense of the world." If the "disaster" is, as *The Writing of the Disaster* constantly entails,

something that pertains to the domain of passivity, it surely doesn't happen as a consecrated end, as an apocalypse conceived, in religious terms, as a revelation. By contrast, Nancy's idea of "adoration" could indeed satisfy what a revelation entails. In *Adoration*, Nancy states that adoration "is, in a way, the praise of infinite sense" (2012, 13). Yet for Nancy this sense is not something that can be given. Rather than a revelation (something that comes from outside), "adoration" is an "address turned toward an outside that is not exterior to the world in itself" (5). In fact, without being turned to an object of the world, something that could be attested to, that could be present, it is turned toward the opening of the world (without this opening being necessarily accessible). "Adoration is addressed to this opening," writes Nancy (15). Thus, delving into the precise meanings of Blanchot's and Nancy's terminologies, we can say that adoration and disaster, although not opposed, can indeed be taken as divergent forces: one relating to the opening of the world, the other relating to what makes the world impossible.

21. "The world," Nancy writes in *Adoration*, "is the exposition of what exists to the touch [*la touche*] of sense, which opens within it the infinity of an 'outside'" (2012, 3).

22. "There is no sense of sense: this is not, ultimately, a negative proposition. It is the affirmation of sense itself—of sensibility, sentiment, significance: the affirmation according to which the world's existents, by referring to one another, open onto the inexhaustible play of their references" (Nancy 2012, 12–13).

23. "The sense of the world is nothing that is guaranteed, nor can we know in advance that it has been lost: it plays itself out entirely in the common echoing and referring that is somehow proposed to us. It is not a 'sense' that has references, axioms, or semiologies outside of the world. It is in play insofar as existents both—ones who speak and others—make circulate within it the possibility of an opening, a breathing, an address that is, strictly speaking, the being-world of the world" (Nancy 2012, 4).

24. Blanchot's and Nancy's relations to Heidegger have been analyzed by Christopher Fynsk in a very relevant chapter of *Last Steps: Maurice Blanchot's Exilic Writings* titled "Perhaps Already a Thought of Community" (2013, 144–60). While it is known that Nancy's relation to Heidegger is crucial for his thinking of community and of the world, Fynsk argues that Blanchot's relation to Heidegger is also crucial for an understanding of Blanchot's ethical and political thought. For Fynsk, Blanchot's critical point of view on Heidegger's understanding of death and of being does not lead him out of the realm of being, and hence out of the political, but instead aims at thinking what fails the human realm in political terms. As Fynsk states, "what is in 'common' is a *failing* in being that can never be an 'event' or can only ever cease to be such for the subject of this passage whose being (which Heidegger defined as a being-able) lapses there" (147). I completely agree with Fynsk that Blanchot's ethics is an ethics of the failure. However, I will discuss in the section titled "Politics" the limits of Blanchot's political thinking of such failure.

25. We find in fact that this sentence appears several times in *The Writing of the Disaster* (in particular, Blanchot 1986, 72) and in Nancy's *Adoration* (2012, 14).

26. In relation to the "collapse of every language" evoked in *The Step Not Beyond*, we can also evoke Blanchot's idea of a "writing outside language," developed in particular in "Atheism and Writing, Humanism and the Cry" in *The Infinite Conversation*. Blanchot's gesture consists not in leaving the realm of language, in making a step into the "Outside," as if something as such could (and should) be reached; rather, Blanchot's writing experiments with a form of bilingualism where language relates to a nonspeaking word (*une parole non parlante*). Yet, if it's crucial to recall that writing does not consist in leaving the world (leaving the world of language), Blanchot's writing, being turned toward the outside of language, prevents the world from being reflected and therefore built.

27. In the original version of *The Writing of the Disaster*, we can read "Nous parlons sur une perte de parole" (Blanchot 1980, 39). This can be translated either as "It is upon losing what we have to say that we speak" (Blanchot 1986, 21), as Ann Smock has translated it, or as "It is upon a loss of speech that we speak." In my opinion, *perte de parole* in French means losing speech rather than losing a determined meaning or intention to speak.

28. This point can be made clearer if we understand consolation not as what silences pain but as what restitutes it to a world. I am here thinking of Michaël Foessel's beautiful book *Le temps de la consolation*, where he argues that "consolation is from one end to the other, a way of learning alterity" (2015, 25). In this sense, for Foessel, consolation is what makes possible another sight (*regard*) within affliction. Thus, consolation is not an opiate against pain. It is rather what allows one to open one's eyes anew, on and with pain.

29. This article will be abbreviated as "Politique au-delà du politique."

30. Nancy says, for instance: "In reading the text in this way, I should also admit that what is written withdraws in offering itself, the writing misleading me [*m'égare*] and dragging me along [*m'entraînant*] with it. No doubt this is the same consent that numerous readers will have given to this book, entering into its community according to the dissolution and disappearance of the bond that forms a community. Right from the beginning, its title—*The Unavowable Community*—has firmly established an adherence to something to which it is impossible to adhere other than through a kind of respectful or stunned, speechless [*interdit*], intimidated silence" (55).

31. In "Notes et contre notes sur *La communauté désavouée*," Danielle Cohen-Levinas suggests this way of responding to the one who cannot respond (because he is dead) is not just a factice circumstance but might be read as a necessity: "S'adresser comme le fait Jean-Luc Nancy (qui écrit à la troisième personne, en se désignant lui-même de son propre nom) à Blanchot—un Blanchot qui n'est plus là pour répondre—relève d'une nécessité supérieure, d'une force qui fait loi" ["To address himself as Jean-Luc Nancy does (who writes in the third person, designat-

ing himself by his own name) to Blanchot—a Blanchot who is no longer there to respond—falls from a higher need, from a ruling force."] (Danielle Cohen-Levinas 2015, 107, translated by Cheryl Emerson).

32. The essential amphibology of the concept of the political has been developed in the article titled "Politique au-delà du politique. Le coeur ou la loi de l'exigence communautaire chez Nancy et Blanchot" (Garrido and Messina 2015, 111).

33. "Blanchot's unavowable avowal comes down to disavowing the community" (Nancy 2016, 58).

34. In *The Disavowed Community*, Nancy describes this presence-absence as follows: "The exemplarity of '68 depends on the real but instantaneous, fleeting nature of this presence, in other words, to the unbinding of community in its own event, in the same way as the lovers expose in it an immemorial escape. The communication of absence (real or imaginary) makes truth [*fait la vérité*] of this co-presence. This extrapolitical truth founds the community out of a foundation that cannot have the constitution of a society "in person" (instituted, not even instituting). This founding derives [*relève*] from myth" (Nancy 2016, 57). For Nancy, Blanchot's focus on May 68's people as absent or contingent amounts to a fascination for absence that posits it as truth. Hence, Nancy's idea that Blanchot's idea of May 68's people derives from myth and that, far from being democratic, it "arises from right-wing thinking": "Defining 'left' or democracy *a minima* by refusing to legitimate, in whatever possible way, an identification or figuration (a work) of the common, of the people (and therefore sovereign), and thus by refusing all types of presentation (symbol, image, instance) of a place that must remain empty or absent—this refusal arises from 'right-wing' thinking from the moment that one offers recourse to a figure, symbol, or myth" (57).

35. "If Nancy can write that there is something sarcastic in the denunciation of the self that Blanchot always puts at stake, it is in that the opening to the Other in the name of which it is promised, operates in the denial of the others who constitute the self" (Garrido and Messina 2015, 129). On Nancy's idea of Blanchot's sarcasm, see *The Disavowed Community* (2016, 77).

36. In other words, whereas we can indeed find a democratic demand in Blanchot, the problem is that democracy, thought of as what is beyond language, cannot be articulated politically. Toward this question, in "D'un extrême à l'autre: par quelle 'conversion,'" Balibar has objected to Nancy that the "political" is essentially ambivalent. In fact, Balibar writes: "La politique n'existe jamais sans une autre scène qui est comme son envers, son envers impolitique" ["The political never exists without another scene that's like its reverse, its impolitical reverse"] (2014, 16, translated by Cheryl Emerson). In line with this point, Balibar insists that Blanchot's writing affirms this ambivalence, and hence it would not depart from the political. However, Nancy's point is that *the way* Blanchot plays with this ambivalence ends up being apolitical in that, in maintaining itself in secret, it ends up refusing language, meaning, world.

37. On this topic, see my article "'Before the Law' or Before the Other: Rethinking the 'Paradox of Sovereignty' in the Light of Lévinas's Thora of Life" (2014), where I show that the Levinassian idea of commandment entails an inspiration, and hence a breath of life, whereas Saint Paul's idea of law is concomitant with a condemnation to death.

38. On Nancy and Lyotard's understanding of the hyphen entailed by the "Judeo-Christian," see chapter two, note 21, this book.

39. On *The Last Man*'s division into two, see chapter four of this book.

40. On this point, see also "Politique au-delà du politique" (Garrido and Messina 2015, 131).

41. See our previous note on Balibar's reading of Blanchot, note 36, this chapter.

42. For a lengthier discussion, see the introduction to this book (28).

43. On this point, see my introduction to the dossier "Maurice Blanchot: Ecriture et pouvoir" (Messina 2019b, 23–25), where I analyze Blanchot's *multipe* relations to silence and his worries about De Gaulle's political uses of silence (24).

44. In "D'un extrême à l'autre: par quelle 'conversion,'" Étienne Balibar questions Nancy's use of the word "extreme" when he suggests that Blanchot's political thought would move from one extreme to another. He observes that "extreme" is related either to the idea of a limit or to the idea of exceeding the limit (Balibar 2004, 9–10). If Blanchot moves from one extreme to another, in the first sense of the term, then the question is whether these two extremes (extreme left and extreme right) do not end up being the same. Balibar's very interesting point is that in order to posit these two extremes, there has to be a center—which is not the case in Blanchot. Hence, what interests Balibar is the second sense of the word "extreme." He thinks that, in this second sense, Blanchot's thought could be democratic in that democracy "always exceeds institution by an essential relation to insurrection" (12). We will see later in this chapter why this last argument is debatable.

45. See, for instance, "An Experience of the Heart" in Nancy's first volume on *The Deconstruction of Christianity* (2008a), where Nancy argues that in Nietzsche, redemption and divinity are notions meant to "save man from God" (79).

46. "The horizon of a subtraction, a retreat, an absence, or even the horizon of what I once called 'absentheism,' to oppose it to atheism, continues to form a horizon. That is to say, it forms a limit, a dead end, an end of the world. That horizon surrounds our thinking all the more in that world, in effect, everywhere touches its confines, and this in a physical mode as well as in a metaphysical one. It can no longer be a matter of getting out of the world, but that is not a reason to consider the world a horizon" (Nancy 2008a, 18).

47. In *The Infinite Conversation*, Blanchot writes: "Already for Nietzsche the problem poses itself in the most radical manner, in the sense that for him atheism is always problematic, and is itself an anachronistic expression. It would be a question, therefore, as Karl Lowith says very well, of passing from the a-Theism of the

nineteenth century to A-theism, which is what occurs with a recognition of the world as the 'play of the world' " (Blanchot 1993, 457n6).

48. Interestingly, when Blanchot and Nancy happen to speak of "A-theism" and "absentheism," their positions regarding the world seem inverted: Blanchot thinks of "A-theism" in relation to Nietzsche's idea of a "play of the world" (Blanchot 1993, 457) while Nancy states: "The horizon of a subtraction, a retreat, an absence, or even the horizon of what I once called 'absentheism,' to oppose it to atheism, continues to form a horizon. That is to say, it forms a limit, a dead end, an end of the world" (Nancy 2008a, 18). In this case, what Blanchot, in the wake of Nietzsche, calls "the play of the world" is the fragmentary, thought of as the impossibility of any unity (and hence of a world). What on his side Nancy calls "the end of the world" "continues to form a horizon" and, hence, to open onto a world. As we stated, the world in Nancy is not a metaphysical notion, but is inseparable from its end. What matters is that in Blanchot, A-theism is not the negation of God but the opening of an absence that entails a radical modification. To negate God is a human possibility. By contrast, to think of God's absence is beyond human power. It thus entails that we cannot rely on any subject, any base, on any fixed conception of the world, on any secure use of language. Nancy certainly agrees with this idea. In *Dis-Enclosure*, and in particular in the chapter "The Name *God* in Blanchot," Nancy relates "atheism" to the topic of the "absent sense" in Blanchot. He states: "This is what is at stake in an 'atheism' that owes it to itself to deny itself the position of the negation it proffers, and the assurance of every sort of presence that could substitute for that of God—that is, the presence of the signifier of absolute signification or significability" (2008a, 86).

49. "On the horizon—a far horizon, perhaps, but not necessarily—there could be for Blanchot a question about 'God.' If 'God' names the unnamable, Blanchot does in fact name it, and this (un)designation [(in) nomination] signals a hyperbolic vanishing point, in infinite excess [*excé-dence*], according to which the encounter with the other [*autrui*] cannot take place without escaping further. A kind of ultratheology triumphs over all possibility of relation (but would there be a relation with 'God'?)" (2016, 40).

References

Acosta López, María del Rosario. 2019. "Grammars of Listening: Philosophical Approaches to the Construction of Historical Memory." *Ideas y Valores* 68 (5): 59–79.
Agamben, Giorgio. 1993. *The Coming Community*. Translated by Michael Hardt. Minneapolis: University of Minnesota Press.
———. 2005a. *State of Exception*. Translated by Kevin Attell. Chicago: University of Chicago Press.
———. 2005b. *The Time That Remains: A Commentary on the Letter to the Romans*. Translated by Patricia Dailey. Stanford, CA: Stanford University Press.
Allen, William S. 2018. *Blanchot and the Outside of Literature*. New York: Bloomsbury Academic.
Alliez, Eric. 2018. "1968–2018 or 'From the Revolution Impossible' to the Impossibility of Revolution. Variations on the Object Petit s." *Crisis and Critique* 5 (2): 31–50.
Anders, Günther. 2006. *Le temps de la fin*. Paris: L'Herne.
Arendt, Hannah. 2006. *Eichmann in Jerusalem: A Report on the Banality of Evil*. London: Penguin.
Augustine. 1952. *Fathers of the Church*. Translated by Gerald G. Walsh, S. J., and Grace Monohan. Vol. 14. Washington, DC: The Catholic University of America Press.
———. 1954. *Fathers of the Church*. Translated by Gerald G. Walsh, S. J., and Grace Monohan. Vol. 23. Washington, DC: The Catholic University of America Press.
Balibar, Étienne. 2014. "D'un extrême à l'autre: par quelle conversion?" *Cahiers Maurice Blanchot*, no. 3 (Fall): 9–19.
Banon, David. 1987. *La lecture infinie: Les voies de l'interprétation midrachique*. Paris: Seuil.
Barth, Karl. 1956. *Christ and Adam: Man and Humanity in Romans 5*. Translated by T. A. Smail. New York: Harper & Bros.
———. 1968. *The Epistle to the Romans*. Translated by Edwyn C. Hoskyns. Oxford: Oxford University Press.

REFERENCES

Basterra, Gabriela. 2005. *Seductions of Fate: Tragic Subjectivity, Ethics, Politics*. London: Palgrave Macmillan.

Bataille, Georges. 1998. *The College of Sociology (1937–1939)*. Edited by Dennis Hollier. Translated by Betsy Wing. Minneapolis: University of Minnesota Press.

Bident, Christophe. 2009. "De la chronique à la théorisation." In *Blanchot dans son siècle—Colloque de Cerisy*, 104–17. Lyon: Parangon/Vs.

———. 2018. *Maurice Blanchot: A Critical Biography*. Translated by John McKeane. New York: Fordham University Press.

Blanchot, Maurice. 1980. *L'écriture du désastre*. Paris: Gallimard.

———. 1981. *The Madness of the Day*. Translated by Lydia Davia. Barrytown, NY: Station Hill Press.

———. 1982. *The Space of Literature*. Translated by Ann Smock. Lincoln: University of Nebraska Press.

———. 1985. "Paix, paix au lointain et au proche." *Le nouvel observateur*, Mai–6 Juin 1985.

———. 1987. *The Last Man*. Translated by Lydia Davis. New York: Columbia University Press.

———. 1990. *The Unavowable Community*. Translated by Pierre Joris. Barrytown, NY: Station Hill Press.

———. 1992. *The Step Not Beyond*. Translated by Lycette Nelson. New York: State University of New York Press.

———. 1995a. "Literature and the Right to Death." In *The Work of Fire*, 300–344. Translated by Charlotte Mandell. Stanford, CA: Stanford University Press.

———. 1995b. *The Writing of the Disaster*. Translated by Ann Smock. Lincoln: University of Nebraska Press.

———. 1996. *The Most High*. Translated by Allan Stoekl. Lincoln: University of Nebraska Press.

———. 2000. *The Instant of My Death*. Translated by Elizabeth Rottenberg. Stanford, CA: Stanford University Press.

———. 2007. "Une étude sur L'Apocalypse." In *Chroniques littéraires*, 486–93. Paris: Gallimard.

———. 1993. *The Infinite Conversation*. Translated by Susan Hanson. Minneapolis: University of Minnesota Press.

Bourgeois, Bernard. 2000. *Hegel à Francfort: Judaïsme, christianisme, hegelianisme*. Paris: J. Vrin.

Brémondy, François. 2014. "Enquête historique et réflexions critiques sur l'itinéraire politique de Maurice Blancho." *Lignes* 43 (1): 63–121.

Camus, Albert. 1989. *The Stranger*. Translated by Matthew Ward. New York: Vintage Books.

Chiesa, Lorenzo, and Frank Ruda. 2011. "The Event of Language as Force of Life: Agamben's Linguistic Vitalism." *Angelaki* 16 (3): 163–80.

Cecire, Natalia. 2015. "Environmental Innocence and Slow Violence." *Women's Studies Quarterly* 43 (1–2): 164–80.
Cohen-Levinas, Danielle. 2009. "Entre eux. Maurice Blanchot et Emmanuel Levinas . . . Là où ils sont, se rendre à l'impossible." In *Blanchot dans son siècle. Colloque de Cerisy*, 69–84. Lyon: Parangon/Vs.
———. 2015. "Notes et contre notes sur *La communauté désavouée*." *Cahiers Maurice Blanchot*, no. 4: 95–100.
———. 2019. "Au commencement était 'Il faut'. Politique comme littérature première." *Cahiers Maurice Blanchot*, no. 6: 101–9.
Cools, Arthur. 2007. *Langage et subjectivité: Vers une approche du différend entre Maurice Blanchot et Emmanuel Lévinas*. Louvain: Éditions de l'Institut Supérieur de Philosophie de Louvain.
———. 2011. "Disastrous Responsibility: Blanchot's Criticism of Levinas' Concept of Subjectivity in *The Writing of the Disaster*." *Levinas Studies* 6: 113–30.
Danta, Chris. 2011. *Literature Suspends Death: Sacrifice and Storytelling in Kierkegaard, Kafka, and Blanchot*. London: Bloomsbury.
Derrida, Jacques. 1992. "Force of Law: The 'Mystical Foundation of Authority.'" In *Deconstruction and the Possibility of Justice*, edited by Drucilla Cornell, Michel Rosenfeld, and David Gray Carlson, translated by Mary Quaintance, 3–67. New York: Routledge.
———. 2001. *The Work of Mourning*. Translated by Pascale-Anne Brault and Michael Naas. Chicago: University of Chicago Press.
———. 2005. *On Touching—Jean-Luc Nancy*. Translated by Christine Irizarry. Stanford, CA: Stanford University Press.
———. 2009. *The Beast and the Sovereign, Volume 1*. Edited by Michel Lisse, Marie-Louise Mallet, and Ginette Michaud. Translated by Geoffrey Bennington. Chicago: University of Chicago Press.
———. 2011. *Parages*. Translated by John P. Leavey. Stanford, CA: Stanford University Press.
———. 2014. *The Death Penalty, Volume 1*. Edited by Geoffrey Bennington, Marc Crépon, and Thomas Dutoit. Translated by Peggy Kamuf. Chicago: University of Chicago Press.
———. 2017. *The Gift of Death*. Translated by David Wills. Chicago: University of Chicago Press.
———. 2020. *Life Death*. Translated by Pascale-Anne Brault and Peggy Kamuf. Chicago: University of Chicago Press.
Dostoyevsky, Fyodor. 1992. *The Idiot*. Translated by Alan Myers. Oxford: Oxford University Press.
Esposito, Roberto. 2008. *Bios: Biopolitics and Philosophy*. Translated by Timothy Campbell. Lincoln: University of Minnesota Press.
———. 2009. *Communitas: The Origin and Destiny of Community*. Translated by Timothy Campbell. Stanford, CA: Stanford University Press.

Fabbri, Lorenzo. 2009. "Chronotopologies of the Exceptions: Derrida and Agamben Before the Camps." *diacritics* 39 (3): 77–95.
Fagenblat, Michael. 2005. "Back to the Other Levinas: Reflections Prompted by Alain P. Toumayan's *Encountering the Other*." *Colloqy* 10: 298–313.
Ferrari, Federico, and Jean-Luc Nancy. 2015. *La fin des fins: Scène en deux actes*. Nantes: Éditions Cécile Defaut.
Foessel, Michaël. 2012. *Après la fin du monde: Critique de la raison apocalyptique*. Paris: Seuil.
———. 2014. "Apocalypse et consolation." *Esprit* June (6): 64–74.
———. 2015. *Le temps de la consolation*. Paris: Seuil.
Foucault, Michel. 1987. "Maurice Blanchot: The Thought from Outside." In *Foucault | Blanchot*, translated by Brian Massumi, 7–60. New York: Zone Books.
Fynsk, Christopher. 2000. *Infant Figures: The Death of the Infans and Other Scenes of Origin*. Stanford, CA: Stanford University Press.
———. 2010. "Writing and Sovereignty." In *Clandestine Encounters: Philosophy in the Narratives of Maurice Blanchot*, edited by Kevin Hart, 178–95. Notre Dame, IN: University of Notre Dame Press.
———. 2013. *Last Steps: Maurice Blanchot's Exilic Writing*. New York: Fordham University Press.
Garrido, Juan Manuel, and Aïcha Liviana Messina. 2015. "Politique au-delà du politique: Le cœur ou la loi de l'exigence communautaire chez Nancy et Blanchot." *Cahiers Maurice Blanchot*, no. 4: 123–34.
Gasché, Rodolphe. 2016. *Deconstruction, Its Force, Its Violence: Together with "Have We Done with the Empire of Judgement?"* Albany: State University of New York Press.
———. 2018. *Storytelling: The Destruction of the Inalienable in the Age of the Holocaust*. Albany: State University of New York Press.
Geroulanos, Stefanos. 2010. *An Atheism That Is Not Humanist Emerges in French Thought*. Stanford, CA: Stanford University Press.
Gregg, John. 1994. *Maurice Blanchot and the Literature of Transgression*. Princeton, NJ: Princeton University Press.
Hammerschlag, Sarah. 2010. *The Figural Jew: Politics and Identity in Postwar French Thought*. Chicago: University of Chicago Press.
Hart, Kevin. 2004. *Maurice Blanchot and the Sacred*. Chicago: University of Chicago Press.
———. 2019a. "Levinas, Blanchot, and Art." In *The Oxford Handbook of Levinas*, edited by Michael L. Morgan, 53–71. New York: Oxford University Press.
———. 2019b. "The Aggrieved Community: Nancy and Blanchot in Dialogue." *Journal for Continental Philosophy of Religion*, no. 1: 27–42.
———. 2021. *L'image vulnérable. Sur l'image de Dieu chez Saint Augustin*. Paris: PUF.
Hegel, Georg Wilhelm Friedrich. 1995. *Lectures on the Philosophy of Religion*. Translated by R. F. Brown, P. C. Hodgson, and J. M. Stewart. Vol. 2. New York: Oxford University Press.

———. 2007a. *Lectures on the Philosophy of Religion*. Translated by R. F. Brown, P. C. Hodgson, and J. M. Stewart. Vol. 1. New York: Oxford University Press.
———. 2007b. *Lectures on the Philosophy of Religion*. Translated by R. F. Brown, P. C. Hodgson, and J. M. Stewart. Vol. 3. New York: Oxford University Press.
———. 2018. *The Phenomenology of Spirit*. Edited and translated by Terry Pinkard. Cambridge: Cambridge University Press.
Heidegger, Martin. 1991. *Nietzsche*. Translated by David Farrell Krell. San Francisco: HarperSanFrancisco.
———. 1996. *Being and Time*. Translated by Joan Stambaugh. Albany: State University of New York Press.
Hill, Leslie. 1997. *Blanchot: Extreme Contemporary*. London: Routledge.
———. 2003. "La pensée politique." *Le magazine littéraire* 424 (10): 35–57.
———. 2007. "Le tournant du fragmentaire: prolégomènes." *Europe* 940–941 (August–September): 74–84.
———. 2010. *Radical Indecision: Barthes, Blanchot, Derrida, and the Future of Criticism*. Notre Dame, IN: University of Notre Dame Press.
———. 2012. *Maurice Blanchot and Fragmentary Writing: A Change of Epoch*. New York: Continuum.
———. 2014. "Pour une politique du fragmentaire." *Cahiers Maurice Blanchot*, no. 3: 50–60.
———. 2015. "Du désoeuvrement au désaveu (à propos de La Commnauté désavouée de Jean Luc Nancy)." *Cahiers Maurice Blanchot*, no. 4 (2016): 134–43.
———. 2016. "From Deconstruction to Disaster (Derrida, Blanchot, Hegel)." *Paragraph*, no. 39: 187–201.
———. 2018. *Nancy, Blanchot: A Serious Controversy*. London: Rowman & Littlefield International.
Holland, Michael. 2010. "Space and Beyond: L'attente l'oubli." In *Clandestine Encounters*, edited by Kevin Hart, 263–81. Notre Dame, IN: University of Notre Dame Press.
———. 2014. "N'en déplaise. (Pour une pensée conséquente)." *Cahiers Maurice Blanchot*, no. 3: 149–72.
———. 2015. *Avant dire: Essais sur Blanchot*. Paris: Hermann.
Hoppenot, Eric. 2012. "De l'Apocalypse à Amalek. Esquisse d'une réflexion sur la pensée du mal dans l'œuvre de Maurice Blanchot." In *Maurice Blanchot et la philosophie*, edited by Eric Hoppenot and Alain Milon, 157–78. Paris: Presse Universitaire de Paris Ouest.
———. 2015. *Maurice Blanchot et La Tradition Juive*. Paris: Kimé.
Hugo, Victor. 2013. *L'homme qui rit*. Paris: Folio classique—Gallimard.
Iyer, Lars. 2003. "The Unbearable Trauma and Witnessing in Blanchot and Lévinas." *Janus Head* 6 (1): 37–63.
———. 2004. *Blanchot's Communism: Art, Philosophy and the Political*. New York: Palgrave Macmillan.
Kafka, Franz. 2000. *The Trial*. Translated by Idris Parry. London: Penguin.

Kant, Immanuel. 1965. *First Introduction to the Critique of Judgment*. Translated by James Haden. Indianapolis, IN: Bobbs-Merrill.

Kierkegaard, Søren. 1980. *The Concept of Anxiety: A Simple Psychologically Orienting Deliberation on the Dogmatic Issue of the Hereditary Sin*. Translated by Reidar Thomte. Princeton, NJ: Princeton University Press.

———. 1985. *Fear and Trembling*. Translated by Alastair Hannay. London: Penguin.

Lacan, Jacques. 2006. *Écrits*. Translated by Bruce Fink. New York: W. W. Norton.

———. 2015. *Ending and Unending Agony: On Maurice Blanchot*. Translated by Hannes Opelz. New York: Fordham University Press.

Langlois, Christopher. 2018. "Literature Outside the Law: Blanchot's The Infinite Conversation." In *Understsanding Blanchot, Understanding Modernism*, edited by Christopher Langlois, 99–119. New York: Bloomsbury Academic.

Levinas, Emmanuel. 1975. "Exercices sur 'la folie du jour.'" In *Sur Maurice Blanchot*, 53–74. Montpellier: Fatamorgana.

———. 1977. *Du sacré au saint: cinq nouvelles lectures talmudiques*. Paris: Minuit.

———. 1989. "Reality and Its Shadow." In *The Levinas Reader*, edited by Seán Hand, translated by Alphonso Lingis, 129–43. London: Basil Blackwell.

———. 1991. *Totality and Infinity: An Essay on Exteriority*. Translated by Alphonso Lingis. Dordrecht: Kluwer Academic Publishers.

———. 1994. *Beyond Verse: Talmudic Readings and Lectures*. Translated by Gary D. Mole. Bloomington, IN: Indiana University Press.

———. 1998. *Otherwise than Being, or Beyond Essence*. Translated by Alphonso Lingis. Pittsburgh, PA: Duquesne University Press.

Lyotard, Jean-François. 1999. *The Hyphen: Between Judaism and Christianity*. Translated by Pascale-Anne Brault and Michael Naas. Amherst, NY: Humanity Books.

Madaule, Pierre. 2009. "La vengeance d'Adam." In *Blanchot dans son siècle—Colloque de Cerisy*, 41–55. Lyon: Parangon/Vs.

Mahn, Jason A. 2011. *Fortunate Fallibility: Kierkegaard and the Power of Sin*. Oxford: Oxford University Press.

Margel, Serge. 2019. "De Blanchot à Blanchot: Les pouvoirs de l'écriture et le droit à la mort." *Cahiers Maurice Blanchot*, no. 6: 77–90.

Marx, Karl. 1963. *The Eighteenth Brumaire of Louis Bonaparte*. Translated by C. P. Dutt. New York: International Publishers.

Matar, Anat. 2018. "Maurice Blanchot: Modernism, Dissidence and the Privilege of Writing." *Critical Horizons* 19: 67–80.

McKeane, John. 2013. "Change in the Archive: Blanchot's *L'entretien infini*." *Forum for Modern Language Studies* 50 (1): 69–81.

Messina, Aïcha Liviana. 2009. "L'hospitalité animale. Faim de l'histoire." *Le portique*, no. 23–24: unpaged.

———. 2014. "'Before the Law' or Before the Other. Rethinking the 'Paradox of Sovereignty' in Light of Lévinas' Thora of Life." *CR: The New Centennial Review* 14 (2): 99–110.

———. 2016. "Souffrance éthique et souffrance tragique: L'élaboration levinassienne de la compassion." *KRITERION* 57 (134): 379–99.

———. 2018. *L'anarchie de la paix: Levinas et la philosophie politique*. Paris: CNRS Éditions.

———. 2019a. "Ambiguïtés du non-pouvoir." *Cahiers Maurice Blanchot*, no. 6: 21–25.

———. 2019b. "Le silence du pouvoir." *Cahiers Maurice Blanchot*, no. 6: 91–101.

Meyer, Eric Daryl. 2014. "The Logos of God and the End of Humanity: Giorgio Agamben and the Gospel of John on Animality as Light and Life." In *Divinanimality: Animal Theory, Creaturely Theology*, edited by Stephen D. Moore, 146–60. New York: Fordham University Press.

Michaelsen, Catherine Bjørnholt. 2014. "Ways of Dying: The Double Death in Kierkegaard and Blanchot." *Kierkegaard Studies Yearbook* 19 (1): 255–83.

Murray, Peter Durno. 2018. *Nietzsche and the Dionysian—A Compulsion to Ethics*. Leiden: Brill and Rodopi.

Nancy, Jean-Luc. 1983. "La communauté désœuvrée." *Alea* 4: 11–49.

———. 1991. *The Inoperative Community*. Translated by Peter Connor, Lisa Garbus, Michael Holland, and Simona Sawhney. Minneapolis: University of Minnesota Press.

———. 1997. *The Sense of the World*. Translated by J. L. Librett. Minneapolis: University of Minnesota Press.

———. 1998. "La déconstruction du christianisme." *Les études philosophiques* 4 (October–December): 503–19.

———. 2003a. "Fin du colloque." In *Maurice Blanchot: Récits critiques*, edited by Christophe Bident and Pierre Vilar, 625–37. Tours: farrago.

———. 2003b. "Le judéo-chrétien." In *Judéités: Questions pour Jacques Derrida*, edited by Joseph Cohen and Raphel Zagury-Orly, 303–22. Paris: Galilée.

———. 2008a. *Dis-Enclosure: The Deconstruction of Christianity*. Translated by Bettina Bergo, Gabriel Malenfant, and Michael B. Smith. New York: Fordham University Press.

———. 2008b. *Philosophical Chronicles*. Translated by Franson Manjali. New York: Fordham University Press.

———. 2012. *Adoration: The Deconstruction of Christianity II*. Translated by John McKeane. New York: Fordham University Press.

———. 2016. *The Disavowed Community*. Translated by Philip Armstrong. New York: Fordham University Press.

Nietzsche, Friedrich. 1996. *Human, All Too Human*. Translated by Gary D. Mole. Cambridge: Cambridge University Press.

———. 2006. *Thus Spoke Zarathustra*. Translated by Robert Pippin. Chicago: University of Chicago Press.

Nioche, Claire. 2013. "Mauric Blanchot, déserter le myth." *Topique* 3 (124): 135–52.

Préli, Georges. 1977. *La force du dehors: Extériorité, limite et non-pouvoir à partir de Maurice Blanchot*. Fontenay-sous-Bois: Recherches.

Quintana, Idoia, and Lisse, Michel. 2014. "Maurice Blanchot: de 'constitution catholique'?" In *L'Herne. Blanchot*, 336–342. Paris, France: Éditions de l'Herne.

Ricoeur, Paul. 1967. *The Symbolism of Evil*. Translated by Emerson Buchanon. Boston: Beacon Press.

Rose, Marika. 2019. *A Theology of Failure: Žižek Against Christian Innocence*. New York: Fordham University Press.

Sheaffer-Jones, Caroline. 2010. "As Though with a New Beginning." In *Clandestine Encounters*, edited by Kevin Hart, 241–61. Notre Dame, IN: University of Notre Dame Press.

Smock, Ann. 1976. "Où Est La Loi? Law and Sovereignty in Aminadab and Le Tres-Haut." *Substance* 5: 99–116.

———. 1984. "Disastrous Responsibility." *L'Esprit Créateur* 24 (3): 5–20.

———. 2003. *What Is There to Say?* Lincoln: University of Nebraska Press.

Stewart, Jon. 2003. *Kierkegaard's Relations to Hegel Reconsidered*. Cambridge: Cambridge University Press.

Surya, Michel. 2014. "L'autre Blanchot." *Lignes* 43 (Special Issue "Les politiques de Maurice Blanchot (1939–1993)"): 7–62.

———. 2015. *L'autre Blanchot: L'écriture du jour, l'écriture de la nuit*. Paris: Gallimard.

Thurschwell, Adam. 2007. "Law and Literature and the Right to Death." In *Figures of Law: Studies of the Interference of Law and Literature*, edited by Gert Hofmann, 45–62. Tübingen: A. Francke.

Toumayan, Alain. 2004. *Encountering the Other: The Artwork and the Problem of Difference in Blanchot and Levinas*. Pittsburgh, PA: Duquesne University Press.

Wall, Thomas Carl. 1999. *Radical Passivity: Lévinas, Blanchot, and Agamben*. Albany: State University of New York Press.

Index

à venir, the (to come), 28, 35, 110, 120, 148n1
action(s), 1–5, 10–11, 107, 119, 137, 157n7, 161n27, 171n8; non-action, 19–20, 75; of grace, 50–52, 174n4
activity, 17, 23, 39–40, 79, 85, 99, 107; criminal, 5; of the spirit, 170n30; of thinking, 13; inactivity, 79
Adam, xi–xii, xiv–xv, 12, 14, 17, 19, 52–53, 55, 63, 75, 80, 93, 147n25, n27, 151n12, 157–158n11, 168n20; Adamic, 18, 20, 88; and Eve, 12–13, 141n1, 144n16, 158n13. *See also* the Fall; silence, Adam's
adoration, 178–179n20; disaster of, 114; of nothingness, 115; of the world, 116, 120. *See also* Nancy, *Adoration: The Deconstruction of Christianity*
Agamben, Giorgio, 24, 27–39, 41–43, 84, 86, 149n6, 151n13, 151n14, 153n20, 154n22, 154n24, 156n7, 157n10, 169n29; *Homo Sacer*, 36–37, 149n6, 151n14, 153n20, 153n22, 157n10; *The State of Exception*, 169n29, 173n1; *The Time That Remains*, 156n7
amoral, 7; amorality, 72. *See also* moral, morality

Anders, Günther, 4, 90–91, 103, 105, 170n2, 171n3, n4, n5
anguish, 74, 76–78, 80, 87, 166n6
anonymous, 3–4, 10, 16, 34, 48, 67, 84, 87, 103, 141n2, 146n20, 151n11, 157n10; anonymity, 32, 87, 170n34
anxiety, 74, 76–78, 80, 166n6, n7, n8, 167n11. *See also* Kierkegaard, *The Concept of Anxiety*
Apocalypse, xii, xv, 24–26, 89–96, 101–103, 105–106, 114, 117, 119, 132, 148n31, 161n27, 162n30, 165n3, 170n1, 171n3, n5, n7, n8, 179n20; apocalyptic(al), xv, 90, 92, 105, 114–115, 133, 171n6
Arendt, Hannah, 3, 7, 142n7
atheism, 26, 42, 120, 130–131, 133, 145, 161n28, 168n18, 180n26, 182n46, n47, 183n48
Augustine (Saint), xi–xii, xiv–xv, 12–15, 171n8; *The City of God*, 12–14, 159n15, 163n35, 171n8; *Confessions*, 144n16
Auschwitz, 35

bare life, 36–37, 151–152n14, 153n20. *See also* Agamben, *Homo Sacer*
Barth, Karl, 17, 45, 50, 68, 148n2, 153n19, 157n8, 157–158n11, 159n19

193

INDEX

Bataille, Georges, 39, 124, 165n4, 170n33
Benjamin, Walter, 36, 142n9
Bible, xiii, 12, 159n18; Old Testament, xv; New Testament, xv, 63
biopolitical, 143n12, 152n14, 153n20; biopolitics, 8–9. *See also* politics, political
"black writing," 64–65, 68, 161n26, 162n31. *See also* "white writing"; Hart, *The Dark Gaze*
Blanchot, Maurice, works by, *Aminabad*, 31, 149; "Atheism and Writing," 161n28, 180n26; *Death Sentence*, 92; *Friendship*, 128; *The Infinite Conversation*, 30–31, 41–43, 63–66, 100, 141n3, 146n20, 149n4, 154n22, 155n31, n32, 161n28, 162n30, 163n34, 173n18, 180n26, 182n47; *The Instant of My Death*, 167n17; *Literature and the Right to Death*, 18–21, 92, 94–95, 97, 147n25, n26, 149n4, 164n36, 172n10, n14; *The Madness of the Day*, 40–41, 150n8, 154n28, 155n29; *The Most High*, 3, 18–22, 31–36, 44, 46, 92, 149n5, 150n6, n10, 151n11, 170n34; *The Space of Literature*, 173n17; *The Step Not Beyond*, 1, 13–15, 22, 24, 29, 40–41, 46–47, 52, 55–58, 64–65, 74–75, 77–80, 85, 88, 91, 111, 153n21, 156n1, 159n15, n17, n19, 163n33, 168n19, 169n27, 180n26; *Thomas the Obscure*, 147n21; *The Unavowable Community*, 23, 26, 106–107, 109, 112, 121–128, 132, 173n1, 174n2, 177n12, n13, 180n30; *When the Time Comes*, 168n17; *The Work of Fire*, 39, 97, 102, 168n18, 172n10; *The Writing of the Disaster*, 10, 15–16, 18, 22, 39, 75, 81–82, 85–86, 89, 101–102, 116, 118, 151n11, 170n31, 172n16, 178n20, 180n25, n27
Book, the, 63–66, 68, 91–92, 94, 160n20, 161n29, 162n30, n31; law of, 25, 64
Brémondy, François, 23, 148n31, 175n7

Camus, Albert, *The Stranger*, 3–4, 136–139
chance, xiii–xiv, 34, 47–48, 66–67, 72, 131–133; law of, 67; sovereignty of, 45; violence of, 43. *See also* luck
child, 103, 138; being of the, 1; face of the, 173n20; of an era, 136; childhood, 142n8; children, 5, 15, 135, 144n12
Christ, 63, 125, 132, 137, 156n1, 157–158n11
common, the, 37–38, 41, 103, 120, 179n23, 181n34; being-in-common, 8, 26; common good, 150n9; common world, 73; the "in common," 114, 118, 125, 130, 133, 179n24; life in common, 154n24; spacing of, 115; time in, 103
community, 23–24, 38, 49, 51, 100, 106, 108, 112–114, 119, 121–125, 128–130, 153–154n22, 173n20, 173n1, 178n14, 179n24, 180n30, 181n33, n34
consolation, 103, 117–119, 180n28
Corinthians, Paul's Letter to, 49–50, 67, 157n10
Cry, the, 15, 42, 65, 68, 139, 150n10, 161n28, 180n26

Deconstruction of Christianity, the, xiv, 22, 24, 26, 105, 109–110, 112–116, 118–120, 122, 131, 133,

154n23, 164n37, 178n15. *See also*
Nancy, *Adoration: Deconstruction of Christianity*.
De Gaulle, Charles, 126, 129, 182n43
Democracy, 121, 126, 133–134, 152n14, 181n34, n36; antidemocratic, 26, 121; in Blanchot's thought, 26, 130, 182n44; democratic, 26, 123, 126–127, 130, 181n34, n36; 26, nondemocratic, 109
Derrida, Jacques, 24, 27–31, 37–39, 41–43, 86, 118; *The Beast and the Sovereign*, 152n14; *The Gift of Death*, 7, 142n6, 146n24, 148n1, n2, 149n3, 151n13, 152n14, 154n22, n24, 155n29, 158n14, 159n15, n16, n19, 164n36, n2, 168n18, 169n22, 178n15; *The Law of Genre*, 41, 155n29; *Life Death*, 145n17, 153n21, 158n14; *On Touching—Jean-Luc Nancy*, 118; *The Work of Mourning*, 111
desire, xi–xii, xv, 6–7, 53–54
destruction, xi, 4, 15, 22, 33, 72, 82, 90, 96, 110, 120, 130, 143–144, 150n7, 159n15, 165n3, 171n3, n4
death, xi, xiv–xv, 9, 12–15, 26, 34, 37–39, 46–47, 50–63, 66, 68, 79, 82, 91–94, 96–97, 110–113, 118–119, 122, 131, 133, 136, 138, 147n27, 150n10, 152n14, 153n19, 156n3, n5, 157n11, 158n13, 159n15, n16, 161n25, 163n35, 178n18, 179n24, 182n37; of desire, 54; death penalty, 137, 163–164n36; death sentence, 50, 52, 138, 159n16; "the dying," 14; eternal death, 171n8; of eternity, 57, 159n19; of God, 133; law and, 24, 38, 52, 55–56, 59, 127, 148n30;

life and, xi, 48, 50–51, 55–56, 58, 66, 91, 145n17, 153n21, 157n8, 158n14; love of, xiv–xv, 47, 54, 57, 61–62, 66, 106, 163–164n36; of the Other, 111, 122; moment of, 27; negativity of, 54; positivity of, 54; realm of, 50, 55; of the subject, 11; "transcendental dying," 153n19; *See also* Blanchot, "Literature and the Right to Death," *Death Sentence*
"to die," the (*mourir*), xv, 39, 43, 47, 54, 56–58, 60–61, 110–112, 159n16, n19, 161n27, 163n33
disgrace, 12–13, 15, 48, 61, 66–68, 146n21. *See also* grace
Dostoevsky, Fyodor, *The Idiot*, 2
Duras, *The Malady of Death*, 124

Edwarda, Madame, 124–125
Esposito, Roberto, 8, 173n1
eternal, 26, 43, 57, 87, 97–98, 103, 106, 110–111, 132, 159n18, 171n8; return, 91
eternity, xi, 13, 26, 57–58, 61, 66, 98, 101–103, 110–112, 119, 159n18, n19
ethical, xiii–xiv, 2, 15, 18–19, 23–24, 43, 46–47, 74, 77, 80, 103, 106, 122–123, 128, 145n18, 151n11, 154n24, 160n20, 167n12, 179n24
ethics, xiii, 7, 15–18, 22–26, 38, 74, 77, 80–82, 84–88, 106, 132–133, 145n18, 146n21, 151n11, 159n18, 160n20, 161n26, 170n31, n33, 179n24
Eve. *See* Adam and
evil, 3–6, 8–9, 12, 15, 49, 52, 61, 87–88, 90, 171n5; good and, 2, 5, 12, 74, 166n7, 171n4
existence, xi–xv, 2, 12, 19, 21, 37, 45, 76, 78, 93, 100, 107, 118, 136,

existence *(continued)*
  147n25, n26, 151–152n14, 153n20, 158n13, 174n4, 175n7, 178n15
Exposure, xv, 36, 43, 56, 85, 117, 170n30; to the Other, 17

Fall, the, xi–xii, xiv, 11–15, 17–19, 24, 57–58, 73–74, 78, 83–84, 105, 107, 131, 141n1, 144n14, n16, 166n1; before the, 19, 77, 86; of innocence, xii, 11, 14–15, 18, 57, 72, 84, 86–88, 131–133; of the subject, 24; of time, xi, 57, 61, 84–85, 169n27
fate, 11, 20, 66, 94, 96, 121, 141n2, 172n11, n12
finite, 12, 17, 57, 83, 91, 94, 111, 119, 166n7
finitude, 12–13, 24, 26, 37–38, 43, 53, 57, 61, 66–67, 72, 110–116, 118–120, 131, 141n1, 154n24, 158n13, 159n18, n19, 166n7, 169n25
flesh, 12–13, 17, 47–48, 51, 54, 58, 151n12, 156n2
Foessel, Michaël, 103, 180n21
foolishness, 49–50, 52–53, 55
folly, 50–51, 53; of grace, 52, 61
freedom, xi, xiv–xv, 4, 7, 20–22, 24, 32, 36–38, 40–41, 44, 46, 51, 61–62, 67, 78, 94, 143n12, 154–155n28, 164n36, 166n7, 167n15, 168n22, 169n24, 172n12
Freud, Sigmund, 10
Fynsk, Christopher, 23; *Infant Figures*, 142n8, 147n29, 154n28, 160n20, 176n12, 179n24

game, 24, 83, 131, 145n18, 159n16; of the law, 40–41, 43, 45–46, 67, 156n33
Genesis, xii, xv, 11–13, 92–95, 98, 144n16, 158n13

Garrido, Juan Manuel, 121–127, 130, 181n32, n35, 182n40
gift, xi, 46–49, 117, 156n1, 157n11, 172n8; of death, 7, 142n6, 168n18, 169n22; of grace, xiv, 24–25, 48, 54–55, 58, 67, 157n10; gratuity, 24, 45–46; of life, 47
Girard, Réne, 23
God, 9, 12–14, 16–17, 50, 64, 66, 78, 88, 93, 96, 116, 118, 120–121, 138–139, 144n16, 156n1, 157n11, 158n13, 161n26, 163n35, 166n7, 168n18, 170n33, 182n45, 183n48, n49; death of, 133; image of, 136, 144n16; name of, 154n27; silence of, 134
good, 2, 5, 12–13, 15, 40, 47–48, 67, 74, 150n9, 153n20, 166n7, 171n4; Goodness, 8–9, 14, 49, 83, 120, 169n25. *See also* evil, good and
grace, xiv–xv, 8, 24–26, 38, 45–55, 57–63, 66–69, 71, 83–84, 106, 131, 156n1, n5, n7, 157n8, n10, n11, 163n36, 174n4; detour of, xv, 24–25, 47–48, 52, 54, 57–58, 60, 62, 67–68, 131; folly of, 51–53, 61; gift of, xiv, 24–25, 47, 55, 58, 67, 156n1; state of, xi, 67. *See also* action of; disgrace
guilt, 1, 3, 17, 43, 63, 74–75, 77, 80–83, 86–87, 139, 141n1, 154n22, 161n24, 166n7, 168n22, 169n23, n25
guilty, 1–2, 18, 43, 45–46, 71, 74, 77–78, 80–82, 86–87

Hart, Kevin, 130–132, 144n16, 145n18, 159n18, 162n31
Hegel, G.W.F, xii–xiv, 5, 9, 13–16, 18–22, 25, 35, 38–39, 43, 45–46, 56–57, 62, 66, 75–77, 79, 92–96,

98–99, 108, 119, 135–139, 144n16, 146n24, 147n25, n26, 152n14, 154n22, 156n3, 162n31, 164n36, 167n10, n14, 172n16, 174n2; works by, *Encyclopedia of Logic*, 166n9; *The Phenomenology of Spirit*, 1, 75, 135; *Lectures on the Philosophy of Religion*, 13, 166n9, 167n14; *The Spirit of Christianity and its Fate*, 20

Heidegger, Martin, 9, 76, 78, 81–82, 98–99, 116–117, 153, 169n22, 172n16, 173n17, 176n10, 178n18, 179n24; *Being and Time*, 167n11, n15; *Nietzsche*, 9

Hill, Leslie, 130, 143n10, 146n24, 148n2, 151n11, 154n22, 155n30, 176n12, 177n13, n14, 178n18; "La pensée politique," 129; *Maurice Blanchot and Fragmentary Writing*, 41, 101

history, xi–xii, 1–2, 4, 6–9, 11, 13–15, 17–18, 20–22, 25–26, 29–32, 34–35, 45–46, 65–66, 68, 82, 84, 89–99, 101–103, 105–106, 132, 136, 139, 141n1, n2, n5, 142n9, 143n10, 147n27 28, 161n29, 162n31, n32, 165n3, 166n7, 172n12, n15, n16, 173n17, n19, n1, 178n15; beginning of, 2, 84, 166n7; of the Book, 66, 162n32; end of, 20–22, 29–30, 32, 34–35, 45–46, 90–92, 96–97, 101–102, 147n28, 165n3

historical, 2, 6, 8, 11, 25, 68, 83, 87, 92–95, 98, 106, 109, 132, 136, 141n1, 142n9, 158n11

historicity, 4, 68, 83–84, 102, 120; ahistoricity, 6–7, 11, 20

Hugo, Victor, *The Man Who Laughs*, 2

idiot, the, 2–3, 6. See also Dostoevsky, *The Idiot*

ignorance, 3, 5, 74–76, 78–81, 86
immortal, xv, 13, 34, 58, 167n14; immortality, xv, 13, 110–111. See also mortal, mortality
impure, 20, 28, 162n32; impurity, 74, 86, 153n20. See also pure, purity
inexistence, 167n14; and innocence, xi, xv
infinity, 56–58, 60–61, 111, 117, 119, 141n2, 179n21, infinite, 16, 41–42, 100, 116; infinitesimal, 113. See also Blanchot, *The Infinite Conversation*
inoperative, 79, 157n10, inoperativity, 10, 46. See also Nancy, *The Inoperative Community*
Iyer, Lars, 23, 148n31, 152n19, 170n30

John (Saint), 102; Apocalypse of, 90, 95, 171n8
Judaism, xiii–xiv, 18, 22–23, 43, 61–62, 107–108, 124, 127–128, 132–133, 143n11, 146n22, 147–148n29, 148n30, 160n20, n21, 163n32, 175n5
Judeo-Christian, 1–2, 8–9, 18, 62, 82, 128, 132, 160n21, 182n38
judgment, 7, 25, 48, 90, 96, 103, 137, 142n7, 171n8; final, 25, 90; last, 132, 171–172n8; suspension of, 3. See also Kant, *The Critique of Judgment*
juridical, 1–2, 5, 28–29, 48, 51, 143n12, 157n7
justice, xiv, 4, 23, 25, 28, 35–36, 46, 48–49, 51, 62, 67, 69, 71, 90, 96, 107, 109, 125, 156n5, 160n20

Kafka, Franz, 27, 39, 46, 60–61, 69, 71; *The Penal Colony*, 51; *The Trial*, 27, 45, 60

Kant, Immanuel, 7; *The Critique of Judgment*, 142n7
Kierkegaard, Søren, xiii, 25, 74–83, 87–88, 166n6, n7, n8, 167n9, n10, n11, n14, n17, 168n18, n20, 170n33; *The Concept of Anxiety*, 74, 76–77, 166n6, n7, 167n9; *Fear and Trembling*, 79, 87, 168n18
knowledge, 1–8, 12–13, 16, 20–21, 28–29, 75–76, 78–81, 84, 87–88, 92, 100, 108, 135, 139, 142n6, n8, 143n12, 149n2, 168n18, 172n16; absolute, 20–21, 135, 139, 144n16; power of, 75; suspension of, 6, 79, 168n18; tree of, 12

Lang, Fritz, 5
language, 5, 17, 19–21, 25–26, 28–31, 36–39, 42–44, 46, 49–51, 63, 65, 68, 71–73, 75, 88, 92–97, 99–100, 102, 105, 117–119, 122–123, 126–130, 132–134, 139, 141n3, 142n8, 143n10, 146n21, 147n26, 149n3, 152n19, 153n20, 154n22, n27, 155n33, 157n7, 161n26, n28, 163n32, n33, n34, 169n26, 170n30, n33, 172n13, n14, n15, 173n17, 176n10, 177n13, 180n26, 181n36, 183n48; outside of, 2, 132, 133, 180n26
Labarthe, Lacoue, 56, 153n19, 159n19
Laporte, Roger, 107, 174n4, 176n9
Levinas, Immanuel, 4, 15–18, 21, 23, 37–38, 81–82, 85, 94, 107, 122, 137, 141n2, 133n11, 144n13, 145n18, n19, 146n20, n22, 150n8, 151n11, 152n18, n19, 153n20, 158n13, 159n18, 160n20, 165n5, 168n22, 169n24, 170n30, n33, 172n10, n11, 176n8, 177n12, 178n18, 182n37; *Totality and Infinity*, 141n1; *Otherwise Than Being*, 37, 152n19, 168n22, 169n24
life, tree of, 12–13. *See also* death, life and
literature, xii, 2, 19–22, 29, 39, 46, 91–97, 102, 107–109, 124, 147n25, n26, 149n3, n4, 150n10, 154n22, n27, 158n14, 160n20, 164n36, 168n17, 170n30n33, 172n9, n13, n14, n15, 176n10, 177n13; *See also* Blanchot, *Literature and the Right to Death*
love, xiv–xv, 20–23, 43, 46, 50, 55, 62, 78, 124–125, 127–128, 144n16, 152n19, 156n3, 161n26, 174n2, 181n34; *See also* death, love of
luck, 47–48, 66–67. *See also* chance
Lyotard, Jean-François, 62, 160n21, 182n38
Luther, Martin, 20

Margel, Serge, 155n33, 156n33
Marx, Karl, 7–8, 49, 143n10, n11, 156n5
Melville, Herman, *Billy Budd*, 3, 72–73, 82–83, 88, 164n1
Messianic, 35, 157n7; Messianism, 35
monster, 5, 7; monstrous, 2
Montaigne, Michel de, 27
moral, 3–4, 6, 8, 141n5, 176n10; morality, 7, 35, 152n14. *See also* amoral, amorality
mortal, 13, 53, 63, 132, mortality, 36–37, 39, 46–47, 50–51, 156n5, 161n26, 171n8. *See also* immortality
mourir, xv, 39, 57, 110, 152. *See also* Death, the "to die"
mute, 4, 15, 147n26; muteness, 25, 89, 105–106
myth, 1–2, 4–5, 7, 73, 76, 83–84, 88, 108–109, 124, 131, 135, 141n1,

174n4, 177n13, 181n34; mythical, 6, 13, 19, 72, 89, 124, 141n1; mythography, 124; mythopoesis, 124

Nancy, Jean-Luc, works by, *Adoration: Deconstruction of Christianity*, 68, 112, 114, 116, 159n19, 178n20, 179n21, 180n25, 182n45; *The Disavowed Community*, vii, 23, 26, 106, 108, 112, 114, 121–122, 133, 173n1, 174n3, 176n12, 177n13, 181n34, n35; *The Inoperative Community*, 122, 153n22, 177n13; *Noli me tangere*, 112; *The Sense of the World*, 115

nature, xv, 2, 32–33, 65, 99, 106, 137, 163n34, 166n8, 167n9, 171n4, 181n34; of the book, 122; divine, 55; evil, 4, 171n4; human, 47–49, 67–68; of the law, 28, 33; of writing, 33

natural, 152n14, 153n20; condition, xii, 9; entity, xii, 9; life, 152n14, 153n20

neuter, the, 22, 40, 43, 145n18, 154n27

Nietzsche, Friedrich, 1, 9, 25, 27, 49–50, 62–63, 65, 68–69, 72–74, 131, 141n5, 160n23, 161n24, n25, n26, 165n3, n4, 168n18, 178n16, 182n45, n47, 183n48; *Human, All Too Human*, 1, 27, 141n5; *Thus Spoke Zarathustra*, 45, 50, 65, 73, 156n6, 160n22

negation, xii–xiii, 9, 34, 66, 68, 77, 79, 94–95, 116, 149n2, 168n18, 183n48; negative, xii–xv, 1–2, 7, 10, 15, 18–19, 21, 25, 39, 51, 54, 79, 92, 95, 98, 128, 165n4, 179n22; negativity, xii–x,iii, xv, 1, 3, 9–11, 13–16, 21, 39, 53–54, 97, 133

nothing, 5, 19, 25–26, 33–34, 40, 55, 60, 67, 69, 76, 88–90, 95–97, 100–103, 115–121, 123, 135, 138–139, 141n4, 142n9, 150n7, 154n27, 155n29, n32, 166n7, 167n10, n11, n14, 169n25, 172n9, 173n19, 179n23

nothingness, 25, 39, 74–78, 94–96, 115–117, 119, 135, 172n15, n16

ontology, 9, 26, 72, 116, 153; ontological, 1–2, 6, 15, 117

Other(s), the, 16–17, 22, 37, 43, 81–83, 85, 106, 111, 117, 123, 127, 130, 141n3, 145n18, 151n11, 159n18, 170n30, 181n35, 183n49; before the, 105, 182n37; death of, 111, 122, 126; face of, xiv; history, 89, 97, 98, 101–103, 105, 132, 173n19; Otherness, 46, 87, 127, 132; than Human Being, 66–67, 69; of the world, 111. *See also* Levinas, *Otherwise than Being*

Outside, the, 10, 16, 42, 45–46, 73, 136, 147n28, 149n4, 151n10, 154n22, 158n13; of history, 6; of language, 180n26; of law, 42, 66; spacing of, 41; of language; of the world, 116

Overman (Übermensch), 65, 74

paradise, 1, 12–13, 15, 73, 88; state of, 84, 89

passivity, 16–18, 24, 33–34, 39–40, 42, 81–82, 84–85, 99–101, 145n19, 153n20, 161n27, 175n8, 179n20; and activity, 17; combat of, 39–43

Paul (Saint), xii–xv, 20, 22, 24–25, 38, 40, 43, 46–59, 61–68, 86, 125, 127, 132, 148n30, 152n14, 156n5, n7, 157n10, n11, 158n21, 161n26,

Paul (Saint) *(continued)*
182n37; Epistles of, xii, 48, 86, 127. *See also* Corinthians, Romans
Pascal, Blaise, 27, 86
penalty, of sin, 163. *See also* death penalty
Plato, 11, 173n18
politics, 8–9, 23, 38, 107, 109, 120–124, 134, 142n7, 151–152n14, 177n12, 179n24; atheism and, 130; Blanchot's, 23, 129–130, 174n3; ethics and, 132–133; of innocence, 126; subject of, 126; writing and, 148n31
political thought, 107–109, 121; Agamben's, 152; Arendt's, 7; Blanchot's, 23, 26, 106, 127, 133, 177n12, 179n24, 182n44; left-wing, 23, 108, 121, 127, 129–130, 174n3, 181n34, 182n44; right-wing, 23, 107–109, 121, 123–124, 127, 129–130, 174n3, 175n7, 181n34, 182n44; *See also* biopolitical
pure, 9, 13, 20, 28, 56, 72, 74, 76, 83, 87, 111, 129, 162n32; absence, 130; being, 153n20, 167n10; exteriority, 63 form of the law, 27, 86, 149n4, 152n14; gift, 172n8; "pure heart," 5–6, 74; of language, 153n20; life, 37–39, 152n14, 153n20; passion, 137, 139; power, 157n7; violence, 169n29; purity, 3, 8, 153n20. *See also* impure, impurity
redeem(ed), 8, 24, 47, 61, 66, 71, 79, 82, 84, 119, 137, 139, 154n22; redemption, 8–9, 14–15, 17, 20–21, 57, 61, 71–72, 74, 82–83, 87–88, 111, 139, 163n35, 182n45
responsibility, 4–5, 8, 11, 15–18, 22, 24–25, 27, 30, 38, 72–73, 85, 88, 96, 102–103, 105, 132, 136, 139, 142n6, 146n21, 162n32, 168n22, 169n23, 170n31, 171n5, 176n10;

responsible, 2, 16, 88, 90, 143n12, 149n2, 151n11; 170n31; subject, 17, 137
resurrection, 26, 26, 92,m 112, 118–119 171n8, 178n17; of Christ, 68
revolution(ary), 6–8, 49, 51–52, 92, 142–143n9, 143n10, n11, 151n10, 156n5, 164n36, 175n7
Ricœur, Paul, *Finitude and Guilt*, 141n1, 166n7, 169n25
Romans, Epistle to the, xiii–xiv, 45–47, 50, 53, 156n2, 156n7, 157–158n11. *See also* Paul (Saint)

sacrifice, 122, 125, 168n17; sacrificial, 109
salvation, 14, 18–19, 21, 55, 61, 63, 66, 82, 84, 111, 118
sense, *sens*, 19, 39, 49–50, 71, 115, 133, 162n32; absent, 183n48; infinite, 117, 179n20; non-sense, 116; of the world, 114–115, 178n20, 179n21, n22, n23; *See also* Nancy, *The Sense of the World*
Schmitt, Karl, 27, 86
silence, 19–20, 52, 71–73, 108, 113, 122, 124, 127, 129, 158n12, 175n7, 180n28, n30; Adam's, 20, 147n27; Blanchot's, 123, 125, 127, 129, 176n10, 182n43; of God, 134; Heidegger's, 176n10; of innocence, 11, 73, 75; of language, 142n8, 147n26, 169n26, 176n10; of "the last man," 20; of the law, 31, 149n3, 150n10; Nancy's, 122; of speech, 130; of writing, 127, 134; silent(ly), 19, 25, 73, 126, 127, 129, 178n14; cry, 139
sin, xiv, 13, 17, 45–47, 50, 57, 73–74, 163n35, 166n7; condition of, 17, 81; fall into, 73, 78, 86; original, 77, 131, 139; sinner, 17, 163n35

sovereign, 32, 34, 51, 71, 88, 149n4, 164n36, 181n34; act, 29; gift, 48; of the state, 32; sovereignty, 29, 36, 149n4, 164n36; of God, 66; of the law, 27, 36, 45, 51, 71, 86, 150n10; paradox of, 182n37; writing and, 154n28
spirit, 10, 47, 51, 58, 75, 95–96, 136, 139, 156n1, 168n20; and grace, xiv; language of the, 50; and law, xiv; life of the, 39; temporalization of, 98–99; and nonspirit, 10. *See also* Hegel, *The Phenomenology of Spirit*; *The Spirit of Christianity and its Fate*
state of exception, 28, 35–36, 84, 150n6. *See also* Agamben, *The State of Exception*
stutter(ing), 72, 75, 89; Billy Budd's, 73
suffering, 17–18, 34, 82, 145n19, 146n20, 161n24; passivity of, 81
Surya, Michel, 23, 174n4, 176n10

time, xi, 14–15, 25–26, 49, 55–57, 59–61, 79, 83–84, 90–103, 106, 109–111, 113, 120–121, 127, 131–132, 139, 142n9, 155n30, n32, 159n17, 165n2, 167n14, 169n23, n27, 172n11, 174n3, 175n7; before history, xi; of captivity, 93; of death, 12; end of, 25–26, 90, 92, 96–97, 102, 106, 132, 171n8; of eternity, 13, 103; fall of, xi, 24, 57, 61, 84–85, 169n27; finite, 119, 159n18; immortal, 13; impossibility of, 25, 89, 110, 159n19; loss of, 83; Messianic, 35; outside of, 15, 67, 169n27; public, 34. *See also,* Heidegger, *Being and Time*
truth, xv, 4, 9–10, 13, 20–21, 34, 65, 69, 80, 88, 91–92, 95–97, 102–103, 108, 121, 123–124, 132, 161n25, 168n19, 181n34

violence, 2, 8, 21, 73, 114, 129, 143n12, 169n29, 175n8; of chance, 43; hermeneutical, 177n12; of the law, 24, 27–30, 35–40, 43, 46, 84, 149n4, 154n22; lawless, 21; of life, 38; and writing, 24, 42, 65
vitalism, 72; vitalistic, 8–9, 153n20
void, the, 10, 21, 28, 33–34, 128; of God, 121; of language, 20, 28–29, 38–39, 42, 46; of law, 58, 151n12; of literature, 21; of meaning, 43, 99; of the subject, 11, 16; of non-place, 89, 101, 173n19; of time, 15; of writing, 64
Von Trier, Lars, *Melancholia*, 103

wandering *(errance)*, 10, 83, 87, 94, 98–100, 106
"white writing," 25, 64–65, 68, 127, 130, 161n26, 162n31. *See also* "black writing"; Hart, *The Dark Gaze*
world, end of, xv, 4, 90–91, 93–94, 96–97, 103, 111, 114, 115–120, 139, 178n20, 182n46, 183n48

www.ingramcontent.com/pod-product-compliance
Lightning Source LLC
Chambersburg PA
CBHW030652230426
43665CB00011B/1062